Everyday

EMOTIONAL
INTELLIGENCE

Harvard Business Review's 10 Must Reads

HBR's 10 Must Reads series is the definitive collection of ideas and best practices for aspiring and experienced leaders alike. These books offer essential reading selected from the pages of *Harvard Business Review* on topics critical to the success of every manager.

Titles include:

HBR's 10 Must Reads 2015
HBR's 10 Must Reads 2016
HBR's 10 Must Reads 2017
HBR's 10 Must Reads 2018
HBR's 10 Must Reads for New Managers
HBR's 10 Must Reads on Change Management
HBR's 10 Must Reads on Collaboration
HBR's 10 Must Reads on Communication
HBR's 10 Must Reads on Emotional Intelligence
HBR's 10 Must Reads on Innovation
HBR's 10 Must Reads on Leadership
HBR's 10 Must Reads on Making Smart Decisions
HBR's 10 Must Reads on Managing Across Cultures
HBR's 10 Must Reads on Managing People
HBR's 10 Must Reads on Managing Yourself
HBR's 10 Must Reads on Sales
HBR's 10 Must Reads on Strategic Marketing
HBR's 10 Must Reads on Strategy
HBR's 10 Must Reads on Teams
HBR's 10 Must Reads: The Essentials

Harvard Business Review Guides

Arm yourself with the advice you need to succeed on the job, from the most trusted brand in business. Packed with how-to essentials from leading experts, the HBR Guides provide smart answers to your most pressing work challenges.

Titles include:

HBR Guide to Being More Productive
HBR Guide to Better Business Writing
HBR Guide to Building Your Business Case
HBR Guide to Buying a Small Business
HBR Guide to Coaching Employees
HBR Guide to Data Analytics Basics for Managers
HBR Guide to Dealing with Conflict
HBR Guide to Delivering Effective Feedback
HBR Guide to Emotional Intelligence
HBR Guide to Finance Basics for Managers
HBR Guide to Getting the Right Work Done
HBR Guide to Leading Teams
HBR Guide to Making Every Meeting Matter
HBR Guide to Managing Up and Across
HBR Guide to Negotiating
HBR Guide to Office Politics
HBR Guide to Performance Management
HBR Guide to Persuasive Presentations
HBR Guide to Project Management

Everyday
EMOTIONAL
INTELLIGENCE

*Big Ideas and Practical Advice
on How to Be Human at Work*

Including:

DANIEL GOLEMAN
ANNIE McKEE
SHAWN ACHOR

HARVARD BUSINESS REVIEW PRESS
Boston, Massachusetts

Copyright 2018 Harvard Business School Publishing Corporation
All rights reserved
Printed in the United States of America
10 9 8 7 6 5 4 3 2 1

No part of this publication may be reproduced, stored in or introduced into a retrieval system, or transmitted, in any form, or by any means (electronic, mechanical, photocopying, recording, or otherwise), without the prior permission of the publisher. Requests for permission should be directed to permissions@hbsp.harvard.edu, or mailed to Permissions, Harvard Business School Publishing, 60 Harvard Way, Boston, Massachusetts 02163.

The web addresses referenced in this book were live and correct at the time of the book's publication but may be subject to change.

Library of Congress cataloging-in-publication data is forthcoming.

ISBN: 9781633694118
eISBN: 9781633694125

The paper used in this publication meets the requirements of the American National Standard for Permanence of Paper for Publications and Documents in Libraries and Archives Z39.48-1992.

Contents

HBR Guide to Emotional Intelligence 163

SECTION FOUR

Everyday Emotional Intelligence

SECTION EIGHT

Developing Emotional Intelligence on Your Team

Editor's Note

This combined edition of *HBR's 10 Must Reads on Emotional Intelligence* and the *HBR Guide to Emotional Intelligence* brings together the definitive ideas that HBR has published on managing an active emotional life at work alongside the most practical articles about how to apply those ideas to yourself, your interactions with your colleagues, and your team.

For the concepts and the research behind emotional intelligence—including Daniel Goleman's seminal article that first connected the topic to management thinking in the pages of HBR—turn to the Must Reads section of the book. There you'll learn about the components and competencies that make up emotional intelligence; you'll also find Goleman's work on "primal leadership," research on how to build the emotional intelligence of groups, a framework for developing EQ in your direct reports, and other big ideas.

The Guide section of the volume gets straight to practical how-tos for handling the daily challenges you face at work: how to deal with difficult people; how to manage your own energy in the face of setbacks; how to run better meetings; how to make smarter decisions; and how to persuade and inspire those around you. The Guide section also includes a quiz you can take to better understand how you view your own EI strengths and weaknesses.

Emotional intelligence is increasingly being recognized as a core professional and leadership competence. Use this volume to learn the concepts and frameworks—and how to apply them to build your effectiveness and influence.

**HBR'S
10
MUST
READS**

On
Emotional
Intelligence

HARVARD BUSINESS REVIEW PRESS
Boston, Massachusetts

What Makes a Leader?

by Daniel Goleman

EVERY BUSINESSPERSON KNOWS a story about a highly intelligent, highly skilled executive who was promoted into a leadership position only to fail at the job. And they also know a story about someone with solid—but not extraordinary—intellectual abilities and technical skills who was promoted into a similar position and then soared.

Such anecdotes support the widespread belief that identifying individuals with the "right stuff" to be leaders is more art than science. After all, the personal styles of superb leaders vary: Some leaders are subdued and analytical; others shout their manifestos from the mountaintops. And just as important, different situations call for different types of leadership. Most mergers need a sensitive negotiator at the helm, whereas many turnarounds require a more forceful authority.

I have found, however, that the most effective leaders are alike in one crucial way: They all have a high degree of what has come to be known as *emotional intelligence*. It's not that IQ and technical skills are irrelevant. They do matter, but mainly as "threshold capabilities"; that is, they are the entry-level requirements for executive positions. But my research, along with other recent studies, clearly shows that emotional intelligence is the sine qua non of leadership. Without it, a person can have the best training in the world, an incisive, analytical mind, and an endless supply of smart ideas, but he still won't make a great leader.

In the course of the past year, my colleagues and I have focused on how emotional intelligence operates at work. We have examined the relationship between emotional intelligence and effective performance, especially in leaders. And we have observed how emotional intelligence shows itself on the job. How can you tell if someone has high emotional intelligence, for example, and how can you recognize it in yourself? In the following pages, we'll explore these questions, taking each of the components of emotional intelligence—self-awareness, self-regulation, motivation, empathy, and social skill—in turn.

Evaluating Emotional Intelligence

Most large companies today have employed trained psychologists to develop what are known as "competency models" to aid them in identifying, training, and promoting likely stars in the leadership firmament. The psychologists have also developed such models for lower-level positions. And in recent years, I have analyzed competency models from 188 companies, most of which were large and global and included the likes of Lucent Technologies, British Airways, and Credit Suisse.

In carrying out this work, my objective was to determine which personal capabilities drove outstanding performance within these organizations, and to what degree they did so. I grouped capabilities into three categories: purely technical skills like accounting and business planning; cognitive abilities like analytical reasoning; and competencies demonstrating emotional intelligence, such as the ability to work with others and effectiveness in leading change.

To create some of the competency models, psychologists asked senior managers at the companies to identify the capabilities that typified the organization's most outstanding leaders. To create other models, the psychologists used objective criteria, such as a division's profitability, to differentiate the star performers at senior levels within their organizations from the average ones. Those individuals were then extensively interviewed and tested, and their capabilities were compared. This process resulted in the creation

Idea in Brief

What distinguishes great leaders from merely good ones? It isn't IQ or technical skills, says Daniel Goleman. It's **emotional intelligence:** a group of five skills that enable the best leaders to maximize their own *and* their followers' performance. When senior managers at one company had a critical mass of EI capabilities, their divisions outperformed yearly earnings goals by 20%.

The EI skills are:

- *Self-awareness*—knowing one's strengths, weaknesses, drives, values, and impact on others

- *Self-regulation*—controlling or redirecting disruptive impulses and moods

- *Motivation*—relishing achievement for its own sake

- *Empathy*—understanding other people's emotional makeup

- *Social skill*—building rapport with others to move them in desired directions

We're each born with certain levels of EI skills. But we can strengthen these abilities through persistence, practice, and feedback from colleagues or coaches.

---

of lists of ingredients for highly effective leaders. The lists ranged in length from seven to 15 items and included such ingredients as initiative and strategic vision.

When I analyzed all this data, I found dramatic results. To be sure, intellect was a driver of outstanding performance. Cognitive skills such as big-picture thinking and long-term vision were particularly important. But when I calculated the ratio of technical skills, IQ, and emotional intelligence as ingredients of excellent performance, emotional intelligence proved to be twice as important as the others for jobs at all levels.

Moreover, my analysis showed that emotional intelligence played an increasingly important role at the highest levels of the company, where differences in technical skills are of negligible importance. In other words, the higher the rank of a person considered to be a star performer, the more emotional intelligence capabilities showed up as the reason for his or her effectiveness. When I compared star performers with average ones in senior leadership positions, nearly 90% of the difference in their profiles was attributable to emotional intelligence factors rather than cognitive abilities.

Idea in Practice

Understanding EI's Components

EI Component	Definition	Hallmarks	Example
Self-awareness	Knowing one's emotions, strengths, weaknesses, drives, values, and goals—and their impact on others	• Self-confidence • Realistic self-assessment • Self-deprecating sense of humor • Thirst for constructive criticism	A manager knows tight deadlines bring out the worst in him. So he plans his time to get work done well in advance.
Self-regulation	Controlling or redirecting disruptive emotions and impulses	• Trustworthiness • Integrity • Comfort with ambiguity and change	When a team botches a presentation, its leader resists the urge to scream. Instead, she considers possible reasons for the failure, explains the consequences to her team, and explores solutions with them.
Motivation	Being driven to achieve for the sake of achievement	• A passion for the work itself and for new challenges • Unflagging energy to improve • Optimism in the face of failure	A portfolio manager at an investment company sees his fund tumble for three consecutive quarters. Major clients defect. Instead of blaming external circumstances, she decides to learn from the experience— and engineers a turnaround.

EI Component	Definition	Hallmarks	Example
Empathy	Considering others' feelings, especially when making decisions	• Expertise in attracting and retaining talent • Ability to develop others • Sensitivity to cross-cultural differences	An American consultant and her team pitch a project to a potential client in Japan. Her team interprets the client's silence as disapproval, and prepares to leave. The consultant reads the client's body language and senses interest. She continues the meeting, and her team gets the job.
Social Skill	Managing relationships to move people in desired directions	• Effectiveness in leading change • Persuasiveness • Extensive networking • Expertise in building and leading teams	A manager wants his company to adopt a better Internet strategy. He finds kindred spirits and assembles a de facto team to create a prototype Web site. He persuades allies in other divisions to fund the company's participation in a relevant convention. His company forms an Internet division— and puts him in charge of it.

Strengthening Your EI

Use practice and feedback from others to strengthen specific EI skills.

Example: An executive learned from others that she lacked empathy, especially the ability to listen. She wanted to fix the problem, so she asked a coach to tell her when she exhibited poor listening skills. She then role-played incidents to practice giving better responses; for example, not interrupting. She also began observing executives skilled at listening—and imitated their behavior.

The five components of emotional intelligence at work

	Definition	Hallmarks
Self-awareness	The ability to recognize and understand your moods, emotions, and drives, as well as their effect on others	Self-confidence Realistic self-assessment Self-deprecating sense of humor
Self-regulation	The ability to control or redirect disruptive impulses and moods The propensity to suspend judgment—to think before acting	Trustworthiness and integrity Comfort with ambiguity Openness to change
Motivation	A passion to work for reasons that go beyond money or status A propensity to pursue goals with energy and persistence	Strong drive to achieve Optimism, even in the face of failure Organizational commitment
Empathy	The ability to understand the emotional makeup of other people Skill in treating people according to their emotional reactions	Expertise in building and retaining talent Cross-cultural sensitivity Service to clients and customers
Social skill	Proficiency in managing relationships and building networks An ability to find common ground and build rapport	Effectiveness in leading change Persuasiveness Expertise in building and leading teams

Other researchers have confirmed that emotional intelligence not only distinguishes outstanding leaders but can also be linked to strong performance. The findings of the late David McClelland, the renowned researcher in human and organizational behavior, are a good example. In a 1996 study of a global food and beverage company, McClelland found that when senior managers had a critical mass of emotional intelligence capabilities, their divisions outperformed yearly earnings goals by 20%. Meanwhile, division leaders without that critical mass underperformed by almost the same amount. McClelland's findings, interestingly, held as true in the company's U.S. divisions as in its divisions in Asia and Europe.

In short, the numbers are beginning to tell us a persuasive story about the link between a company's success and the emotional intelligence of its leaders. And just as important, research is also demonstrating that people can, if they take the right approach, develop their emotional intelligence. (See the sidebar "Can Emotional Intelligence Be Learned?")

Self-Awareness

Self-awareness is the first component of emotional intelligence—which makes sense when one considers that the Delphic oracle gave the advice to "know thyself" thousands of years ago. Self-awareness means having a deep understanding of one's emotions, strengths, weaknesses, needs, and drives. People with strong self-awareness are neither overly critical nor unrealistically hopeful. Rather, they are honest—with themselves and with others.

People who have a high degree of self-awareness recognize how their feelings affect them, other people, and their job performance. Thus, a self-aware person who knows that tight deadlines bring out the worst in him plans his time carefully and gets his work done well in advance. Another person with high self-awareness will be able to work with a demanding client. She will understand the client's impact on her moods and the deeper reasons for her frustration. "Their trivial demands take us away from the real work that needs

Can Emotional Intelligence Be Learned?

FOR AGES, PEOPLE HAVE DEBATED if leaders are born or made. So too goes the debate about emotional intelligence. Are people born with certain levels of empathy, for example, or do they acquire empathy as a result of life's experiences? The answer is both. Scientific inquiry strongly suggests that there is a genetic component to emotional intelligence. Psychological and developmental research indicates that nurture plays a role as well. How much of each perhaps will never be known, but research and practice clearly demonstrate that emotional intelligence can be learned.

One thing is certain: Emotional intelligence increases with age. There is an old-fashioned word for the phenomenon: maturity. Yet even with maturity, some people still need training to enhance their emotional intelligence. Unfortunately, far too many training programs that intend to build leadership skills—including emotional intelligence—are a waste of time and money. The problem is simple: They focus on the wrong part of the brain.

Emotional intelligence is born largely in the neurotransmitters of the brain's limbic system, which governs feelings, impulses, and drives. Research indicates that the limbic system learns best through motivation, extended practice, and feedback. Compare this with the kind of learning that goes on in the neocortex, which governs analytical and technical ability. The neocortex grasps concepts and logic. It is the part of the brain that figures out how to use a computer or make a sales call by reading a book. Not surprisingly—but mistakenly—it is also the part of the brain targeted by most training programs aimed at enhancing emotional intelligence. When such programs take, in effect, a neocortical approach, my research with the Consortium for Research on Emotional Intelligence in Organizations has shown they can even have a *negative* impact on people's job performance.

To enhance emotional intelligence, organizations must refocus their training to include the limbic system. They must help people break old behavioral habits and establish new ones. That not only takes much more time than conventional training programs, it also requires an individualized approach.

Imagine an executive who is thought to be low on empathy by her colleagues. Part of that deficit shows itself as an inability to listen; she interrupts people and doesn't pay close attention to what they're saying. To fix the problem, the executive needs to be motivated to change, and then she needs practice and feedback from others in the company. A colleague or coach could be tapped to let the executive know when she has been observed failing to listen. She would then have to replay the incident and give a better response; that is, demonstrate her ability to absorb what others are saying. And the executive could be directed to observe certain executives who listen well and to mimic their behavior.

With persistence and practice, such a process can lead to lasting results. I know one Wall Street executive who sought to improve his empathy— specifically his ability to read people's reactions and see their perspectives. Before beginning his quest, the executive's subordinates were terrified of working with him. People even went so far as to hide bad news from him. Naturally, he was shocked when finally confronted with these facts. He went home and told his family—but they only confirmed what he had heard at work. When their opinions on any given subject did not mesh with his, they, too, were frightened of him.

Enlisting the help of a coach, the executive went to work to heighten his empathy through practice and feedback. His first step was to take a vacation to a foreign country where he did not speak the language. While there, he monitored his reactions to the unfamiliar and his openness to people who were different from him. When he returned home, humbled by his week abroad, the executive asked his coach to shadow him for parts of the day, several times a week, to critique how he treated people with new or different perspectives. At the same time, he consciously used on-the-job interactions as opportunities to practice "hearing" ideas that differed from his. Finally, the executive had himself videotaped in meetings and asked those who worked for and with him to critique his ability to acknowledge and understand the feelings of others. It took several months, but the executive's emotional intelligence did ultimately rise, and the improvement was reflected in his overall performance on the job.

It's important to emphasize that building one's emotional intelligence cannot—will not—happen without sincere desire and concerted effort. A brief seminar won't help; nor can one buy a how-to manual. It is much harder to learn to empathize—to internalize empathy as a natural response to people—than it is to become adept at regression analysis. But it can be done. "Nothing great was ever achieved without enthusiasm," wrote Ralph Waldo Emerson. If your goal is to become a real leader, these words can serve as a guidepost in your efforts to develop high emotional intelligence.

to be done," she might explain. And she will go one step further and turn her anger into something constructive.

Self-awareness extends to a person's understanding of his or her values and goals. Someone who is highly self-aware knows where he is headed and why; so, for example, he will be able to be firm in turning down a job offer that is tempting financially but does not fit with his principles or long-term goals. A person who lacks self-awareness is apt to make decisions that bring on inner turmoil by treading on buried values. "The money looked good so I signed on," someone might say two years into a job, "but the work means so little to me that I'm constantly bored." The decisions of self-aware people mesh with their values; consequently, they often find work to be energizing.

How can one recognize self-awareness? First and foremost, it shows itself as candor and an ability to assess oneself realistically. People with high self-awareness are able to speak accurately and openly—although not necessarily effusively or confessionally—about their emotions and the impact they have on their work. For instance, one manager I know of was skeptical about a new personal-shopper service that her company, a major department-store chain, was about to introduce. Without prompting from her team or her boss, she offered them an explanation: "It's hard for me to get behind the roll-out of this service," she admitted, "because I really wanted to run the project, but I wasn't selected. Bear with me while I deal with that." The manager did indeed examine her feelings; a week later, she was supporting the project fully.

Such self-knowledge often shows itself in the hiring process. Ask a candidate to describe a time he got carried away by his feelings and did something he later regretted. Self-aware candidates will be frank in admitting to failure—and will often tell their tales with a smile. One of the hallmarks of self-awareness is a self-deprecating sense of humor.

Self-awareness can also be identified during performance reviews. Self-aware people know—and are comfortable talking about—their limitations and strengths, and they often demonstrate a thirst for constructive criticism. By contrast, people with low self-awareness interpret the message that they need to improve as a threat or a sign of failure.

Self-aware people can also be recognized by their self-confidence. They have a firm grasp of their capabilities and are less likely to set themselves up to fail by, for example, overstretching on assignments. They know, too, when to ask for help. And the risks they take on the job are calculated. They won't ask for a challenge that they know they can't handle alone. They'll play to their strengths.

Consider the actions of a midlevel employee who was invited to sit in on a strategy meeting with her company's top executives. Although she was the most junior person in the room, she did not sit there quietly, listening in awestruck or fearful silence. She knew she had a head for clear logic and the skill to present ideas persuasively, and she offered cogent suggestions about the company's strategy. At the same time, her self-awareness stopped her from wandering into territory where she knew she was weak.

Despite the value of having self-aware people in the workplace, my research indicates that senior executives don't often give self-awareness the credit it deserves when they look for potential leaders. Many executives mistake candor about feelings for "wimpiness" and fail to give due respect to employees who openly acknowledge their shortcomings. Such people are too readily dismissed as "not tough enough" to lead others.

In fact, the opposite is true. In the first place, people generally admire and respect candor. Furthermore, leaders are constantly required to make judgment calls that require a candid assessment of capabilities—their own and those of others. Do we have the management expertise to acquire a competitor? Can we launch a new product within six months? People who assess themselves honestly—that is, self-aware people—are well suited to do the same for the organizations they run.

Self-Regulation

Biological impulses drive our emotions. We cannot do away with them—but we can do much to manage them. Self-regulation, which is like an ongoing inner conversation, is the component of emotional

13

intelligence that frees us from being prisoners of our feelings. People engaged in such a conversation feel bad moods and emotional impulses just as everyone else does, but they find ways to control them and even to channel them in useful ways.

Imagine an executive who has just watched a team of his employees present a botched analysis to the company's board of directors. In the gloom that follows, the executive might find himself tempted to pound on the table in anger or kick over a chair. He could leap up and scream at the group. Or he might maintain a grim silence, glaring at everyone before stalking off.

But if he had a gift for self-regulation, he would choose a different approach. He would pick his words carefully, acknowledging the team's poor performance without rushing to any hasty judgment. He would then step back to consider the reasons for the failure. Are they personal—a lack of effort? Are there any mitigating factors? What was his role in the debacle? After considering these questions, he would call the team together, lay out the incident's consequences, and offer his feelings about it. He would then present his analysis of the problem and a well-considered solution.

Why does self-regulation matter so much for leaders? First of all, people who are in control of their feelings and impulses—that is, people who are reasonable—are able to create an environment of trust and fairness. In such an environment, politics and infighting are sharply reduced and productivity is high. Talented people flock to the organization and aren't tempted to leave. And self-regulation has a trickle-down effect. No one wants to be known as a hothead when the boss is known for her calm approach. Fewer bad moods at the top mean fewer throughout the organization.

Second, self-regulation is important for competitive reasons. Everyone knows that business today is rife with ambiguity and change. Companies merge and break apart regularly. Technology transforms work at a dizzying pace. People who have mastered their emotions are able to roll with the changes. When a new program is announced, they don't panic; instead, they are able to suspend judgment, seek out information, and listen to the executives as they explain the new program. As the initiative moves forward, these people are able to move with it.

Sometimes they even lead the way. Consider the case of a manager at a large manufacturing company. Like her colleagues, she had used a certain software program for five years. The program drove how she collected and reported data and how she thought about the company's strategy. One day, senior executives announced that a new program was to be installed that would radically change how information was gathered and assessed within the organization. While many people in the company complained bitterly about how disruptive the change would be, the manager mulled over the reasons for the new program and was convinced of its potential to improve performance. She eagerly attended training sessions— some of her colleagues refused to do so—and was eventually promoted to run several divisions, in part because she used the new technology so effectively.

I want to push the importance of self-regulation to leadership even further and make the case that it enhances integrity, which is not only a personal virtue but also an organizational strength. Many of the bad things that happen in companies are a function of impulsive behavior. People rarely plan to exaggerate profits, pad expense accounts, dip into the till, or abuse power for selfish ends. Instead, an opportunity presents itself, and people with low impulse control just say yes.

By contrast, consider the behavior of the senior executive at a large food company. The executive was scrupulously honest in his negotiations with local distributors. He would routinely lay out his cost structure in detail, thereby giving the distributors a realistic understanding of the company's pricing. This approach meant the executive couldn't always drive a hard bargain. Now, on occasion, he felt the urge to increase profits by withholding information about the company's costs. But he challenged that impulse—he saw that it made more sense in the long run to counteract it. His emotional self-regulation paid off in strong, lasting relationships with distributors that benefited the company more than any short-term financial gains would have.

The signs of emotional self-regulation, therefore, are easy to see: a propensity for reflection and thoughtfulness; comfort with ambiguity and change; and integrity—an ability to say no to impulsive urges.

Like self-awareness, self-regulation often does not get its due. People who can master their emotions are sometimes seen as cold fish—their considered responses are taken as a lack of passion. People with fiery temperaments are frequently thought of as "classic" leaders—their outbursts are considered hallmarks of charisma and power. But when such people make it to the top, their impulsiveness often works against them. In my research, extreme displays of negative emotion have never emerged as a driver of good leadership.

Motivation

If there is one trait that virtually all effective leaders have, it is motivation. They are driven to achieve beyond expectations—their own and everyone else's. The key word here is *achieve*. Plenty of people are motivated by external factors, such as a big salary or the status that comes from having an impressive title or being part of a prestigious company. By contrast, those with leadership potential are motivated by a deeply embedded desire to achieve for the sake of achievement.

If you are looking for leaders, how can you identify people who are motivated by the drive to achieve rather than by external rewards? The first sign is a passion for the work itself—such people seek out creative challenges, love to learn, and take great pride in a job well done. They also display an unflagging energy to do things better. People with such energy often seem restless with the status quo. They are persistent with their questions about why things are done one way rather than another; they are eager to explore new approaches to their work.

A cosmetics company manager, for example, was frustrated that he had to wait two weeks to get sales results from people in the field. He finally tracked down an automated phone system that would beep each of his salespeople at 5 p.m. every day. An automated message then prompted them to punch in their numbers—how many calls and sales they had made that day. The system shortened the feedback time on sales results from weeks to hours.

That story illustrates two other common traits of people who are driven to achieve. They are forever raising the performance bar, and they like to keep score. Take the performance bar first. During performance reviews, people with high levels of motivation might ask to be "stretched" by their superiors. Of course, an employee who combines self-awareness with internal motivation will recognize her limits—but she won't settle for objectives that seem too easy to fulfill.

And it follows naturally that people who are driven to do better also want a way of tracking progress—their own, their team's, and their company's. Whereas people with low achievement motivation are often fuzzy about results, those with high achievement motivation often keep score by tracking such hard measures as profitability or market share. I know of a money manager who starts and ends his day on the Internet, gauging the performance of his stock fund against four industry-set benchmarks.

Interestingly, people with high motivation remain optimistic even when the score is against them. In such cases, self-regulation combines with achievement motivation to overcome the frustration and depression that come after a setback or failure. Take the case of another portfolio manager at a large investment company. After several successful years, her fund tumbled for three consecutive quarters, leading three large institutional clients to shift their business elsewhere.

Some executives would have blamed the nosedive on circumstances outside their control; others might have seen the setback as evidence of personal failure. This portfolio manager, however, saw an opportunity to prove she could lead a turnaround. Two years later, when she was promoted to a very senior level in the company, she described the experience as "the best thing that ever happened to me; I learned so much from it."

Executives trying to recognize high levels of achievement motivation in their people can look for one last piece of evidence: commitment to the organization. When people love their jobs for the work itself, they often feel committed to the organizations that make that work possible. Committed employees are likely to stay with an organization even when they are pursued by headhunters waving money.

It's not difficult to understand how and why a motivation to achieve translates into strong leadership. If you set the performance bar high for yourself, you will do the same for the organization when you are in a position to do so. Likewise, a drive to surpass goals and an interest in keeping score can be contagious. Leaders with these traits can often build a team of managers around them with the same traits. And of course, optimism and organizational commitment are fundamental to leadership—just try to imagine running a company without them.

Empathy

Of all the dimensions of emotional intelligence, empathy is the most easily recognized. We have all felt the empathy of a sensitive teacher or friend; we have all been struck by its absence in an unfeeling coach or boss. But when it comes to business, we rarely hear people praised, let alone rewarded, for their empathy. The very word seems unbusiness-like, out of place amid the tough realities of the marketplace.

But empathy doesn't mean a kind of "I'm OK, you're OK" mushi-ness. For a leader, that is, it doesn't mean adopting other people's emotions as one's own and trying to please everybody. That would be a nightmare—it would make action impossible. Rather, empathy means thoughtfully considering employees' feelings—along with other factors—in the process of making intelligent decisions.

For an example of empathy in action, consider what happened when two giant brokerage companies merged, creating redundant jobs in all their divisions. One division manager called his people together and gave a gloomy speech that emphasized the number of people who would soon be fired. The manager of another division gave his people a different kind of speech. He was up-front about his own worry and confusion, and he promised to keep people informed and to treat everyone fairly.

The difference between these two managers was empathy. The first manager was too worried about his own fate to consider the feelings of his anxiety-stricken colleagues. The second knew intuitively what his people were feeling, and he acknowledged their fears with his words. Is it any surprise that the first manager saw his division sink as many demoralized people, especially the most talented, departed? By contrast, the second manager continued to be a strong leader, his best people stayed, and his division remained as productive as ever.

Empathy is particularly important today as a component of leadership for at least three reasons: the increasing use of teams; the rapid pace of globalization; and the growing need to retain talent.

Consider the challenge of leading a team. As anyone who has ever been a part of one can attest, teams are cauldrons of bubbling emotions. They are often charged with reaching a consensus—which is hard enough with two people and much more difficult as the numbers increase. Even in groups with as few as four or five members, alliances form and clashing agendas get set. A team's leader must be able to sense and understand the viewpoints of everyone around the table.

That's exactly what a marketing manager at a large information technology company was able to do when she was appointed to lead a troubled team. The group was in turmoil, overloaded by work and missing deadlines. Tensions were high among the members. Tinkering with procedures was not enough to bring the group together and make it an effective part of the company.

So the manager took several steps. In a series of one-on-one sessions, she took the time to listen to everyone in the group—what was frustrating them, how they rated their colleagues, whether they felt they had been ignored. And then she directed the team in a way that brought it together: She encouraged people to speak more openly about their frustrations, and she helped people raise constructive complaints during meetings. In short, her empathy allowed her to understand her team's emotional makeup. The result was not just heightened collaboration among members but also added business, as the team was called on for help by a wider range of internal clients.

Globalization is another reason for the rising importance of empathy for business leaders. Cross-cultural dialogue can easily lead to miscues and misunderstandings. Empathy is an antidote. People who have it are attuned to subtleties in body language; they can hear the message beneath the words being spoken. Beyond that, they have a deep understanding of both the existence and the importance of cultural and ethnic differences.

Consider the case of an American consultant whose team had just pitched a project to a potential Japanese client. In its dealings with Americans, the team was accustomed to being bombarded with questions after such a proposal, but this time it was greeted with a long silence. Other members of the team, taking the silence as disapproval, were ready to pack and leave. The lead consultant gestured them to stop. Although he was not particularly familiar with Japanese culture, he read the client's face and posture and sensed not rejection but interest—even deep consideration. He was right: When the client finally spoke, it was to give the consulting firm the job.

Finally, empathy plays a key role in the retention of talent, particularly in today's information economy. Leaders have always needed empathy to develop and keep good people, but today the stakes are higher. When good people leave, they take the company's knowledge with them.

That's where coaching and mentoring come in. It has repeatedly been shown that coaching and mentoring pay off not just in better performance but also in increased job satisfaction and decreased turnover. But what makes coaching and mentoring work best is the nature of the relationship. Outstanding coaches and mentors get inside the heads of the people they are helping. They sense how to give effective feedback. They know when to push for better performance and when to hold back. In the way they motivate their protégés, they demonstrate empathy in action.

In what is probably sounding like a refrain, let me repeat that empathy doesn't get much respect in business. People wonder how leaders can make hard decisions if they are "feeling" for all the people who will be affected. But leaders with empathy do more than sympathize with people around them: They use their knowledge to improve their companies in subtle but important ways.

Social Skill

The first three components of emotional intelligence are self-management skills. The last two, empathy and social skill, concern a person's ability to manage relationships with others. As a component of emotional intelligence, social skill is not as simple as it sounds. It's not just a matter of friendliness, although people with high levels of social skill are rarely mean-spirited. Social skill, rather, is friendliness with a purpose: moving people in the direction you desire, whether that's agreement on a new marketing strategy or enthusiasm about a new product.

Socially skilled people tend to have a wide circle of acquaintances, and they have a knack for finding common ground with people of all kinds—a knack for building rapport. That doesn't mean they socialize continually; it means they work according to the assumption that nothing important gets done alone. Such people have a network in place when the time for action comes.

Social skill is the culmination of the other dimensions of emotional intelligence. People tend to be very effective at managing relationships when they can understand and control their own emotions and can empathize with the feelings of others. Even motivation contributes to social skill. Remember that people who are driven to achieve tend to be optimistic, even in the face of setbacks or failure. When people are upbeat, their "glow" is cast upon conversations and other social encounters. They are popular, and for good reason.

Because it is the outcome of the other dimensions of emotional intelligence, social skill is recognizable on the job in many ways that will by now sound familiar. Socially skilled people, for instance, are adept at managing teams—that's their empathy at work. Likewise, they are expert persuaders—a manifestation of self-awareness, self-regulation, and empathy combined. Given those skills, good persuaders know when to make an emotional plea, for instance, and when an appeal to reason will work better. And motivation, when publicly visible, makes such people excellent collaborators; their passion for the work spreads to others, and they are driven to find solutions.

But sometimes social skill shows itself in ways the other emotional intelligence components do not. For instance, socially skilled people may at times appear not to be working while at work. They seem to be idly schmoozing—chatting in the hallways with colleagues or joking around with people who are not even connected to their "real" jobs. Socially skilled people, however, don't think it makes sense to arbitrarily limit the scope of their relationships. They build bonds widely because they know that in these fluid times, they may need help someday from people they are just getting to know today.

For example, consider the case of an executive in the strategy department of a global computer manufacturer. By 1993, he was convinced that the company's future lay with the Internet. Over the course of the next year, he found kindred spirits and used his social skill to stitch together a virtual community that cut across levels, divisions, and nations. He then used this de facto team to put up a corporate Web site, among the first by a major company. And, on his own initiative, with no budget or formal status, he signed up the company to participate in an annual Internet industry convention. Calling on his allies and persuading various divisions to donate funds, he recruited more than 50 people from a dozen different units to represent the company at the convention.

Management took notice: Within a year of the conference, the executive's team formed the basis for the company's first Internet division, and he was formally put in charge of it. To get there, the executive had ignored conventional boundaries, forging and maintaining connections with people in every corner of the organization.

Is social skill considered a key leadership capability in most companies? The answer is yes, especially when compared with the other components of emotional intelligence. People seem to know intuitively that leaders need to manage relationships effectively; no leader is an island. After all, the leader's task is to get work done through other people, and social skill makes that possible. A leader who cannot express her empathy may as well not have it at all. And a leader's motivation will be useless if he cannot communicate his passion to the organization. Social skill allows leaders to put their emotional intelligence to work.

It would be foolish to assert that good-old-fashioned IQ and technical ability are not important ingredients in strong leadership. But the recipe would not be complete without emotional intelligence. It was once thought that the components of emotional intelligence were "nice to have" in business leaders. But now we know that, for the sake of performance, these are ingredients that leaders "need to have."

It is fortunate, then, that emotional intelligence can be learned. The process is not easy. It takes time and, most of all, commitment. But the benefits that come from having a well-developed emotional intelligence, both for the individual and for the organization, make it worth the effort.

Originally published in June 1996. Reprint R0401H

Primal Leadership

The Hidden Driver of Great Performance.
*by Daniel Goleman, Richard Boyatzis,
and Annie McKee*

WHEN THE THEORY OF EMOTIONAL intelligence at work began to receive widespread attention, we frequently heard executives say—in the same breath, mind you—"That's incredible," and, "Well, I've known that all along." They were responding to our research that showed an incontrovertible link between an executive's emotional maturity, exemplified by such capabilities as self-awareness and empathy, and his or her financial performance. Simply put, the research showed that "good guys"—that is, emotionally intelligent men and women—finish first.

We've recently compiled two years of new research that, we suspect, will elicit the same kind of reaction. People will first exclaim, "No way," then quickly add, "But of course." We found that of all the elements affecting bottom-line performance, the importance of the leader's mood and its attendant behaviors are most surprising. That powerful pair set off a chain reaction: The leader's mood and behaviors drive the moods and behaviors of everyone else. A cranky and ruthless boss creates a toxic organization filled with negative underachievers who ignore opportunities; an inspirational, inclusive leader spawns acolytes for whom any challenge is surmountable. The final link in the chain is performance: profit or loss.

Our observation about the overwhelming impact of the leader's "emotional style," as we call it, is not a wholesale departure from our research into emotional intelligence. It does, however, represent a deeper analysis of our earlier assertion that a leader's emotional intelligence creates a certain culture or work environment. High levels of emotional intelligence, our research showed, create climates in which information sharing, trust, healthy risk-taking, and learning flourish. Low levels of emotional intelligence create climates rife with fear and anxiety. Because tense or terrified employees can be very productive in the short term, their organizations may post good results, but they never last.

Our investigation was designed in part to look at how emotional intelligence drives performance—in particular, at how it travels from the leader through the organization to bottom-line results. "What mechanism," we asked, "binds the chain together?" To answer that question, we turned to the latest neurological and psychological research. We also drew on our work with business leaders, observations by our colleagues of hundreds of leaders, and Hay Group data on the leadership styles of thousands of executives. From this body of research, we discovered that emotional intelligence is carried through an organization like electricity through wires. To be more specific, the leader's mood is quite literally contagious, spreading quickly and inexorably throughout the business.

We'll discuss the science of mood contagion in more depth later, but first let's turn to the key implications of our finding. If a leader's mood and accompanying behaviors are indeed such potent drivers of business success, then a leader's premier task—we would even say his primal task—is emotional leadership. A leader needs to make sure that not only is he regularly in an optimistic, authentic, high-energy mood, but also that, through his chosen actions, his followers feel and act that way, too. Managing for financial results, then, begins with the leader managing his inner life so that the right emotional and behavioral chain reaction occurs.

Managing one's inner life is not easy, of course. For many of us, it's our most difficult challenge. And accurately gauging how one's emotions affect others can be just as difficult. We know of one CEO, for example, who was certain that everyone saw him as upbeat and reliable; his direct reports told us they found his cheerfulness strained, even fake, and his decisions erratic. (We call this common

Idea in Brief

What *most* influences your company's bottom-line performance? The answer will surprise you—*and* make perfect sense: It's a leader's own mood.

Executives' emotional intelligence—their self-awareness, empathy, rapport with others—has clear links to their own performance. But new research shows that a leader's emotional style also drives everyone *else*'s moods and behaviors—through a neurological process called **mood contagion**. It's akin to "Smile and the whole world smiles with you."

Emotional intelligence travels through an organization like electricity over telephone wires. Depressed, ruthless bosses create toxic organizations filled with negative underachievers. But if you're an upbeat, inspirational leader, you cultivate positive employees who embrace and surmount even the toughest challenges.

Emotional leadership isn't just putting on a game face every day. It means understanding your impact on others—then adjusting your style accordingly. A difficult process of self-discovery—but essential *before* you can tackle your leadership responsibilities.

---

disconnect "CEO disease.") The implication is that primal leadership demands more than putting on a game face every day. It requires an executive to determine, through reflective analysis, how his emotional leadership drives the moods and actions of the organization, and then, with equal discipline, to adjust his behavior accordingly.

That's not to say that leaders can't have a bad day or week: Life happens. And our research doesn't suggest that good moods have to be high-pitched or nonstop—optimistic, sincere, and realistic will do. But there is no escaping the conclusion that a leader must first attend to the impact of his mood and behaviors before moving on to his wide panoply of other critical responsibilities. In this article, we introduce a process that executives can follow to assess how others experience their leadership, and we discuss ways to calibrate that impact. But first, we'll look at why moods aren't often discussed in the workplace, how the brain works to make moods contagious, and what you need to know about CEO disease.

Idea in Practice

Strengthening Your Emotional Leadership

Since few people have the guts to tell you the truth about your emotional impact, you must discover it on your own. The following process can help. It's based on brain science, as well as years of field research with executives. Use these steps to rewire your brain for greater emotional intelligence.

1. **Who do you want to be?** Imagine yourself as a highly effective leader. What do you see?

   Example: Sofia, a senior manager, often micromanaged others to ensure work was done "right." So she *imagined* herself in the future as an effective

leader of her own company, enjoying trusting relationships with coworkers. She saw herself as relaxed, happy, and empowering. The exercise revealed gaps in her current emotional style.

2. **Who are you now?** To see your leadership style as others do, gather 360-degree feedback, especially from peers and subordinates. Identify your weaknesses *and* strengths.

3. **How do you get from here to there?** Devise a plan for closing the gap between who you are and who you want to be.

   Example: Juan, a marketing executive, was intimidating,

No Way! Yes Way

When we said earlier that people will likely respond to our new finding by saying "No way," we weren't joking. The fact is, the emotional impact of a leader is almost never discussed in the workplace, let alone in the literature on leadership and performance. For most people, "mood" feels too personal. Even though Americans can be shockingly candid about personal matters—witness the *Jerry Springer Show* and its ilk—we are also the most legally bound. We can't even ask the age of a job applicant. Thus, a conversation about an executive's mood or the moods he creates in his employees might be construed as an invasion of privacy.

We also might avoid talking about a leader's emotional style and its impact because, frankly, the topic feels soft. When was the last time you evaluated a subordinate's mood as part of her performance impossible to please—a grouch. Charged with growing his company, he *needed* to be encouraging, optimistic—a coach with a vision. Setting out to understand others, he coached soccer, volunteered at a crisis center, and got to know subordinates by meeting outside of work. These new situations stimulated him to break old habits and try new responses.

4. **How do you make change stick?** Repeatedly rehearse new behaviors—physically *and* mentally—until they're automatic.

Example: Tom, an executive, wanted to learn how to coach

rather than castigate struggling employees. Using his commuting time to visualize a difficult meeting with one employee, he envisioned asking questions and listening, and mentally rehearsed how he'd handle feeling impatient. This exercise prepared him to adopt new behaviors at the actual meeting.

5. **Who can help you?** Don't try to build your emotional skills alone—identify others who can help you navigate this difficult process. Managers at Unilever formed learning groups that helped them strengthen their leadership abilities by exchanging frank feedback and developing strong mutual trust.

appraisal? You may have alluded to it—"Your work is hindered by an often negative perspective," or "Your enthusiasm is terrific"—but it is unlikely you mentioned mood outright, let alone discussed its impact on the organization's results.

And yet our research undoubtedly will elicit a "But of course" reaction, too. Everyone knows how much a leader's emotional state drives performance because everyone has had, at one time or another, the inspirational experience of working for an upbeat manager or the crushing experience of toiling for a sour-spirited boss. The former made everything feel possible, and as a result, stretch goals were achieved, competitors beaten, and new customers won. The latter made work grueling. In the shadow of the boss's dark mood, other parts of the organization became "the enemy," colleagues became suspicious of one another, and customers slipped away.

Our research, and research by other social scientists, confirms the verity of these experiences. (There are, of course, rare cases when a brutal boss produces terrific results. We explore that dynamic in the sidebar "Those Wicked Bosses Who Win.") The studies are too numerous to mention here but, in aggregate, they show that when the leader is in a happy mood, the people around him view everything in a more positive light. That, in turn, makes them optimistic about achieving their goals, enhances their creativity and the efficiency of their decision making, and predisposes them to be helpful. Research conducted by Alice Isen at Cornell in 1999, for example, found that an upbeat environment fosters mental efficiency, making people better at taking in and understanding information, at using decision rules in complex judgments, and at being flexible in their thinking. Other research directly links mood and financial performance. In 1986, for instance, Martin Seligman and Peter Schulman of the University of Pennsylvania demonstrated that insurance agents who had a "glass half-full" outlook were far more able than their more pessimistic peers to persist despite rejections, and thus, they closed more sales. (For more information on these studies and a list of our research base, visit www.eiconsortium.org.)

Many leaders whose emotional styles create a dysfunctional environment are eventually fired. (Of course, that's rarely the stated reason; poor results are.) But it doesn't have to end that way. Just as a bad mood can be turned around, so can the spread of toxic feelings from an emotionally inept leader. A look inside the brain explains both why and how.

The Science of Moods

A growing body of research on the human brain proves that, for better or worse, leaders' moods affect the emotions of the people around them. The reason for that lies in what scientists call the open-loop nature of the brain's limbic system, our emotional center. A closed-loop system is self-regulating, whereas an open-loop system depends on external sources to manage itself. In other words, we rely on connections with other people to determine our moods. The

Those Wicked Bosses Who Win

EVERYONE KNOWS OF a rude and coercive CEO who, by all appearances, epitomizes the antithesis of emotional intelligence yet seems to reap great business results. If a leader's mood matters so much, how can we explain those mean-spirited, successful SOBs?

First, let's take a closer look at them. Just because a particular executive is the most visible, he may not actually lead the company. A CEO who heads a conglomerate may have no followers to speak of; it's his division heads who actively lead people and affect profitability.

Second, sometimes an SOB leader has strengths that counterbalance his caustic behavior, but they don't attract as much attention in the business press. In his early days at GE, Jack Welch exhibited a strong hand at the helm as he undertook a radical company turnaround. At that time and in that situation, Welch's firm, top-down style was appropriate. What got less press was how Welch subsequently settled into a more emotionally intelligent leadership style, especially when he articulated a new vision for the company and mobilized people to follow it.

Those caveats aside, let's get back to those infamous corporate leaders who seem to have achieved sterling business results despite their brutish approaches to leadership. Skeptics cite Bill Gates, for example, as a leader who gets away with a harsh style that should theoretically damage his company.

But our leadership model, which shows the effectiveness of specific leadership styles in specific situations, puts Gates's supposedly negative behaviors in a different light. (Our model is explained in detail in the HBR article "Leadership That Gets Results," which appeared in the March–April 2000 issue.) Gates is the achievement-driven leader par excellence, in an organization that has cherry-picked highly talented and motivated people. His apparently harsh leadership style—baldly challenging employees to surpass their past performance—can be quite effective when employees are competent, motivated, and need little direction—all characteristics of Microsoft's engineers.

In short, it's all too easy for a skeptic to argue against the importance of leaders who manage their moods by citing a "rough and tough" leader who achieved good business results despite his bad behavior. We contend that there are, of course, exceptions to the rule, and that in some specific business cases, an SOB boss resonates just fine. But in general, leaders who are jerks must reform or else their moods and actions will eventually catch up with them.

open-loop limbic system was a winning design in evolution because it let people come to one another's emotional rescue—enabling a mother, for example, to soothe her crying infant.

The open-loop design serves the same purpose today as it did thousands of years ago. Research in intensive care units has shown, for example, that the comforting presence of another person not only lowers the patient's blood pressure but also slows the secretion of fatty acids that block arteries. Another study found that three or more incidents of intense stress within a year (for example, serious financial trouble, being fired, or a divorce) triples the death rate in socially isolated middle-aged men, but it has no impact on the death rate of men with many close relationships.

Scientists describe the open loop as "interpersonal limbic regulation"; one person transmits signals that can alter hormone levels, cardiovascular functions, sleep rhythms, even immune functions, inside the body of another. That's how couples are able to trigger surges of oxytocin in each other's brains, creating a pleasant, affectionate feeling. But in all aspects of social life, our physiologies intermingle. Our limbic system's open-loop design lets other people change our very physiology and hence, our emotions.

Even though the open loop is so much a part of our lives, we usually don't notice the process. Scientists have captured the attunement of emotions in the laboratory by measuring the physiology—such as heart rate—of two people sharing a good conversation. As the interaction begins, their bodies operate at different rhythms. But after 15 minutes, the physiological profiles of their bodies look remarkably similar.

Researchers have seen again and again how emotions spread irresistibly in this way whenever people are near one another. As far back as 1981, psychologists Howard Friedman and Ronald Riggio found that even completely nonverbal expressiveness can affect other people. For example, when three strangers sit facing one another in silence for a minute or two, the most emotionally expressive of the three transmits his or her mood to the other two—without a single word being spoken.

Smile and the World Smiles with You

REMEMBER THAT OLD cliché? It's not too far from the truth. As we've shown, mood contagion is a real neurological phenomenon, but not all emotions spread with the same ease. A 1999 study conducted by Sigal Barsade at the Yale School of Management showed that, among working groups, cheerfulness and warmth spread easily, while irritability caught on less so, and depression least of all.

It should come as no surprise that laughter is the most contagious of all emotions. Hearing laughter, we find it almost impossible not to laugh or smile, too. That's because some of our brain's open-loop circuits are designed to detect smiles and laughter, making us respond in kind. Scientists theorize that this dynamic was hardwired into our brains ages ago because smiles and laughter had a way of cementing alliances, thus helping the species survive.

The main implication here for leaders undertaking the primal task of managing their moods and the moods of others is this: Humor hastens the spread of an upbeat climate. But like the leader's mood in general, humor must resonate with the organization's culture and its reality. Smiles and laughter, we would posit, are only contagious when they're genuine.

The same holds true in the office, boardroom, or shop floor; group members inevitably "catch" feelings from one another. In 2000, Caroline Bartel at New York University and Richard Saavedra at the University of Michigan found that in 70 work teams across diverse industries, people in meetings together ended up sharing moods—both good and bad—within two hours. One study asked teams of nurses and accountants to monitor their moods over weeks; researchers discovered that their emotions tracked together, and they were largely independent of each team's shared hassles. Groups, therefore, like individuals, ride emotional roller coasters, sharing everything from jealousy to angst to euphoria. (A good mood, incidentally, spreads most swiftly by the judicious use of humor. For more on this, see the sidebar "Smile and the World Smiles with You.")

Moods that start at the top tend to move the fastest because everyone watches the boss. They take their emotional cues from him. Even when the boss isn't highly visible—for example, the CEO

Get Happy, Carefully

GOOD MOODS GALVANIZE good performance, but it doesn't make sense for a leader to be as chipper as a blue jay at dawn if sales are tanking or the business is going under. The most effective executives display moods and behaviors that match the situation at hand, with a healthy dose of optimism mixed in. They respect how other people are feeling—even if it is glum or defeated—but they also model what it looks like to move forward with hope and humor.

This kind of performance, which we call resonance, is for all intents and purposes the four components of emotional intelligence in action.

Self-awareness, perhaps the most essential of the emotional intelligence competencies, is the ability to read your own emotions. It allows people to know their strengths and limitations and feel confident about their self-worth. Resonant leaders use self-awareness to gauge their own moods accurately, and they intuitively know how they are affecting others.

Self-management is the ability to control your emotions and act with honesty and integrity in reliable and adaptable ways. Resonant leaders don't let their occasional bad moods seize the day; they use self-management to leave it outside the office or to explain its source to people in a reasonable manner, so they know where it's coming from and how long it might last.

Social awareness includes the key capabilities of empathy and organizational intuition. Socially aware executives do more than sense other people's emotions, they show that they care. Further, they are experts at reading the currents of office politics. Thus, resonant leaders often keenly understand how their words and actions make others feel, and they are sensitive enough to change them when that impact is negative.

Relationship management, the last of the emotional intelligence competencies, includes the abilities to communicate clearly and convincingly,

---

who works behind closed doors on an upper floor—his attitude affects the moods of his direct reports, and a domino effect ripples throughout the company.

Call That CEO a Doctor

If the leader's mood is so important, then he or she had better get into a good one, right? Yes, but the full answer is more complicated than that. A leader's mood has the greatest impact on performance disarm conflicts, and build strong personal bonds. Resonant leaders use these skills to spread their enthusiasm and solve disagreements, often with humor and kindness.

As effective as resonant leadership is, it is just as rare. Most people suffer through dissonant leaders whose toxic moods and upsetting behaviors wreak havoc before a hopeful and realistic leader repairs the situation.

Consider what happened recently at an experimental division of the BBC, the British media giant. Even though the group's 200 or so journalists and editors had given their best effort, management decided to close the division.

The shutdown itself was had enough, but the brusque, contentious mood and manner of the executive sent to deliver the news to the assembled staff incited something beyond the expected frustration. People became enraged—at both the decision and the bearer of the news. The executive's cranky mood and delivery created an atmosphere so threatening that he had to call security to be ushered from the room.

The next day, another executive visited the same staff. His mood was somber and respectful, as was his behavior. He spoke about the importance of journalism to the vibrancy of a society and of the calling that had drawn them all to the field in the first place. He reminded them that no one goes into journalism to get rich—as a profession its finances have always been marginal, job security ebbing and flowing with the larger economic tides. He recalled a time in his own career when he had been let go and how he had struggled to find a new position—but how he had stayed dedicated to the profession. Finally, he wished them well in getting on with their careers.

The reaction from what had been an angry mob the day before? When this resonant leader finished speaking, the staff cheered.

---

when it is upbeat. But it must also be in tune with those around him. We call this dynamic *resonance*. (For more on this, see the sidebar "Get Happy, Carefully.")

We found that an alarming number of leaders do not really know if they have resonance with their organizations. Rather, they suffer from CEO disease; its one unpleasant symptom is the sufferer's near-total ignorance about how his mood and actions appear to the organization. It's not that leaders don't care how they are perceived; most do. But they incorrectly assume that they can decipher this information themselves. Worse, they think that if they are having a negative effect, someone will tell them. They're wrong.

As one CEO in our research explains, "I so often feel I'm not getting the truth. I can never put my finger on it, because no one is actually lying to me. But I can sense that people are hiding information or camouflaging key facts. They aren't lying, but neither are they telling me everything I need to know. I'm always second-guessing."

People don't tell leaders the whole truth about their emotional impact for many reasons. Sometimes they are scared of being the bearer of bad news—and getting shot. Others feel it isn't their place to comment on such a personal topic. Still others don't realize that what they really want to talk about is the effects of the leader's emotional style—that feels too vague. Whatever the reason, the CEO can't rely on his followers to spontaneously give him the full picture.

Taking Stock

The process we recommend for self-discovery and personal reinvention is neither newfangled nor born of pop psychology, like so many self-help programs offered to executives today. Rather, it is based on three streams of research into how executives can improve the emotional intelligence capabilities most closely linked to effective leadership. (Information on these research streams can also be found at www.eiconsortium.org.). In 1989, one of us (Richard Boyatzis) began drawing on this body of research to design the five-step process itself, and since then, thousands of executives have used it successfully.

Unlike more traditional forms of coaching, our process is based on brain science. A person's emotional skills—the attitude and abilities with which someone approaches life and work—are not genetically hardwired, like eye color and skin tone. But in some ways they might as well be, because they are so deeply embedded in our neurology.

A person's emotional skills do, in fact, have a genetic component. Scientists have discovered, for instance, the gene for shyness—which is not a mood, per se, but it can certainly drive a person toward a persistently quiet demeanor, which may be read as a "down" mood.

Other people are preternaturally jolly—that is, their relentless cheerfulness seems preternatural until you meet their peppy parents. As one executive explains, "All I know is that ever since I was a baby, I have always been happy. It drives some people crazy, but I couldn't get blue if I tried. And my brother is the exact same way; he saw the bright side of life, even during his divorce."

Even though emotional skills are partly inborn, experience plays a major role in how the genes are expressed. A happy baby whose parents die or who endures physical abuse may grow into a melancholy adult. A cranky toddler may turn into a cheerful adult after discovering a fulfilling avocation. Still, research suggests that our range of emotional skills is relatively set by our mid-20s and that our accompanying behaviors are, by that time, deep-seated habits. And therein lies the rub: The more we act a certain way—be it happy, depressed, or cranky—the more the behavior becomes ingrained in our brain circuitry, and the more we will continue to feel and act that way.

That's why emotional intelligence matters so much for a leader. An emotionally intelligent leader can monitor his or her moods through self-awareness, change them for the better through self-management, understand their impact through empathy, and act in ways that boost others' moods through relationship management.

The following five-part process is designed to rewire the brain toward more emotionally intelligent behaviors. The process begins with imagining your ideal self and then coming to terms with your real self, as others experience you. The next step is creating a tactical plan to bridge the gap between ideal and real, and after that, to practice those activities. It concludes with creating a community of colleagues and family—call them change enforcers—to keep the process alive. Let's look at the steps in more detail.

"Who do I want to be?"

Sofia, a senior manager at a northern European telecommunications company, knew she needed to understand how her emotional leadership affected others. Whenever she felt stressed, she tended to communicate poorly and take over subordinates' work so that the job would be done "right." Attending leadership seminars hadn't changed her habits, and neither had reading management books or working with mentors.

When Sofia came to us, we asked her to imagine herself eight years from now as an effective leader and to write a description of a typical day. "What would she be doing?" we asked. "Where would she live? Who would be there? How would it feel?" We urged her to consider her deepest values and loftiest dreams and to explain how those ideals had become a part of her everyday life.

Sofia pictured herself leading her own tight-knit company staffed by ten colleagues. She was enjoying an open relationship with her daughter and had trusting relationships with her friends and coworkers. She saw herself as a relaxed and happy leader and parent, and as loving and empowering to all those around her.

In general, Sofia had a low level of self-awareness: She was rarely able to pinpoint why she was struggling at work and at home. All she could say was, "Nothing is working right." This exercise, which prompted her to picture what life would look like if everything were going right, opened her eyes to the missing elements in her emotional style. She was able to see the impact she had on people in her life.

"Who am I now?"

In the next step of the discovery process, you come to see your leadership style as others do. This is both difficult and dangerous. Difficult, because few people have the guts to tell the boss or a colleague what he's really like. And dangerous, because such information can sting or even paralyze. A small bit of ignorance about yourself isn't always a bad thing: Ego-defense mechanisms have their advantages. Research by Martin Seligman shows that high-functioning people generally feel more optimistic about their prospects and possibilities than average performers. Their rose-colored lenses, in fact, fuel the enthusiasm and energy that make the unexpected and the extraordinary achievable. Playwright Henrik Ibsen called such self-delusions "vital lies," soothing mistruths we let ourselves believe in order to face a daunting world.

But self-delusion should come in very small doses. Executives should relentlessly seek the truth about themselves, especially since it is sure to be somewhat diluted when they hear it anyway. One way to get the truth is to keep an extremely open attitude toward critiques. Another is to seek out negative feedback, even cultivating a colleague or two to play devil's advocate.

We also highly recommend gathering feedback from as many people as possible—including bosses, peers, and subordinates. Feedback from subordinates and peers is especially helpful because it most accurately predicts a leader's effectiveness, two, four, and even seven years out, according to research by Glenn McEvoy at Utah State and Richard Beatty at Rutgers University.

Of course, 360-degree feedback doesn't specifically ask people to evaluate your moods, actions, and their impact. But it does reveal how people experience you. For instance, when people rate how well you listen, they are really reporting how well they think you hear them. Similarly, when 360-degree feedback elicits ratings about coaching effectiveness, the answers show whether or not people feel you understand and care about them. When the feedback uncovers low scores on, say, openness to new ideas, it means that people experience you as inaccessible or unapproachable or both. In sum, all you need to know about your emotional impact is in 360-degree feedback, if you look for it.

One last note on this second step. It is, of course, crucial to identify your areas of weakness. But focusing only on your weaknesses can be dispiriting. That's why it is just as important, maybe even more so, to understand your strengths. Knowing where your real self overlaps with your ideal self will give you the positive energy you need to move forward to the next step in the process—bridging the gaps.

"How do I get from here to there?"
Once you know who you want to be and have compared it with how people see you, you need to devise an action plan. For Sofia, this meant planning for a real improvement in her level of self-awareness. So she asked each member of her team at work to give

her feedback—weekly, anonymously, and in written form—about her mood and performance and their affect on people. She also committed herself to three tough but achievable tasks: spending an hour each day reflecting on her behavior in a journal, taking a class on group dynamics at a local college, and enlisting the help of a trusted colleague as an informal coach.

Consider, too, how Juan, a marketing executive for the Latin American division of a major integrated energy company, completed this step. Juan was charged with growing the company in his home country of Venezuela as well as in the entire region—a job that would require him to be a coach and a visionary and to have an encouraging, optimistic outlook. Yet 360-degree feedback revealed that Juan was seen as intimidating and internally focused. Many of his direct reports saw him as a grouch—impossible to please at his worst, and emotionally draining at his best.

Identifying this gap allowed Juan to craft a plan with manageable steps toward improvement. He knew he needed to hone his powers of empathy if he wanted to develop a coaching style, so he committed to various activities that would let him practice that skill. For instance, Juan decided to get to know each of his subordinates better; if he understood more about who they were, he thought, he'd be more able to help them reach their goals. He made plans with each employee to meet outside of work, where they might be more comfortable revealing their feelings.

Juan also looked for areas outside of his job to forge his missing links—for example, coaching his daughter's soccer team and volunteering at a local crisis center. Both activities helped him to experiment with how well he understood others and to try out new behaviors.

Again, let's look at the brain science at work. Juan was trying to overcome ingrained behaviors—his approach to work had taken hold over time, without his realizing it. Bringing them into awareness was a crucial step toward changing them. As he paid more attention, the situations that arose—while listening to a colleague, coaching soccer, or talking on the phone to someone who was distraught—all became cues that stimulated him to break old habits and try new responses.

Resonance in Times of Crisis

WHEN TALKING ABOUT LEADERS' moods, the importance of resonance cannot be overstated. While our research suggests that leaders should generally be upbeat, their behavior must be rooted in realism, especially when faced with a crisis.

Consider the response of Bob Mulholland, senior VP and head of the client relations group at Merrill Lynch, to the terrorist attacks in New York. On September 11, 2001, Mulholland and his staff in Two World Financial Center felt the building rock, then watched as smoke poured out of a gaping hole in the building directly across from theirs. People started panicking: Some ran frantically from window to window. Others were paralyzed with fear. Those with relatives working in the World Trade Center were terrified for their safety. Mulholland knew he had to act: "When there's a crisis, you've got to show people the way, step by step, and make sure you're taking care of their concerns."

He started by getting people the information they needed to "unfreeze." He found out, for instance, which floors employees' relatives worked on and assured them that they'd have enough time to escape. Then he calmed the panic-stricken, one at a time. "We're getting out of here now," he said quietly, "and you're coming with me. Not the elevator, take the stairs." He remained calm and decisive, yet he didn't minimize people's emotional responses. Thanks to him, everyone escaped before the towers collapsed.

Mulholland's leadership didn't end there. Recognizing that this event would touch each client personally, he and his team devised a way for financial consultants to connect with their clients on an emotional level. They called every client to ask, "How are you? Are your loved ones okay? How are you feeling?" As Mulholland explains, "There was no way to pick up and do business as usual. The first order of 'business' was letting our clients know we really do care."

Bob Mulholland courageously performed one of the most crucial emotional tasks of leadership: He helped himself and his people find meaning in the face of chaos and madness. To do so, he first attuned to and expressed the shared emotional reality. That's why the direction he eventually articulated resonated at the gut level. His words and his actions reflected what people were feeling in their hearts.

This cueing for habit change is neural as well as perceptual. Researchers at the University of Pittsburgh and Carnegie Mellon University have shown that as we mentally prepare for a task, we activate the prefrontal cortex—the part of the brain that moves us into action. The greater the prior activation, the better we do at the task.

Such mental preparation becomes particularly important when we're trying to replace an old habit with a better one. As neuroscientist Cameron Carter at the University of Pittsburgh found, the prefrontal cortex becomes particularly active when a person prepares to overcome a habitual response. The aroused prefrontal cortex marks the brain's focus on what's about to happen. Without that arousal, a person will reenact tried-and-true but undesirable routines: The executive who just doesn't listen will once again cut off his subordinate, a ruthless leader will launch into yet another critical attack, and so on. That's why a learning agenda is so important. Without one, we literally do not have the brainpower to change.

"How do I make change stick?"

In short, making change last requires practice. The reason, again, lies in the brain. It takes doing and redoing, over and over, to break old neural habits. A leader must rehearse a new behavior until it becomes automatic—that is, until he's mastered it at the level of implicit learning. Only then will the new wiring replace the old.

While it is best to practice new behaviors, as Juan did, sometimes just envisioning them will do. Take the case of Tom, an executive who wanted to close the gap between his real self (perceived by colleagues and subordinates to be cold and hard driving) and his ideal self (a visionary and a coach).

Tom's learning plan involved finding opportunities to step back and coach his employees rather than jumping down their throats when he sensed they were wrong. Tom also began to spend idle moments during his commute thinking through how to handle encounters he would have that day. One morning, while en route to a breakfast meeting with an employee who seemed to be bungling a project, Tom ran through a positive scenario in his mind. He asked questions and listened to be sure he fully understood the situation before trying to solve the problem. He anticipated feeling impatient, and he rehearsed how he would handle these feelings.

Studies on the brain affirm the benefits of Tom's visualization technique: Imagining something in vivid detail can fire the same brain cells actually involved in doing that activity. The new brain circuitry appears to go through its paces, strengthening connections, even when we merely repeat the sequence in our minds. So to alleviate the fears associated with trying out riskier ways of leading, we should first visualize some likely scenarios. Doing so will make us feel less awkward when we actually put the new skills into practice.

Experimenting with new behaviors and seizing opportunities inside and outside of work to practice them—as well as using such methods as mental rehearsal—eventually triggers in our brains the neural connections necessary for genuine change to occur. Even so, lasting change doesn't happen through experimentation and brainpower alone. We need, as the song goes, a little help from our friends.

"Who can help me?"

The fifth step in the self-discovery and reinvention process is creating a community of supporters. Take, for example, managers at Unilever who formed learning groups as part of their executive development process. At first, they gathered to discuss their careers and how to provide leadership. But because they were also charged with discussing their dreams and their learning goals, they soon realized that they were discussing both their work and their personal lives. They developed a strong mutual trust and began relying on one another for frank feedback as they worked on strengthening their leadership abilities. When this happens, the business benefits through stronger performance. Many professionals today have created similar groups, and for good reason. People we trust let us try out unfamiliar parts of our leadership repertoire without risk.

We cannot improve our emotional intelligence or change our leadership style without help from others. We not only practice with other people but also rely on them to create a safe environment in which to experiment. We need to get feedback about how our actions affect others and to assess our progress on our learning agenda.

In fact, perhaps paradoxically, in the self-directed learning process we draw on others every step of the way—from articulating and refining our ideal self and comparing it with the reality to the final assessment that affirms our progress. Our relationships offer us the very context in which we understand our progress and comprehend the usefulness of what we're learning.

Mood over Matter

When we say that managing your mood and the moods of your followers is the task of primal leadership, we certainly don't mean to suggest that mood is all that matters. As we've noted, your actions are critical, and mood and actions together must resonate with the organization and with reality. Similarly, we acknowledge all the other challenges leaders must conquer—from strategy to hiring to new product development. It's all in a long day's work.

But taken as a whole, the message sent by neurological, psychological, and organizational research is startling in its clarity. Emotional leadership is the spark that ignites a company's performance, creating a bonfire of success or a landscape of ashes. Moods matter that much.

Originally published in December 2001. Reprint Ro111C

Why It's So Hard to Be Fair

by Joel Brockner

WHEN COMPANY A HAD TO DOWNSIZE, it spent considerable amounts of money providing a safety net for its laid-off workers. The severance package consisted of many weeks of pay, extensive outplacement counseling, and the continuation of health insurance for up to one year. But senior managers never explained to their staff why these layoffs were necessary or how they chose which jobs to eliminate. What's more, the midlevel line managers who delivered the news to terminated employees did so awkwardly, mumbling a few perfunctory words about "not wanting to do this" and then handing them off to the human resources department. Even the people who kept their jobs were less than thrilled about the way things were handled. Many of them heard the news while driving home on Friday and had to wait until Monday to learn that their jobs were secure. Nine months later, the company continued to sputter. Not only did it have to absorb enormous legal costs defending against wrongful termination suits, but it also had to make another round of layoffs, in large part because employee productivity and morale plummeted after the first round was mishandled.

When Company B downsized, by contrast, it didn't offer nearly as generous a severance package. But senior managers there explained the strategic purpose of the layoffs multiple times before they were implemented, and executives and middle managers alike made themselves available to answer questions and express regret both to those who lost their jobs and to those who remained. Line managers worked with HR to tell people that their jobs were being eliminated, and they expressed genuine concern while doing so. As a result, virtually none of the laid-off employees filed a wrongful termination lawsuit. Workers took some time to adjust to the loss of their former colleagues, but they understood why the layoffs had happened. And within nine months, Company B's performance was better than it had been before the layoffs occurred.

Although Company A spent much more money during its restructuring, Company B exhibited much greater *process fairness*. In other words, employees at Company B believed that they had been treated justly. From minimizing costs to strengthening performance, process fairness pays enormous dividends in a wide variety of organizational and people-related challenges. Studies show that when managers practice process fairness, their employees respond in ways that bolster the organization's bottom line both directly and indirectly. Process fairness is more likely to generate support for a new strategy, for instance, and to foster a culture that promotes innovation. What's more, it costs little financially to implement. In short, fair process makes great business sense. So why don't more companies practice it consistently? This article examines that paradox and offers advice on how to promote greater process fairness in your organization.

The Business Case for Fair Process

Ultimately, each employee decides for him or herself whether a decision has been made fairly. But broadly speaking, there are three drivers of process fairness. One is how much input employees believe they have in the decision-making process: Are their opinions requested and given serious consideration? Another is how employees believe decisions are made and implemented: Are they consistent? Are they based on accurate information? Can mistakes be corrected? Are the personal biases of the decision maker minimized? Is ample advance

Idea in Brief

There are myriad ways a company can lose money if it doesn't practice process fairness, including employee theft and turnover, legal costs incurred by defending against wrongful termination suits, and implementing expensive solutions aimed at helping employees cope with the stresses of modern work.

Many executives turn to money first when solving problems, but asking employees for their opinions on a new initiative or explaining to them why you're giving a choice assignment to someone else doesn't cost much money and results in more-satisfied employees. From minimizing costs to strengthening performance, process fairness pays enormous dividends in a wide variety challenges.

Good organizations care not only about the outcomes their managers produce but also about the fairness of the process they use to achieve them. The sooner they minimize the costs of decisions that might threaten employees and maximize the benefits of decisions that may be sources of opportunity for them, the better off they will be.

notice given? Is the decision process transparent? The third factor is how managers behave: Do they explain why a decision was made? Do they treat employees respectfully, actively listening to their concerns and empathizing with their points of view?

It's worth noting that process fairness is distinct from outcome fairness, which refers to employees' judgments of the bottom-line results of their exchanges with their employers. Process fairness doesn't ensure that employees will always get what they want; but it does mean that they will have a chance to be heard. Take the case of an individual who was passed over for a promotion. If he believes that the chosen candidate was qualified, and if his manager has had a candid discussion with him about how he can be better prepared for the next opportunity, chances are he'll be a lot more productive and engaged than if he believes the person who got the job was the boss's pet, or if he received no guidance on how to move forward.

When people feel hurt by their companies, they tend to retaliate. And when they do, it can have grave consequences. A study of nearly 1,000 people in the mid-1990s, led by Duke's Allan Lind and Ohio State's Jerald Greenberg, found that a major determinant of whether employees sue for wrongful termination is their perception of how fairly the termination process was carried out. Only 1% of ex-employees who felt that they were treated with a high degree of process fairness filed a wrongful termination lawsuit versus 17% of those who believed they were treated with a low degree of process fairness. To put that in monetary terms, the expected cost savings of practicing process fairness is $1.28 million for every 100 employees dismissed. That figure—which was calculated using the 1988 rate of $80,000 as the cost of legal defense—is a conservative estimate, since inflation alone has caused legal fees to swell to more than $120,000 today. So, although we can't calculate the precise financial cost of practicing fair process, it's safe to say that expressing genuine concern and treating dismissed employees with dignity is a good deal more affordable than not doing so.

Customers, too, are less likely to file suit against a service provider if they believe they've been treated with process fairness. In 1997, medical researcher Wendy Levinson and her colleagues found that patients typically do not sue their doctors for malpractice simply because they believe that they received poor medical care. A more telling factor is whether the doctor took the time to explain the treatment plan and to answer the patient's questions with consideration—in short, to treat patients with process fairness. Doctors who fail to do so are far more likely to be slapped with malpractice suits when problems arise.

In addition to reducing legal costs, fair process cuts down on employee theft and turnover. A study by management and human resources professor Greenberg examined how pay cuts were handled at two manufacturing plants. At one, a vice president called a meeting at the end of the workweek and announced that the company would implement a 15% pay cut, across the board, for ten weeks. He very briefly explained why, thanked employees, and answered a few questions—the whole thing was over in 15 minutes. The other plant implemented an identical pay cut, but the company president made the announcement to the employees. He told them that other cost-saving options, like layoffs, had been considered but that the pay cuts seemed to be the least unpalatable choice. The president took an hour and a half to address employees' questions and concerns, and he repeatedly expressed regret about having to take this step. Greenberg found that during the ten-week period, employee theft was nearly 80% lower at the second plant than at the first, and employees were 15 times less likely to resign.

Many executives turn to money first to solve problems. But my research shows that companies can reduce expenses by routinely practicing process fairness. Think about it: Asking employees for their opinions on a new initiative or explaining to someone why you're giving a choice assignment to her colleague doesn't cost much money. Of course, companies should continue to offer tangible assistance to employees as well. Using process fairness, however, companies could spend a lot less money and still have more satisfied employees.

Consider the financial fallout that occurs when expatriates leave their overseas assignments prematurely. Conventional wisdom says that expats are more likely to leave early when they or their family members don't adjust well to their new living conditions. So companies often go to great expense to facilitate their adjustment—picking up the tab for housing costs, children's schooling, and the like. In a 2000 study of 128 expatriates, human resources consultant Ron Garonzik, Rutgers Business School professor Phyllis Siegel, and I found that the expats' adjustment to various aspects of their lives outside work had no effect on their intentions to depart prematurely if they believed that their bosses generally treated them fairly. In other words, high process fairness induced expats to stick with an overseas assignment even when they were not particularly enthralled with living abroad.

In a similar vein, some companies have devised expensive solutions to help employees cope with the stress of modern work. They've set up on-site day care centers and sponsored stress management workshops to help reduce absenteeism and burnout. Those efforts are laudable, but process fairness is also an effective strategy. When Phyllis Siegel and I surveyed nearly 300 employees from dozens of organizations, we found that work/life conflict had no measurable effect on employees' commitment—as long as they felt that senior executives provided good reasons for their decisions and treated them with dignity and respect.

Of course, executives should not simply emphasize process fairness over tangible support. Determining exactly how much tangible support to provide is perhaps best captured by the law of diminishing returns. Beyond a moderate level of financial assistance, practicing process fairness proves much more cost effective because, although money does talk, it doesn't say it all.

Fair Process as a Performance Booster

Process fairness can not only minimize costs but can also help to increase value, inspiring operational managers to carry out a well-founded strategic plan eagerly or embrace, rather than sabotage, an organizational change. This form of value is less tangible than direct reduction of expenses, but it affects the bottom line nonetheless.

The fact is, most strategic and organizational change initiatives fail in their implementation, not in their conception. Several years ago, I worked with the CEO of a financial services institution that needed a major restructuring. The bank's operational managers, however, were showing signs of resistance that threatened to stop the process dead in its tracks. I advised the CEO and his senior management team to conduct several town hall–type meetings and to hold informal focus groups with the operational managers. During those talks, it became clear that the managers felt that the CEO and senior executives failed to appreciate the magnitude of the change they were asking for. Interestingly, the managers didn't request additional resources; they simply wanted those at the top to recognize their difficult plight. By expressing authentic interest, senior executives created a trusting environment in which managers felt they could safely voice their true objections to the change effort. That enabled senior managers to respond to the root problem. Moreover, since the operational managers felt respected, they showed a similar level of process fairness with *their* direct reports during the actual restructuring, making the change go more smoothly.

Michael Beer, of Harvard Business School, and Russell Eisenstat, president of the Center for Organizational Fitness, recently provided evidence of how systematically practiced process fairness (embedded in an action-learning methodology known as the strategic fitness process, or SFP) has helped numerous organizations capture value by getting employees to buy in to strategies. A critical element of SFP is the appointment of a task force consisting of eight well-respected managers from one or two levels below senior management. Their job is to interview roughly 100 employees from different parts of the company to learn about the organizational strengths that are apt to facilitate strategy implementation as well as the shortcomings that could hinder it. Task force members distill the information they gain from these interviews into major themes and feed them back to senior management. Then they discuss how the strategy could be rolled out most effectively. SFP is a model for process fairness: More than 25 companies—including Becton, Dickinson; Honeywell; JPMorgan Chase; Hewlett-Packard; and Merck—have used it with great success to hone the substance of their strategic initiatives and, probably more important, to gain employees' commitment to making those initiatives happen.

Most companies say that they want to promote creativity and innovation, but few use process fairness to achieve those ends. They're missing out on a great opportunity to create value. Harvard Business School professor Teresa Amabile has conducted extensive research on employees working in creative endeavors in order to understand how work environments foster or impede creativity and innovation. She has consistently found that work environments in which employees have a high degree of operational autonomy lead to the highest degree of creativity and innovation. Operational autonomy, of course, can be seen as the extreme version of process fairness.

The nature of organizations, though, means that few (if any) employees can have complete operational autonomy—just about everyone has a boss. Creativity and innovation tend to suffer in work environments characterized by low levels of process fairness, such as when employees believe that the organization is strictly controlled by upper management or when they believe that their ideas will be summarily dismissed. When employees believe that their supervisor is open to new ideas and that he or she values their contributions to projects, however, creativity and innovation are more likely to flourish. Two examples illustrate how process fairness creates value by attracting innovative employees or additional customers.

The CEO of a renowned electrical-engineering firm, for instance, wanted to change the corporate culture to be more receptive to new ideas, so he separated a large group of workers into teams of ten, asking each team to come up with ten ideas for improving the business. Then the team leaders were brought into a room where the company's executives were gathered and were asked to "sell" as many of their team's ideas as possible. The executives, for their part, had been instructed to "buy" as many ideas as possible. The team leaders swarmed like bees to honey to the few executives who had reputations for being good listeners and open to new ideas. The other executives stood by idly because team leaders assumed from past experience that they wouldn't listen.

One company that used process fairness to create value is Progressive Casualty Insurance. In 1994, the firm began to give potential customers comparison rates from two competitors along with its own quotes for auto insurance. Even though Progressive's rates weren't always the lowest, the very act of delivering this information created goodwill. Potential customers felt that they were being treated honestly, and the practice drew many new sales.

Why Isn't Everybody Doing It?

With all that process fairness has going for it, one might expect that executives would practice it regularly. Unfortunately, many (if not most) don't. They'd do well to follow the example of Winston Churchill, who keenly understood the cost-effectiveness of process fairness. On the day after the bombing of Pearl Harbor, Churchill wrote a declaration of war to the Japanese, ending it as follows: "I have the honour to be, with high consideration, Sir, Your obedient servant, Winston S. Churchill." After being castigated by his countrymen for the letter's deferential tone, Churchill is said to have retorted, "When you have to kill a man, it costs nothing to be polite."

In a change management seminar I've taught to more than 400 managers, I ask participants to rate themselves on how well they plan and implement organizational change. I also ask the managers' bosses, peers, direct reports, and customers to rate them. The measure contains more than 30 items, and managers consistently give themselves the highest marks on the item that measures process fairness: "When managing change, I make extra efforts to treat people with dignity and respect." Those rating them, however, are not nearly as positive. In fact, this is the only item in which managers' self-assessments are significantly higher than the ratings they receive from each of their groups. It's not entirely clear why this perceptual gap exists. Perhaps managers are tuned in to their intentions to treat others respectfully, but they aren't as good at reading how those intentions come across to others. Or maybe it's just wishful— and self-serving—thinking.

Some managers wrongly believe that tangible resources are always more meaningful to employees than being treated decently. At a cocktail party, the CEO of a major international bank proudly told me about the hefty severance pay his company gave to its laid-off employees. I expressed admiration for his organization's show of concern toward the people who lost their jobs and then asked what had been done for those who remained. Somewhat defensively, he said that it was only necessary to do something for the employees who were "affected" by the layoffs. The others were "lucky enough to still have their jobs." But economically supporting those who lost their jobs doesn't cancel out the need to show process fairness to those affected by the change—which, incidentally, includes everyone. Ironically, the fact that process fairness is relatively inexpensive financially may be why this numbers-oriented executive undervalued it.

Another reason process fairness may be overlooked is because some of its benefits aren't obvious to executives. Social psychologist Marko Elovainio of the University of Helsinki and his colleagues recently conducted a study of more than 31,000 Finnish employees, examining the relationship between employees' negative life events (such as the onset of a severe illness or death of a spouse) and the frequency of sickness-related absences from work for the subsequent 30 months. The study showed that the tendency for negative life events to translate into sickness-related absences depended on how much process fairness employees experienced before the events occurred. That is, *not* being pretreated with process fairness led to absences waiting to happen.

Sometimes corporate policies hinder fair process. The legal department may discourage managers from explaining their decisions, for instance, on the grounds that disclosure of information could make the company vulnerable to lawsuits. Better not to say anything at all, the thinking goes, than to risk having the information come back to haunt the organization in the courtroom. Clearly, legal considerations about what to communicate are important, but they should not be taken to unnecessary extremes. All too often organizations withhold information (such as the alternatives to downsizing that have been considered) when revealing it would have done far more good.

Legal and medical advocates in Hawaii, for instance, are currently drafting a statute that would allow health care professionals to apologize for medical errors without increasing the risk of lawsuits. Doctors often refrain from apologizing for mistakes because they fear that admitting them will anger their patients, who will then be more likely to file malpractice suits. In fact, the opposite is true: Patients who feel they've been treated disrespectfully file *more* malpractice suits than those who feel they have been treated with dignity. By making apologies for medical mistakes inadmissible during a trial, the law would let doctors express regrets without worrying that doing so would hurt them in court.

Managers who unwaveringly believe that knowledge is power may fear that engaging in process fairness will weaken their power. After all, if employees have a voice in deciding how things should be run, who needs a manager? Managers sometimes do run the risk of losing power when they involve others in decision making. But usually the practice of process fairness increases power and influence. When employees feel that they are heard in the decision-making process, they are more likely to support—rather than merely comply with—those decisions, their bosses, and the organization as a whole.

The desire to avoid uncomfortable situations is another reason managers fail to practice process fairness. As Robert Folger of the University of Central Florida has suggested, managers who plan and implement tough decisions often experience conflicting emotions. They might want to approach the affected parties out of sympathy and to explain the thinking behind a decision, but the desire to avoid them is also strong. Andy Molinsky at Brandeis University and Harvard Business School's Joshua Margolis analyzed why managers find it so hard to perform necessary evils (such as laying off employees and delivering other bad news) with interpersonal sensitivity, which is an important element of process fairness. Leaders in this situation have to manage their own internal dramas, including feelings of guilt (for, say, making poor strategic decisions that led to the downsizing) and anxiety (about having sufficient interpersonal sensitivity to accomplish the task gracefully). Instead of wrestling with those uncomfortable emotions, many managers find it easier to sidestep the issue—and the people affected by it—altogether.

"Emotional contagion" also comes into play in these situations. Just as we tend to laugh when we see others laugh, even when we don't know why, we also involuntarily feel anxious or sad when those around us feel that way—and that's uncomfortable. No wonder so many managers avoid people in emotional pain. Unfortunately, such avoidance makes it very unlikely that they will practice process fairness.

I can understand how managers feel. Several years ago, I was working with a telecommunications organization after the first layoffs in the company's history. The CEO and his senior management team wanted me to talk to the midlevel managers about how the layoffs would affect the people who remained and what they could do to help their direct reports "get over it." Feeling betrayed and fearful, however, the midlevel managers were in no mood to help others return to business as usual. They identified me with the problem and implied that I was partly responsible for the decision to downsize. That was a moment of real insight for me: Trying to counsel this unhappy and suspicious group, I completely understood the discomfort that managers experience when they're called on to act compassionately toward people who feel aggrieved. It was much harder than I expected.

The senior managers of the company admitted to me that they were tempted to avoid the rank and file—partly out of guilt and partly because they doubted whether they would be able to keep a cool enough head to practice process fairness. That's a natural response, but ignoring negative emotions only keeps them swirling around longer. When senior managers made themselves more accessible to their workforce, employees reacted positively, and the organization developed a renewed sense of purpose.

Toward Process Fairness

Companies can take several steps to make fair process the norm.

Address the knowledge gaps

Managers need to be warned about the negative emotions they might experience when practicing fair process. Merely acknowledging that it is legitimate to feel like fleeing the scene can help managers withstand the impulse to do so. Studies have shown that people can tolerate negative experiences more easily when they expect them. Just as forewarned surgical patients have been found to experience less postoperative pain, forewarned managers may be better able to cope with (and hence not act on) their negative emotions.

Furthermore, managers are more likely to endure a difficult process when they know that the effort will have a tangible payoff. But it's not enough for managers to be vaguely aware that process fairness is cost effective. Corporate executives should educate them about all the financial benefits, using charts and figures, just as they would when making a business case for other important organizational initiatives.

Invest in training

Study after study has shown that fair-process training can make a big difference. Subordinates of the trained managers, for instance, are not only significantly less likely to steal or to resign from the organization, but they are also more likely to go the extra mile—aiding coworkers who have been absent, helping orient new employees, assisting supervisors with their duties, and working overtime. Several studies by Jerald Greenberg have even found that employees whose managers underwent process fairness training suffered significantly less insomnia when coping with stressful work conditions.

Daniel Skarlicki, of the University of British Columbia's Sauder School of Business, and Gary Latham, of the University of Toronto's Joseph L. Rotman School of Management, have identified some factors of an effective process fairness training program. Participants respond better to active guidance than to a lecture on the benefits of improved process fairness. That's why it's particularly effective to give trainees specific instructions on what they need to do and how they need to do it, such as how to detect resistance to a new strategic initiative. After the participants have practiced these behaviors, give them feedback and let them try again.

When I was working with an executive at a utility company several years ago, for example, I noticed that she made a common mistake: She didn't tell others that she had seriously considered their opinions before making her decisions, even though she had. I advised her to preface her explanations by saying explicitly that she had "given their input some serious thought." Six months later, she told me my advice had been priceless. She learned that it's not enough for executives just to *be* fair, they also have to be *seen* as fair.

Training is most effective when it's delivered in several installments rather than all at once. For example, one successful program consisted of a two-hour session each week for eight weeks, along with assigned role-playing homework. That way, participants could receive feedback from instructors during the formal training sessions and from their peers in between meetings. As with most constructive feedback, referring to behaviors ("You never explained why you made this decision") rather than to traits ("You came across as condescending") proved to be most compelling.

Both the process and the outcome of the training need to be communicated to participants—but not at the same time. Before the sessions begin, focus on the outcome. Participants are likely to be far more engaged if they are told that the program will help them gain their employees' commitment to strategy implementation than if they are told it will help them communicate that they've seriously considered other people's points of view. During the course, however, focus on process. Thinking about expected outcomes (improved strategy implementation, for instance) can distract people from learning the specific practical skills they need (such as how to involve people in decision making) to achieve the desired results.

Finally, it is important for trainees to maintain expectations that are both optimistic and realistic. Once again, the distinction between outcome and process is useful to keep in mind. You can generate optimism by focusing on the outcomes: Touting the improvements that previous trainees have made should help people feel positive about their own chances for growth. And you can inject realism by focusing on the process: Behavioral change is difficult and rarely takes a linear course. Trainees shouldn't expect to get better at process fairness day by day; but, if they keep working at it, they will improve. I suggest trainees ask themselves three months after the program if they are practicing process fairness more on average than they were three months prior to it. Conducting after-action reviews also helps managers continue to hone their skills long after the training sessions are over.

Make process fairness a top priority

Like most managerial behaviors, the practice of process fairness must begin at the top. When senior managers explain why they have made certain strategic decisions, make themselves available for honest two-way communication with the rank and file, involve employees in decision making, provide ample advance notice of change, and treat people's concerns with respect, the practice of process fairness is likely to spread like wildfire throughout the rest of the organization.

By modeling process fairness, senior management does more than communicate organizational values; it also sends a message about "the art of the possible." People are more likely to try to tackle difficult challenges when they see others whom they respect doing so. In one company that was trying to implement a much-needed restructuring, senior executives effectively served as role models not only by describing the mixed feelings they had about practicing process fairness but also by articulating the process they went through that ultimately convinced them to do so. The message they sent was that it was legitimate for operational managers to have mixed emotions, but, at the end of the day, the reasons in favor of practicing process fairness prevailed.

In addition to acting as role models, senior managers may communicate the value they place on process fairness by making its practice a legitimate topic of conversation throughout the organization. I worked with one company, for example, that selected its employee of the month based on process fairness skills as well as bottom-line results. Other organizations have made managers' annual pay raises partly dependent on 360-degree feedback about how they plan and implement decisions, in which perceptions of process fairness figure prominently.

Recent corporate scandals show that giving workforces outcome-only directives ("I don't care how you get there, just get there") can be disastrous. Forward-thinking organizations care not only about the outcomes their managers produce but also about the fairness of the process they use to achieve them. This is not a call for micro-management. Just as there is usually more than one way to produce financial results, there is more than one way to involve people in decision making, to communicate why certain actions are being undertaken, and to express thoughtfulness and concern.

There is a moral imperative for companies to practice process fairness. It is, simply put, the right thing to do. As such, process fairness is the responsibility of all executives, at all levels, and in all functions; it cannot be delegated to HR. But with that moral responsibility comes business opportunity. An executive must minimize the costs of decisions that might threaten employees and maximize the benefits of decisions that may be sources of opportunity for them. In both instances, practicing process fairness will help get you there. The sooner you realize it, the better off you and your company will be.

Originally published in March 2006. Reprint R0603H

Why Good Leaders Make Bad Decisions

by Andrew Campbell, Jo Whitehead,
and Sydney Finkelstein

DECISION MAKING LIES AT THE HEART of our personal and professional lives. Every day we make decisions. Some are small, domestic, and innocuous. Others are more important, affecting people's lives, livelihoods, and well-being. Inevitably, we make mistakes along the way. The daunting reality is that enormously important decisions made by intelligent, responsible people with the best information and intentions are sometimes hopelessly flawed.

Consider Jürgen Schrempp, CEO of Daimler-Benz. He led the merger of Chrysler and Daimler against internal opposition. Nine years later, Daimler was forced to virtually give Chrysler away in a private equity deal. Steve Russell, chief executive of Boots, the UK drugstore chain, launched a health care strategy designed to differentiate the stores from competitors and grow through new health care services such as dentistry. It turned out, though, that Boots managers did not have the skills needed to succeed in health care services, and many of these markets offered little profit potential. The strategy contributed to Russell's early departure from the top job. Brigadier General Matthew Broderick, chief of the Homeland Security Operations Center, who was responsible for alerting

President Bush and other senior government officials if Hurricane Katrina breached the levees in New Orleans, went home on Monday, August 29, 2005, after reporting that they seemed to be holding, despite multiple reports of breaches.

All these executives were highly qualified for their jobs, and yet they made decisions that soon seemed clearly wrong. Why? And more important, how can we avoid making similar mistakes? This is the topic we've been exploring for the past four years, and the journey has taken us deep into a field called decision neuroscience. We began by assembling a database of 83 decisions that we felt were flawed at the time they were made. From our analysis of these cases, we concluded that flawed decisions start with errors of judgment made by influential individuals. Hence we needed to understand how these errors of judgment occur.

In the following pages, we will describe the conditions that promote errors of judgment and explore ways organizations can build protections into the decision-making process to reduce the risk of mistakes. We'll conclude by showing how two leading companies applied the approach we describe. To put all this in context, however, we first need to understand just how the human brain forms its judgments.

How the Brain Trips Up

We depend primarily on two hardwired processes for decision making. Our brains assess what's going on using pattern recognition, and we react to that information—or ignore it—because of emotional tags that are stored in our memories. Both of these processes are normally reliable; they are part of our evolutionary advantage. But in certain circumstances, both can let us down.

Pattern recognition is a complex process that integrates information from as many as 30 different parts of the brain. Faced with a new situation, we make assumptions based on prior experiences and judgments. Thus a chess master can assess a chess game and choose a high-quality move in as little as six seconds by drawing on patterns he or she has seen before. But pattern recognition can also

Idea in Brief

- Leaders make decisions largely through unconscious processes that neuroscientists call pattern recognition and emotional tagging. These processes usually make for quick, effective decisions, but they can be distorted by self-interest, emotional attachments, or misleading memories.

- Managers need to find systematic ways to recognize

the sources of bias—what the authors call "red flag conditions"—and then design safeguards that introduce more analysis, greater debate, or stronger governance.

- By using the approach described in this article, companies will avoid many flawed decisions that are caused by the way our brains operate.

mislead us. When we're dealing with seemingly familiar situations, our brains can cause us to think we understand them when we don't.

What happened to Matthew Broderick during Hurricane Katrina is instructive. Broderick had been involved in operations centers in Vietnam and in other military engagements, and he had led the Homeland Security Operations Center during previous hurricanes. These experiences had taught him that early reports surrounding a major event are often false: It's better to wait for the "ground truth" from a reliable source before acting. Unfortunately, he had no experience with a hurricane hitting a city built below sea level.

By late on August 29, some 12 hours after Katrina hit New Orleans, Broderick had received 17 reports of major flooding and levee breaches. But he also had gotten conflicting information. The Army Corps of Engineers had reported that it had no evidence of levee breaches, and a late afternoon CNN report from Bourbon Street in the French Quarter had shown city dwellers partying and claiming they had dodged the bullet. Broderick's pattern-recognition process told him that these contrary reports were the ground truth he was looking for. So before going home for the night, he issued a situation report stating that the levees had not been breached, although he did add that further assessment would be needed the next day.

Idea in Practice

Leaders make quick decisions by recognizing patterns in the situations they encounter, bolstered by emotional associations attached to those patterns. Most of the time, the process works well, but it can result in serious mistakes when judgments are biased.

Example: When Wang Laboratories launched its own personal computer, founder An Wang chose to create a proprietary operating system even though the IBM PC was clearly becoming the standard. This blunder was influenced by his belief that IBM had cheated him early in his career, which made him reluctant to consider using a system linked to an IBM product.

To guard against distorted decision making and strengthen the decision process, get the help of an independent person to identify which decision makers are likely to be affected by self-interest, emotional attachments, or misleading memories.

Example: The about-to-be-promoted head of the cosmetics business at one Indian company was considering whether to appoint her number two as her successor. She recognized that her judgment might be distorted by her attachment to her colleague and by her vested interest in keeping her workload down during her transition. The executive asked a headhunter to evaluate her colleague and to determine whether better candidates could be found externally.

If the risk of distorted decision making is high, companies need to build safeguards into the decision process: Expose decision makers to additional experience and analysis, design in more debate and opportunities for challenge, and add more oversight.

Example: In helping the CEO make an important strategic decision, the chairman of one global chemical company encouraged the chief executive to seek advice from investment bankers, set up a project team to analyze options, and create a steering committee that included the chairman and the CFO to generate the decision.

Emotional tagging is the process by which emotional information attaches itself to the thoughts and experiences stored in our memories. This emotional information tells us whether to pay attention to something or not, and it tells us what sort of action we should be contemplating (immediate or postponed, fight or flight). When the parts of our brains controlling emotions are damaged, we can see how important emotional tagging is: Neurological research shows that we become slow and incompetent decision makers even though we can retain the capacity for objective analysis.

Like pattern recognition, emotional tagging helps us reach sensible decisions most of the time. But it, too, can mislead us. Take the case of Wang Laboratories, the top company in the word-processing industry in the early 1980s. Recognizing that his company's future was threatened by the rise of the personal computer, founder An Wang built a machine to compete in this sector. Unfortunately, he chose to create a proprietary operating system despite the fact that the IBM PC was clearly becoming the dominant standard in the industry. This blunder, which contributed to Wang's demise a few years later, was heavily influenced by An Wang's dislike of IBM. He believed he had been cheated by IBM over a new technology he had invented early in his career. These feelings made him reject a software platform linked to an IBM product even though the platform was provided by a third party, Microsoft.

Why doesn't the brain pick up on such errors and correct them? The most obvious reason is that much of the mental work we do is unconscious. This makes it hard to check the data and logic we use when we make a decision. Typically, we spot bugs in our personal software only when we see the results of our errors in judgment. Matthew Broderick found out that his ground-truth rule of thumb was an inappropriate response to Hurricane Katrina only after it was too late. An Wang found out that his preference for proprietary software was flawed only after Wang's personal computer failed in the market.

Compounding the problem of high levels of unconscious thinking is the lack of checks and balances in our decision making. Our brains do not naturally follow the classical textbook model: Lay out the options, define the objectives, and assess each option against each objective. Instead, we analyze the situation using pattern recognition and arrive at a decision to act or not by using emotional tags. The two processes happen almost instantaneously. Indeed, as the research of psychologist Gary Klein shows, our brains leap to conclusions and are reluctant to consider alternatives. Moreover, we are particularly bad at revisiting our initial assessment of a situation—our initial frame.

An exercise we frequently run at Ashridge Business School shows how hard it is to challenge the initial frame. We give students a case that presents a new technology as a good business opportunity. Often, a team works many hours before it challenges this frame and starts, correctly, to see the new technology as a major threat to the company's dominant market position. Even though the financial model consistently calculates negative returns from launching the new technology, some teams never challenge their original frame and end up proposing aggressive investments.

Raising the Red Flag

In analyzing how it is that good leaders made bad judgments, we found they were affected in all cases by three factors that either distorted their emotional tags or encouraged them to see a false pattern. We call these factors "red flag conditions."

The first and most familiar red flag condition, *the presence of inappropriate self-interest*, typically biases the emotional importance we place on information, which in turn makes us readier to perceive the patterns we want to see. Research has shown that even well-intentioned professionals, such as doctors and auditors, are unable to prevent self-interest from biasing their judgments of which medicine to prescribe or opinion to give during an audit.

The second, somewhat less familiar condition is *the presence of distorting attachments*. We can become attached to people, places, and things, and these bonds can affect the judgments we form about both the situation we face and the appropriate actions to take. The reluctance executives often feel to sell a unit they've worked in nicely captures the power of inappropriate attachments.

The final red flag condition is *the presence of misleading memories*. These are memories that seem relevant and comparable to the current situation but lead our thinking down the wrong path. They can cause us to overlook or undervalue some important differentiating factors, as Matthew Broderick did when he gave too little thought to the implications of a hurricane hitting a city below sea level. The chance of being misled by memories is intensified by any emotional tags we have attached to the past experience. If our decisions in the previous similar experience worked well, we'll be all the more likely to overlook key differences.

That's what happened to William Smithburg, former chairman of Quaker Oats. He acquired Snapple because of his vivid memories of Gatorade, Quaker's most successful deal. Snapple, like Gatorade, appeared to be a new drinks company that could be improved with Quaker's marketing and management skills. Unfortunately, the similarities between Snapple and Gatorade proved to be superficial, which meant that Quaker ended up destroying rather than creating value. In fact, Snapple was Smithburg's worst deal.

Of course, part of what we are saying is common knowledge: People have biases, and it's important to manage decisions so that these biases balance out. Many experienced leaders do this already. But we're arguing here that, given the way the brain works, we cannot rely on leaders to spot and safeguard against their own errors in judgment. For important decisions, we need a deliberate, structured way to identify likely sources of bias—those red flag conditions—and we need to strengthen the group decision-making process.

Consider the situation faced by Rita Chakra, head of the cosmetics business of Choudry Holdings (the names of the companies and people cited in this and the following examples have been disguised). She was promoted head of the consumer products division and needed to decide whether to promote her number two into her cosmetics job or recruit someone from outside. Can we anticipate any potential red flags in this decision? Yes, her emotional tags could be unreliable because of a distorting attachment she may have to her colleague or an inappropriate self-interest she could have in keeping her workload down while changing jobs. Of course we don't know for certain whether Rita feels this attachment or holds that vested interest. And since the greater part of decision making is unconscious, Rita would not know either. What we do know is that there is a risk. So how should Rita protect herself, or how should her boss help her protect herself?

The simple answer is to involve someone else—someone who has no inappropriate attachments or self-interest. This could be Rita's boss, the head of human resources, a headhunter, or a trusted colleague. That person could challenge her thinking, force her to review her logic, encourage her to consider options, and possibly even champion a solution she would find uncomfortable. Fortunately, in this situation, Rita was already aware of some red flag conditions, and so she involved a headhunter to help her evaluate her colleague and external candidates. In the end, Rita did appoint her colleague but only after checking to see if her judgment was biased.

We've found many leaders who intuitively understand that their thinking or their colleagues' thinking can be distorted. But few leaders do so in a structured way, and as a result many fail to provide sufficient safeguards against bad decisions. Let's look now at a couple of companies that approached the problem of decision bias systematically by recognizing and reducing the risk posed by red flag conditions.

Safeguarding Against Your Biases

A European multinational we'll call Global Chemicals had an underperforming division. The management team in charge of the division had twice promised a turnaround and twice failed to deliver. The CEO, Mark Thaysen, was weighing his options.

This division was part of Thaysen's growth strategy. It had been assembled over the previous five years through two large and four smaller acquisitions. Thaysen had led the two larger acquisitions and appointed the managers who were struggling to perform. The chairman of the supervisory board, Olaf Grunweld, decided to consider whether Thaysen's judgment about the underperforming division might be biased and, if so, how he might help. Grunweld was not second-guessing Thaysen's thinking. He was merely alert to the possibility that the CEO's views might be distorted.

Grunweld started by looking for red flag conditions. (For a description of a process for identifying red flags, see the sidebar, "Identifying Red Flags.") Thaysen built the underperforming division, and his attachment to it might have made him reluctant to abandon the strategy or the team he had put in place. What's more, because in the past he had successfully supported the local managers during a tough turnaround in another division, Thaysen ran the risk of seeing the wrong pattern and unconsciously favoring the view that continued support was needed in this situation, too. Thus alerted to Thaysen's possible distorting attachments and potential misleading memories, Grunweld considered three types of safeguards to strengthen the decision process.

Injecting fresh experience or analysis

You can often counteract biases by exposing the decision maker to new information and a different take on the problem. In this instance, Grunweld asked an investment bank to tell Thaysen what value the company might get from selling the underperforming division. Grunweld felt this would encourage Thaysen to at least consider that radical option—a step Thaysen might too quickly dismiss if he had become overly attached to the unit or its management team.

Introducing further debate and challenge

This safeguard can ensure that biases are confronted explicitly. It works best when the power structure of the group debating the issue is balanced. While Thaysen's chief financial officer was a strong individual, Grunweld felt that the other members of the executive group would be likely to follow Thaysen's lead without challenging him. Moreover, the head of the underperforming division was a member of the executive group, making it hard for open debate to occur. So Grunweld proposed a steering committee consisting of himself, Thaysen, and the CFO. Even if Thaysen strongly pushed for a particular solution, Grunweld and the CFO would make sure his reasoning was properly challenged and debated. Grunweld also suggested that Thaysen set up a small project team, led by the head of strategy, to analyze all the options and present them to the steering committee.

Imposing stronger governance

The requirement that a decision be ratified at a higher level provides a final safeguard. Stronger governance does not eliminate distorted thinking, but it can prevent distortions from leading to a bad outcome. At Global Chemicals, the governance layer was the supervisory board. Grunweld realized, however, that its objectivity could be compromised because he was a member of both the board and the steering committee. So he asked two of his board colleagues to be ready to argue against the proposal emanating from the steering committee if they felt uncomfortable.

In the end, the steering committee proposed an outright sale of the division, a decision the board approved. The price received was well above expectations, convincing all that they had chosen the best option.

The chairman of Global Chemicals took the lead role in designing the decision process. That was appropriate given the importance of the decision. But many decisions are made at the operating level, where direct CEO involvement is neither feasible nor desirable. That was the case at Southern Electricity, a division of a larger U.S. utility. Southern consisted of three operating units and two powerful functions. Recent regulatory changes meant that prices could not be raised and might even fall. So managers were looking for ways to cut back on capital expenditures.

Division head Jack Williams recognized that the managers were also risk averse, preferring to replace equipment early with the best upgrades available. This, he realized, was a result of some high-profile breakdowns in the past, which had exposed individuals both to complaints from customers and to criticism from colleagues. Williams believed the emotional tags associated with these experiences might be distorting their judgment.

What could he do to counteract these effects? Williams rejected the idea of stronger governance; he felt that neither his management team nor the parent company's executives knew enough to do the job credibly. He also rejected additional analysis, because Southern's analysis was already rigorous. He concluded that he had to find

Identifying Red Flags

RED FLAGS ARE useful only if they can be spotted before a decision is made. How can you recognize them in complex situations? We have developed the following seven-step process:

1. Lay out the range of options. It's never possible to list them all. But it's normally helpful to note the extremes. These provide boundaries for the decision.

2. List the main decision makers. Who is going to be influential in making the judgment calls and the final choice? There may be only one or two people involved. But there could also be 10 or more.

3. Choose one decision maker to focus on. It's usually best to start with the most influential person. Then identify red flag conditions that might distort that individual's thinking.

4. Check for inappropriate self-interest or distorting attachments. Is any option likely to be particularly attractive or unattractive to the decision maker because of personal interests or attachments to people, places, or things? Do any of these interests or attachments conflict with the objectives of the main stakeholders?

5. Check for misleading memories. What are the uncertainties in this decision? For each area of uncertainty, consider whether the decision maker might draw on potentially misleading memories. Think about past experiences that could mislead, especially ones with strong emotional associations. Think also about previous judgments that could now be unsound, given the current situation.

6. Repeat the analysis with the next most influential person. In a complex case, it may be necessary to consider many more people, and the process may bring to light a long list of possible red flags.

7. Review the list of red flags you have identified and determine whether the brain's normally efficient pattern-recognition and emotional-tagging processes might be biased in favor of or against some options. If so, put one or more safeguards in place.

a way to inject more debate into the decision process and enable people who understood the details to challenge the thinking.

His first thought was to involve himself and his head of finance in the debates, but he didn't have time to consider the merits of hundreds of projects, and he didn't understand the details well enough to effectively challenge decisions earlier in the process than he currently was doing, at the final approval stage. Williams finally decided to get the unit and function heads to challenge one another, facilitated by a consultant. Rather than impose this process on his managers, Williams chose to share his thinking with them. Using the language of red flags, he was able to get them to see the problem without their feeling threatened. The new approach was very successful. The reduced capital-expenditure target was met with room to spare and without Williams having to make any of the tough judgment calls himself.

Because we now understand more about how the brain works, we can anticipate the circumstances in which errors of judgment may occur and guard against them. So rather than rely on the wisdom of experienced chairmen, the humility of CEOs, or the standard organizational checks and balances, we urge all involved in important decisions to explicitly consider whether red flags exist and, if they do, to lobby for appropriate safeguards. Decisions that involve no red flags need many fewer checks and balances and thus less bureaucracy. Some of those resources could then be devoted to protecting the decisions most at risk with more intrusive and robust protections.

Originally published in February 2009. Reprint R0902D

Building the Emotional Intelligence of Groups

by Vanessa Urch Druskat and Steven B. Wolff

WHEN MANAGERS FIRST STARTED HEARING ABOUT the concept of emotional intelligence in the 1990s, scales fell from their eyes. The basic message, that effectiveness in organizations is at least as much about EQ as IQ, resonated deeply; it was something that people knew in their guts but that had never before been so well articulated. Most important, the idea held the potential for positive change. Instead of being stuck with the hand they'd been dealt, people could take steps to enhance their emotional intelligence and make themselves more effective in their work and personal lives.

Indeed, the concept of emotional intelligence had real impact. The only problem is that so far emotional intelligence has been viewed only as an individual competency, when the reality is that most work in organizations is done by teams. And if managers have one pressing need today, it's to find ways to make teams work better.

It is with real excitement, therefore, that we share these findings from our research: individual emotional intelligence has a group analog, and it is just as critical to groups' effectiveness. Teams can develop greater emotional intelligence and, in so doing, boost their overall performance.

Why Should Teams Build Their Emotional Intelligence?

No one would dispute the importance of making teams work more effectively. But most research about how to do so has focused on identifying the task processes that distinguish the most successful teams—that is, specifying the need for cooperation, participation, commitment to goals, and so forth. The assumption seems to be that, once identified, these processes can simply be imitated by other teams, with similar effect. It's not true. By analogy, think of it this way: a piano student can be taught to play Minuet in G, but he won't become a modern-day Bach without knowing music theory and being able to play with heart. Similarly, the real source of a great team's success lies in the fundamental conditions that allow effective task processes to emerge—and that cause members to engage in them wholeheartedly.

Our research tells us that three conditions are essential to a group's effectiveness: trust among members, a sense of group identity, and a sense of group efficacy. When these conditions are absent, going through the motions of cooperating and participating is still possible. But the team will not be as effective as it could be, because members will choose to hold back rather than fully engage. To be most effective, the team needs to create emotionally intelligent norms—the attitudes and behaviors that eventually become habits—that support behaviors for building trust, group identity, and group efficacy. The outcome is complete engagement in tasks. (For more on how emotional intelligence influences these conditions, see the sidebar "A Model of Team Effectiveness.")

Three Levels of Emotional Interaction

Make no mistake: a team with emotionally intelligent members does not necessarily make for an emotionally intelligent group. A team, like any social group, takes on its own character. So creating an upward, self-reinforcing spiral of trust, group identity, and group efficacy requires more than a few members who exhibit emotionally intelligent behavior. It requires a team atmosphere in which the norms build emotional capacity (the ability to respond

Idea in Brief

How does IDEO, the celebrated industrial-design firm, ensure that its teams consistently produce the most innovative products under intense deadline and budget pressures? By focusing on its teams' **emotional intelligence**—that powerful combination of self-management skills and ability to relate to others.

Many executives realize that EQ (emotional quotient) is as critical as IQ to an individual's effectiveness. But *groups'* emotional intelligence may be even more important, since most work gets done in teams.

A group's EI isn't simply the sum of its members'. Instead, it comes from norms that support awareness and regulation of emotions within and outside the team. These norms build trust, group identity, and a sense of group efficacy. Members feel that they work better *together* than individually.

Group EI norms build the foundation for true collaboration and cooperation—helping otherwise skilled teams fulfill their highest potential.

constructively in emotionally uncomfortable situations) and influence emotions in constructive ways.

Team emotional intelligence is more complicated than individual emotional intelligence because teams interact at more levels. To understand the differences, let's first look at the concept of individual emotional intelligence as defined by Daniel Goleman. In his definitive book *Emotional Intelligence*, Goleman explains the chief characteristics of someone with high EI; he or she is *aware* of emotions and able to *regulate* them—and this awareness and regulation are directed both *inward*, to one's self, and *outward*, to others. "Personal competence," in Goleman's words, comes from being aware of and regulating one's own emotions. "Social competence" is awareness and regulation of others' emotions.

A group, however, must attend to yet another level of awareness and regulation. It must be mindful of the emotions of its members, its own group emotions or moods, and the emotions of other groups and individuals outside its boundaries.

In this article, we'll explore how emotional incompetence at any of these levels can cause dysfunction. We'll also show how

Idea in Practice

To build a foundation for emotional intelligence, a group must be aware of and constructively regulate the emotions of:

- individual team members

- the whole group

- other key groups with whom it interacts.

How? By establishing EI norms—rules for behavior that are introduced by group leaders, training, or the larger organizational culture. Here are some examples of norms—and what they look like in action—from IDEO:

Emotions of...	To Hone Awareness...	To Regulate...	IDEO Examples
Individual Team Members	Understand the sources of individuals' behavior and take steps to address problematic behavior. Encourage all group members to share their perspectives before making key decisions.	Handle confrontation constructively. If team members fall short, call them on it by letting them know the group needs them. Treat each other in a caring way—acknowledge when someone is upset; show appreciation and respect.	Awareness: A project leader notices a designer's frustration over a marketing decision and initiates negotiations to resolve the issue. Regulation: During brainstorming sessions, participants pelt colleagues with soft toys if they prematurely judge ideas.

establishing specific group norms that create awareness and regulation of emotion at these three levels can lead to better outcomes. First, we'll focus on the individual level—how emotionally intelligent groups work with their individual members' emotions. Next, we'll focus on the group level. And finally, we'll look at the cross-boundary level.

Working with Individuals' Emotions

Jill Kasper, head of her company's customer service department, is naturally tapped to join a new cross-functional team focused on enhancing the customer experience: she has extensive experience in

Emotions of . . .	To Hone Awareness . . .	To Regulate . . .	IDEO Examples
The Whole Group	Regularly assess the group's strengths, weaknesses, and modes of interaction. Invite reality checks from customers, colleagues, suppliers.	Create structures that let the group express its emotions. Cultivate an affirmative environment. Encourage proactive problem solving.	Awareness: Teams work closely with customers to determine what needs improvement. Regulation: "Finger-blaster" toys scattered around the office let people have fun and vent stress.
Other Key Groups	Designate team members as liaisons to key outside constituencies. Identify and support other groups' expectations and needs.	Develop cross-boundary relationships to gain outsiders' confidence. Know the broader social and political context in which your group must succeed. Show your appreciation of other groups.	Regulation: IDEO built such a good relationship with an outside fabricator that it was able to call on it for help during a crisis—on the weekend.

and a real passion for customer service. But her teammates find she brings little more than a bad attitude to the table. At an early brainstorming session, Jill sits silent, arms crossed, rolling her eyes. Whenever the team starts to get energized about an idea, she launches into a detailed account of how a similar idea went nowhere in the past. The group is confused: this is the customer service star they've been hearing about? Little do they realize she feels insulted by the very formation of the team. To her, it implies she hasn't done her job well enough.

When a member is not on the same emotional wavelength as the rest, a team needs to be emotionally intelligent vis-à-vis that individual. In part, that simply means being aware of the problem. Having a

A Model of Team Effectiveness

STUDY AFTER STUDY has shown that teams are more creative and productive when they can achieve high levels of participation, cooperation, and collaboration among members. But interactive behaviors like these aren't easy to legislate. Our work shows that three basic conditions need to be present before such behaviors can occur: mutual trust among members, a sense of group identity (a feeling among members that they belong to a unique and worthwhile group), and a sense of group efficacy (the belief that the team can perform well and that group members are more effective working together than apart).

At the heart of these three conditions are emotions. Trust, a sense of identity, and a feeling of efficacy arise in environments where emotion is well handled, so groups stand to benefit by building their emotional intelligence.

Group emotional intelligence isn't a question of dealing with a necessary evil—catching emotions as they bubble up and promptly suppressing them. Far from it. It's about bringing emotions deliberately to the surface and understanding how they affect the team's work. It's also about behaving in ways that build relationships both inside and outside the team and that strengthen the team's ability to face challenges. Emotional intelligence means exploring, embracing, and ultimately relying on emotion in work that is, at the end of the day, deeply human.

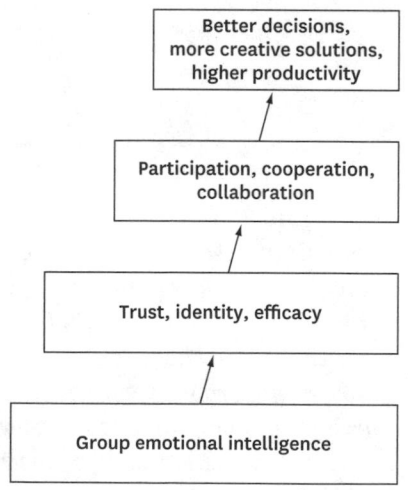

norm that encourages interpersonal understanding might facilitate an awareness that Jill is acting out of defensiveness. And picking up on this defensiveness is necessary if the team wants to make her understand its desire to amplify her good work, not negate it.

Some teams seem to be able to do this naturally. At Hewlett-Packard, for instance, we learned of a team that was attempting to cross-train its members. The idea was that if each member could pinch-hit on everyone else's job, the team could deploy efforts to whatever task required the most attention. But one member seemed very uncomfortable with learning new skills and tasks; accustomed to being a top producer in his own job, he hated not knowing how to do a job perfectly. Luckily, his teammates recognized his discomfort, and rather than being annoyed, they redoubled their efforts to support him. This team benefited from a group norm it had established over time emphasizing interpersonal understanding. The norm had grown out of the group's realization that working to accurately hear and understand one another's feelings and concerns improved member morale and a willingness to cooperate.

Many teams build high emotional intelligence by taking pains to consider matters from an individual member's perspective. Think of a situation where a team of four must reach a decision; three favor one direction and the fourth favors another. In the interest of expedience, many teams in this situation would move directly to a majority vote. But a more emotionally intelligent group would pause first to hear out the objection. It would also ask if everyone were completely behind the decision, even if there appeared to be consensus. Such groups would ask, "Are there any perspectives we haven't heard yet or thought through completely?"

Perspective taking is a team behavior that teamwork experts discuss often—but not in terms of its emotional consequence. Many teams are trained to use perspective-taking techniques to make decisions or solve problems (a common tool is affinity diagramming). But these techniques may or may not improve a group's emotional intelligence. The problem is that many of these techniques consciously attempt to remove emotion from the process by collecting and combining perspectives in a mechanical way. A more effective approach to perspective taking is to ensure that team members see one another making the effort to grapple with perspectives; that way, the team has a better chance of creating the kind of trust that leads to greater participation among members.

An executive team at the Hay Group, a consulting firm, engages in the kind of deep perspective taking we're describing. The team has done role-playing exercises in which members adopt others' opinions and styles of interaction. It has also used a "storyboarding" technique, in which each member creates a small poster representing his or her ideas. As team members will attest, these methods and others have helped the group build trust and increase participation.

Regulating Individuals' Emotions

Interpersonal understanding and perspective taking are two ways that groups can become more aware of their members' perspectives and feelings. But just as important as awareness is the ability to regulate those emotions—to have a positive impact on how they are expressed and even on how individual team members feel. We're not talking about imposing groupthink or some other form of manipulation here—clearly, the goal must be to balance the team's cohesion with members' individuality. We're simply acknowledging that people take their emotional cues from those around them. Something that seems upsetting initially can seem not so bad— or ten times worse—depending on whether one's colleagues are inclined to smooth feathers or fan flames. The most constructive way of regulating team members' emotions is by establishing norms in the group for both confrontation and caring.

It may seem illogical to suggest that an emotionally intelligent group must engage in confrontation, but it's not. Inevitably, a team member will indulge in behavior that crosses the line, and the team must feel comfortable calling the foul. In one manufacturing team we studied, a member told us about the day she selfishly decided to extend her break. Before long, one of her teammates stormed into the break room, saying, "What are you doing in here? Get back out on the floor—your team needs you!" The woman had overstepped the bounds, and she got called on it. There were no hard feelings, because the woman knew the group valued her contributions.

Some teams also find that a little humor helps when pointing out errant behavior. Teasing someone who is habitually late for meetings, for instance, can make that person aware of how important timeliness is to the group. Done right, confrontation can be seen in a positive light; it's a way for the group to say, "We want you in—we need your contribution." And it's especially important when a team must work together on a long-term assignment. Without confrontation, disruptive behavior can fester and erode a sense of trust in a team.

Establishing norms that reinforce caring behavior is often not very difficult and usually a matter of concentrating on little things. When an individual is upset, for example, it may make all the difference to have group members acknowledge that person's feelings. We saw this in a meeting where one team member arrived angry because the time and place of the meeting was very inconvenient for him. When another member announced the sacrifice the man had made to be there, and thanked him, the man's attitude turned around 180 degrees. In general, a caring orientation includes displaying positive regard, appreciation, and respect for group members through behaviors such as support, validation, and compassion.

Interpersonal understanding, perspective taking, confrontation, caring—these norms build trust and a sense of group identity among members. And all of them can be established in teams where they don't arise naturally. You may ask, But is it really worth all the effort? Does it make sense to spend managerial time fostering new norms to accommodate a few prickly personalities? Of course it does. Teams are at the very foundation of an organization, and they won't work effectively without mutual trust and a common commitment to goals.

Working with Group Emotions

Chris couldn't believe it, but he was requesting a reassignment. The team he was on was doing good work, staying on budget, and hitting all its deadlines—though not always elegantly. Its leader, Stan Evans, just got a promotion. So why was being on the team such a downer? At the last major status meeting, they should have been serving champagne—so much had been achieved. Instead, everyone was thoroughly dispirited over a setback they hadn't foreseen, which turned out later to be no big deal. It seemed no matter what happened, the group griped. The team even saw Stan's promotion in a negative light: "Oh, so I guess management wants to keep a closer eye on us" and "I hear Stan's new boss doesn't back this project." Chris had a friend on another team who was happy to put in a good word for him. The work was inherently less interesting—but hey, at least they were having fun.

Some teams suffer because they aren't aware of emotions at the group level. Chris's team, for instance, isn't aware of all it has achieved, and it doesn't acknowledge that it has fallen into a malaise. In our study of effective teams, we've found that having norms for group self-awareness—of emotional states, strengths and weaknesses, modes of interaction, and task processes—is a critical part of group emotional intelligence that facilitates group efficacy. Teams gain it both through self-evaluation and by soliciting feedback from others.

Self-evaluation can take the form of a formal event or a constant activity. At Sherwin Williams, a group of managers was starting a new initiative that would require higher levels of teamwork. Group members hired a consultant, but before the consultant arrived, they met to assess their strengths and weaknesses as a team. They found that merely articulating the issues was an important step toward building their capabilities.

A far less formal method of raising group emotional awareness is through the kind of activity we saw at the Veterans Health Administration's Center for Leadership and Development. Managers there have developed a norm in which they are encouraged to speak up when they feel the group is not being productive. For example, if there's a post-lunch lull and people on the team are low on energy, someone might say, "Don't we look like a bunch of sad sacks?" With attention called to it, the group makes an effort to refocus.

Emotionally competent teams don't wear blinders; they have the emotional capacity to face potentially difficult information and actively seek opinions on their task processes, progress, and performance from the outside. For some teams, feedback may come directly from customers. Others look to colleagues within the company, to suppliers, or to professional peers. A group of designers we studied routinely posts its work in progress on walls throughout the building, with invitations to comment and critique. Similarly, many advertising agencies see annual industry competitions as a valuable source of feedback on their creative teams' work.

Regulating Group Emotions

Many teams make conscious efforts to build team spirit. Team-building outings, whether purely social or Outward Bound–style physical challenges, are popular methods for building this sense of collective enthusiasm. What's going on here is that teams and their leaders recognize they can improve a team's overall attitude—that is, they are regulating group-level emotion. And while the focus of a team-building exercise is often not directly related to a group's actual work, the benefits are highly relevant: teams come away with higher emotional capacity and thus a greater ability to respond to emotional challenges.

The most effective teams we have studied go far beyond the occasional "ropes and rocks" off-site. They have established norms that strengthen their ability to respond effectively to the kind of emotional challenges a group confronts on a daily basis. The norms they favor accomplish three main things: they create resources for working with emotions, foster an affirmative environment, and encourage proactive problem solving.

Teams need resources that all members can draw on to deal with group emotions. One important resource is a common vocabulary. To use an example, a group member at the Veterans Health Administration picked up on another member's bad mood and told him that he was just "cranky" today. The "cranky" term stuck and became the group's gentle way of letting someone know that their negativity was having a bad effect on the group. Other resources may include helpful ways to vent frustrations. One executive team leader we interviewed described his team's practice of making time for a "wailing wall"—a few minutes of whining and moaning about some setback. Releasing and acknowledging those negative emotions, the leader says, allows the group to refocus its attention on the parts of the situation it can control and channel its energy in a positive direction. But sometimes, venting takes more than words. We've seen more than one intense workplace outfitted with toys—like soft projectile shooters—that have been used in games of cube warfare.

Perhaps the most obvious way to build emotional capacity through regulating team-level emotion is simply to create an affirmative environment. Everyone values a team that, when faced with a challenge, responds with a can-do attitude. Again, it's a question of having the right group norms—in this case, favoring optimism, and positive images and interpretations over negative ones. This doesn't always come naturally to a team, as one executive we interviewed at the Hay Group knows. When external conditions create a cycle of negativity among group members, he takes it upon himself to change the atmosphere of the group. He consciously resists the temptation to join the complaining and blaming and instead tries to reverse the cycle with a positive, constructive note.

One of the most powerful norms we have seen for building a group's ability to respond to emotionally challenging situations is an emphasis on proactive problem solving. We saw a lot of this going on in a manufacturing team we observed at AMP Corporation. Much of what this team needed to hit its targets was out of its strict control. But rather than sit back and point fingers, the team worked hard to get what it needed from others, and in some cases, took matters into its own hands. In one instance, an alignment problem in a key machine was creating faulty products. The team studied the problem and approached the engineering group with its own suggested design for a part that might correct the problem. The device worked, and the number of defective products decreased significantly.

This kind of problem solving is valuable for many reasons. It obviously serves the company by removing one more obstacle to profitability. But, to the point of our work, it also shows a team in control of its own emotions. It refused to feel powerless and was eager to take charge.

Working with Emotions Outside the Group

Jim sighed. The "Bugs" team was at it again. Didn't they see that while they were high-fiving one another over their impressive productivity, the rest of the organization was paying for it? This time, in their self-managed wisdom, they'd decided to make a three months' supply of one component. No changeover meant no machine downtime and a record low cost per unit. But now the group downstream was swamped with inventory it didn't need and worried about shortages of something else. Jim braced himself for his visit to the floor. The Bugs didn't take criticism well; they seemed to think they were flawless and that everyone else was just trying to take them down a notch. And what was with that name, anyway? Some kind of inside joke, Jim guessed. Too bad nobody else got it.

The last kind of emotional intelligence any high-performing team should have relates to cross-boundary relationships. Just as individuals should be mindful of their own emotions and others', groups should look both inward and outward emotionally. In the case of the Bugs, the team is acting like a clique—creating close emotional ties within but ignoring the feelings, needs, and concerns of important individuals and teams in the broader organization.

Some teams have developed norms that are particularly helpful in making them aware of the broader organizational context. One practice is to have various team members act as liaisons to important constituencies. Many teams are already made up of members drawn from different parts of an organization, so a cross-boundary perspective comes naturally. Others need to work a little harder. One team we studied realized it would be important to understand the perspective of its labor union. Consequently, a team member from HR went to some lengths to discover the right channels for having a union member appointed to the group. A cross-boundary perspective is especially important in situations where a team's work will have significant impact on others in the organization—for example, where a team is asked to design an intranet to serve everyone's needs. We've seen many situations in which a team is so enamored of its solution that it is caught completely by surprise when others in the company don't share its enthusiasm.

85

Some of the most emotionally intelligent teams we have seen are so attuned to their broader organizational context that it affects how they frame and communicate their own needs and accomplishments. A team at the chemical-processing company KoSa, for example, felt it needed a new piece of manufacturing equipment, but senior management wasn't so sure the purchase was a priority. Aware that the decision makers were still on the fence, the team decided to emphasize the employee safety benefits of the new machine—just one aspect of its desirability to them, but an issue of paramount importance to management. At a plant safety meeting attended by high-level managers, they made the case that the equipment they were seeking would greatly reduce the risk of injury to workers. A few weeks later they got it.

Sometimes, a team must be particularly aware of the needs and feelings of another group within the organization. We worked with an information technology company where the hardware engineers worked separately from the software engineers to achieve the same goal—faster processing and fewer crashes. Each could achieve only so much independently. When finally a hardware team leader went out of his way to build relationships with the software people, the two teams began to cooperate—and together, they achieved 20% to 40% higher performance than had been targeted.

This kind of positive outcome can be facilitated by norms that encourage a group to recognize the feelings and needs of other groups. We saw effective norms for interteam awareness at a division of AMP, where each manufacturing team is responsible for a step in the manufacturing process and they need one another to complete the product on time. Team leaders there meet in the morning to understand the needs, resources, and schedules of each team. If one team is ahead and another is behind, they reallocate resources. Members of the faster team help the team that's behind and do so in a friendly way that empathizes with their situation and builds the relationship.

Most of the examples we've been citing show teams that are not only aware of but also able to influence outsiders' needs and perspectives. This ability to regulate emotion at the cross-boundary level is a group's version of the "social skills" so critical to individual emotional intelligence. It involves developing external relationships and gaining the confidence of outsiders, adopting an ambassadorial role instead of an isolationist one.

A manufacturing team we saw at KoSa displayed very high social skills in working with its maintenance team. It recognized that, when problems occurred in the plant, the maintenance team often had many activities on its plate. All things being equal, what would make the maintenance team consider this particular manufacturing group a high priority? Knowing a good relationship would be a factor, the manufacturing team worked hard to build good ties with the maintenance people. At one point, for instance, the manufacturing team showed its appreciation by nominating the maintenance team for "Team of the Quarter" recognition—and then doing all the letter writing and behind-the-scenes praising that would ultimately help the maintenance team win. In turn, the manufacturing team's good relationship with maintenance helped it become one of the highest producers in the plant.

A Model for Group Emotional Intelligence

We've been discussing the need for teams to learn to channel emotion effectively at the three levels of human interaction important to them: team to individual member, team to itself, and team to outside entities. Together, the norms we've been exploring help groups work with emotions productively and intelligently. Often, groups with emotionally intelligent members have norms like these in place, but it's unlikely any group would unconsciously come up with *all* the norms we have outlined. In other words, this is a model for group emotional intelligence that any work team could benefit from by applying it deliberately.

What would the ultimate emotionally intelligent team look like? Closest to the ideal are some of the teams we've seen at IDEO, the celebrated industrial design firm. IDEO's creative teams are responsible for the look and feel of products like Apple's first mouse, the Crest toothpaste tube, and the Palm V personal digital assistant. The firm routinely wins competitions for the form and function of its designs and even has a business that teaches creative problem-solving techniques to other companies.

The nature of IDEO's work calls for high group emotional intelligence. Under pressure of client deadlines and budget estimates, the company must deliver innovative, aesthetic solutions that balance human needs with engineering realities. It's a deep philosophical belief at IDEO that great design is best accomplished through the creative friction of diverse teams and not the solitary pursuit of brilliant individuals, so it's imperative that the teams at IDEO click. In our study of those teams, we found group norms supporting emotional intelligence at all three levels of our model.

First, the teams at IDEO are very aware of individual team members' emotions, and they are adept at regulating them. For example, an IDEO designer became very frustrated because someone from marketing was insisting a logo be applied to the designer's product, which he felt would ruin it visually. At a meeting about the product, the team's project leader picked up on the fact that something was wrong. The designer was sitting off by himself, and things "didn't look right." The project leader looked into the situation and then initiated a negotiation that led to a mutual solution.

IDEO team members also confront one another when they break norms. This is common during brainstorming sessions, where the rule is that people must defer judgment and avoid shooting down ideas. If someone breaks that norm, the team comes down on him in a playful yet forceful way (imagine being pelted by foam toys). Or if someone is out of line, the norm is to stand up and call her on it immediately. If a client is in the room, the confrontation is subtler—perhaps a kick under the chair.

Teams at IDEO also demonstrate strengths in group-focused emotional intelligence. To ensure they have a high level of self-awareness, teams constantly seek feedback from both inside and outside the organization. Most important, they work very closely with customers. If a design is not meeting customer expectations, the team finds out quickly and takes steps to modify it.

Regulating group emotion at IDEO often means providing outlets for stress. This is a company that believes in playing and having fun.

Several hundred finger blasters (a toy that shoots soft projectiles) have been placed around the building for employees to pick up and start shooting when they're frustrated. Indeed, the design firm's culture welcomes the expression of emotions, so it's not uncommon for someone—whether happy or angry—to stand up and yell. IDEO has even created fun office projects that people can work on if they need a break. For example, they might have a project to design the company holiday card or to design the "tourist stop" displays seen by visitors.

Finally, IDEO teams also have norms to ensure they are aware of the needs and concerns of people outside their boundaries and that they use that awareness to develop relationships with those individuals and groups. On display at IDEO is a curious model: a toy truck with plastic pieces on springs that pop out of the bed of the truck when a button is pressed. It turns out the model commemorates an incident that taught a variety of lessons. The story centers on a design team that had been working for three weeks on a very complex plastic enclosure for a product. Unfortunately, on the Thursday before a Monday client deadline, when an engineer was taking it to be painted, it slipped from his pickup bed and exploded on the road at 70 mph. The team was willing to work through the weekend to rebuild the part but couldn't finish it without the help of the outside fabricator it had used on the original. Because they had taken the time to build a good relationship with the fabricator, its people were willing to go above and beyond the call of duty. The lighthearted display was a way for teammates to show the engineer that all was forgiven—and a reminder to the rest of the organization of how a team in crisis can get by with a little help from its friends.

Where Do Norms Come From?

Not every company is as dependent on teams and their emotional intelligence as IDEO. But now more than ever, we see companies depending on teams for decisions and tasks that, in another time, would have been the work of individuals. And unfortunately, we also see them discovering that a team can have everything going

Building Norms for Three Levels of Group Emotional Intelligence

GROUP EMOTIONAL INTELLIGENCE IS ABOUT the small acts that make a big difference. It is not about a team member working all night to meet a deadline; it is about saying thank you for doing so. It is not about in-depth discussion of ideas; it is about asking a quiet member for his thoughts. It is not about harmony, lack of tension, and all members liking each other; it is about acknowledging when harmony is false, tension is unexpressed, and treating others with respect. The following table outlines some of the small things that groups can do to establish the norms that build group emotional intelligence.

Individual	Group	Cross-Boundary
Norms that create awareness of emotions		
Interpersonal understanding	*Team self-evaluation*	*Organizational understanding*
1. Take time away from group tasks to get to know one another.	1. Schedule time to examine team effectiveness.	1. Find out the concerns and needs of others in the organization.
2. Have a "check in" at the beginning of the meeting—that is, ask how everyone is doing.	2. Create measurable task and process objectives and then measure them.	2. Consider who can influence the team's ability to accomplish its goals.
3. Assume that undesirable behavior takes place for a reason. Find out what that reason is. Ask questions and listen. Avoid negative attributions.	3. Acknowledge and discuss group moods.	3. Discuss the culture and politics in the organization.
	4. Communicate your sense of what is transpiring in the team.	4. Ask whether proposed team actions are congruent with the organization's culture and politics.
4. Tell your teammates what you're thinking and how you're feeling.	5. Allow members to call a "process check." (For instance, a team member might say, "Process check: is this the most effective use of our time right now?")	
Perspective taking	*Seeking feedback*	
1. Ask whether everyone agrees with a decision.	1. Ask your "customers" how you are doing.	
2. Ask quiet members what they think.	2. Post your work and invite comments.	
3. Question decisions that come too quickly.	3. Benchmark your processes.	
4. Appoint a devil's advocate.		

Individual	Group	Cross-Boundary
Norms that help regulate emotions		

Individual	Group	Cross-Boundary
Confronting 1. Set ground rules and use them to point out errant behavior. 2. Call members on errant behavior. 3. Create playful devices for pointing out such behavior. These often emerge from the group spontaneously. Reinforce them. *Caring* 1. Support members: volunteer to help them if they need it, be flexible, and provide emotional support. 2. Validate members' contributions. Let members know they are valued. 3. Protect members from attack. 4. Respect individuality and differences in perspectives. Listen. 5. Never be derogatory or demeaning.	*Creating resources for working with emotion* 1. Make time to discuss difficult issues, and address the emotions that surround them. 2. Find creative, shorthand ways to acknowledge and express the emotion in the group. 3. Create fun ways to acknowledge and relieve stress and tension. 4. Express acceptance of members' emotions. *Creating an affirmative environment* 1. Reinforce that the team can meet a challenge. Be optimistic. For example, say things like, "We can get through this" or "Nothing will stop us." 2. Focus on what you can control. 3. Remind members of the group's important and positive mission. 4. Remind the group how it solved a similar problem before. 5. Focus on problem solving, not blaming. *Solving problems proactively* 1. Anticipate problems and address them before they happen. 2. Take the initiative to understand and get what you need to be effective. 3. Do it yourself if others aren't responding. Rely on yourself, not others.	*Building external relationships* 1. Create opportunities for networking and interaction. 2. Ask about the needs of other teams. 3. Provide support for other teams. 4. Invite others to team meetings if they might have a stake in what you are doing.

for it—the brightest and most qualified people, access to resources, a clear mission—but still fail because it lacks group emotional intelligence.

Norms that build trust, group identity, and group efficacy are the key to making teams click. They allow an otherwise highly skilled and resourced team to fulfill its potential, and they can help a team faced with substantial challenges achieve surprising victories. So how do norms as powerful as the ones we've described in this article come about? In our research, we saw them being introduced from any of five basic directions: by formal team leaders, by informal team leaders, by courageous followers, through training, or from the larger organizational culture. (For more on how to establish the norms described in this article, see the sidebar "Building Norms for Three Levels of Group Emotional Intelligence.")

At the Hay Group, for example, it was the deliberate action of a team leader that helped one group see the importance of emotions to the group's overall effectiveness. Because this particular group was composed of managers from many different cultures, its leader knew he couldn't assume all the members possessed a high level of inter-personal understanding. To establish that norm, he introduced novel-ties like having a meeting without a table, using smaller groups, and conducting an inventory of team members' various learning styles.

Interventions like these can probably be done only by a formal team leader. The ways informal leaders or other team members enhance emotional intelligence are typically more subtle, though often just as powerful. Anyone might advance the cause, for exam-ple, by speaking up if the group appears to be ignoring an important perspective or feeling—or simply by doing his or her part to create an affirmative environment.

Training courses can also go a long way toward increasing emo-tional awareness and showing people how to regulate emotions. We know of many companies that now focus on emotional issues in leadership development courses, negotiation and communication workshops, and employee-assistance programs like those for stress management. These training programs can sensitize team members to the importance of establishing emotionally intelligent norms.

Finally, perhaps more than anything, a team can be influenced by a broader organizational culture that recognizes and celebrates employee emotion. This is clearly the case at IDEO and, we believe, at many of the companies creating the greatest value in the new economy. Unfortunately, it's the most difficult piece of the puzzle to put in place at companies that don't already have it. For organizations with long histories of employees checking their emotions at the door, change will occur, if at all, one team at a time.

Becoming Intelligent About Emotion

The research presented in this article arose from one simple imperative: in an era of teamwork, it's essential to figure out what makes teams work. Our research shows that, just like individuals, the most effective teams are emotionally intelligent ones—and that any team can attain emotional intelligence.

In this article, we've attempted to lay out a model for positive change, containing the most important types of norms a group can create to enhance its emotional intelligence. Teams, like all groups, operate according to such norms. By working to establish norms for emotional awareness and regulation at all levels of interaction, teams can build the solid foundation of trust, group identity, and group efficacy they need for true cooperation and collaboration— and high performance overall.

Originally published in March 2001. Reprint R0103E

The Price of Incivility

Lack of Respect Hurts Morale—and the Bottom Line.
by Christine Porath and Christine Pearson

RUDENESS AT WORK IS RAMPANT, and it's on the rise. Over the past 14 years we've polled thousands of workers about how they're treated on the job, and 98% have reported experiencing uncivil behavior. In 2011 half said they were treated rudely at least once a week—up from a quarter in 1998.

The costs chip away at the bottom line. Nearly everybody who experiences workplace incivility responds in a negative way, in some cases overtly retaliating. Employees are less creative when they feel disrespected, and many get fed up and leave. About half deliberately decrease their effort or lower the quality of their work. And incivility damages customer relationships. Our research shows that people are less likely to buy from a company with an employee they perceive as rude, whether the rudeness is directed at them or at other employees. Witnessing just a single unpleasant interaction leads customers to generalize about other employees, the organization, and even the brand.

We've interviewed employees, managers, HR executives, presidents, and CEOs. We've administered questionnaires, run experiments, led workshops, and spoken with doctors, lawyers, judges, law enforcement officers, architects, engineers, consultants, and coaches about how they've faced and handled incivility. And we've collected data from more than 14,000 people throughout the United States and Canada in order to track the prevalence, types, causes, costs, and cures of incivility at work. We know two things for certain: Incivility is expensive, and few organizations recognize or take action to curtail it.

In this article we'll discuss our findings, detail the costs, and propose some interventions. But first, let's look at the various shapes incivility can take.

Forms of Incivility

We've all heard of (or experienced) the "boss from hell." The stress of ongoing hostility from a manager takes a toll, sometimes a big one. We spoke with a man we'll call Matt, who reported to Larry—a volatile bully who insulted his direct reports, belittled their efforts, and blamed them for things over which they had no control. (The names in this article have been changed and the identities disguised.) Larry was rude to customers, too. When he accompanied Matt to one client's store, he told the owner, "I see you're carrying on your father's tradition. This store looked like sh-- then. And it looks like sh-- in your hands."

Matt's stress level skyrocketed. He took a risk and reported Larry to HR. (He wasn't the first to complain.) Called on the carpet, Larry failed to apologize, saying only that perhaps he "used an atomic bomb" when he "could have used a flyswatter." Weeks later Larry was named district manager of the year. Three days after that, Matt had a heart attack.

The conclusion of Matt's story is unusual, but unchecked rudeness is surprisingly common. We heard of one boss who was so routinely abusive that employees and suppliers had a code for alerting one another to his impending arrival ("The eagle has landed!"). The only positive aspect was that their shared dislike helped the employees forge close bonds. After the company died, in the late 1990s, its alums formed a network that thrives to this day.

In some cases an entire department is infected. Jennifer worked in an industry that attracted large numbers of educated young professionals willing to work for a pittance in order to be in a creative

Idea in Brief

Leaders can counter rudeness at work both by monitoring their own actions and by fostering civility in others.

Strategies for managing yourself include modeling good behavior and asking for feedback. Turn off your iPhone during meetings, pay attention to questions, and follow up on promises.

When it comes to managing the organization, you should hire for civility, teach it, create group norms, reward positive behavior, penalize rudeness, and seek out former employees for an honest assessment of your company's culture.

Failure to keep tabs on behavior can allow incivility to creep into everyday interactions—and could cost your organization millions in lost employees, lost customers, and lost productivity.

field. It was widely accepted that they had to pay their dues. The atmosphere included door slamming, side conversations, exclusion, and blatant disregard for people's time. Years later Jennifer still cringes as she remembers her boss screaming, "You made a mistake!" when she'd overlooked a minor typo in an internal memo. There was lots of attrition among low-level employees, but those who did stay seemed to absorb the behaviors they'd been subjected to, and they put newcomers through the same kind of abuse.

Fran was a senior executive in a global consumer products company. After several quarters of outstanding growth despite a down economy, she found herself confronted by a newcomer in the C-suite, Joe. For six months Fran had to jump through hoops to defend the business, even though it had defied stagnation. She never got an explanation for why she was picked on, and eventually she left, not for another job but to escape what she called "a soul-destroying experience."

Incivility can take much more subtle forms, and it is often prompted by thoughtlessness rather than actual malice. Think of the manager who sends e-mails during a presentation, or the boss who "teases" direct reports in ways that sting, or the team leader who takes credit for good news but points a finger at team members when something goes wrong. Such relatively minor acts can be even more insidious than overt bullying, because they are less obvious and easier to overlook—yet they add up, eroding engagement and morale.

The Costs of Incivility

Many managers would say that incivility is wrong, but not all recognize that it has tangible costs. Targets of incivility often punish their offenders and the organization, although most hide or bury their feelings and don't necessarily think of their actions as revenge. Through a poll of 800 managers and employees in 17 industries, we learned just how people's reactions play out. Among workers who've been on the receiving end of incivility:

- 48% intentionally decreased their work effort.
- 47% intentionally decreased the time spent at work.
- 38% intentionally decreased the quality of their work.
- 80% lost work time worrying about the incident.
- 63% lost work time avoiding the offender.
- 66% said that their performance declined.
- 78% said that their commitment to the organization declined.
- 12% said that they left their job because of the uncivil treatment.
- 25% admitted to taking their frustration out on customers.

Experiments and other reports offer additional insights about the effects of incivility. Here are some examples of what can happen.

Creativity suffers

In an experiment we conducted with Amir Erez, a professor of management at the University of Florida, participants who were treated rudely by other subjects were 30% less creative than others in the study. They produced 25% fewer ideas, and the ones they did come up with were less original. For example, when asked what to do with a brick, participants who had been treated badly proposed logical but not particularly imaginative activities, such as "build a house," "build a wall," and "build a school." We saw more sparks from participants who had been treated civilly; their suggestions included "sell the brick on eBay," "use it as a goalpost for a street soccer game," "hang it on a museum wall and call it abstract art," and "decorate it like a pet and give it to a kid as a present."

Performance and team spirit deteriorate
Survey results and interviews indicate that simply witnessing incivility has negative consequences. In one experiment we conducted, people who'd observed poor behavior performed 20% worse on word puzzles than other people did. We also found that witnesses to incivility were less likely than others to help out, even when the person they'd be helping had no apparent connection to the uncivil person: Only 25% of the subjects who'd witnessed incivility volunteered to help, whereas 51% of those who hadn't witnessed it did.

Customers turn away
Public rudeness among employees is common, according to our survey of 244 consumers. Whether it's waiters berating fellow waiters or store clerks criticizing colleagues, disrespectful behavior makes people uncomfortable, and they're quick to walk out without making a purchase.

We studied this phenomenon with the USC marketing professors Debbie MacInnis and Valerie Folkes. In one experiment, half the participants witnessed a supposed bank representative publicly reprimanding another for incorrectly presenting credit card information. Only 20% of those who'd seen the encounter said that they would use the bank's services in the future, compared with 80% of those who hadn't. And nearly two-thirds of those who'd seen the exchange said that they would feel anxious dealing with *any* employee of the bank.

What's more, when we tested various scenarios, we found that it didn't matter whether the targeted employee was incompetent,

99

whether the reprimand had been delivered behind closed doors (but overheard), or whether the employee had done something questionable or illegal, such as park in a handicapped spot. Regardless of the circumstances, people don't like to see others treated badly.

Managing incidents is expensive

HR professionals say that just one incident can soak up weeks of attention and effort. According to a study conducted by Accountemps and reported in *Fortune,* managers and executives at *Fortune* 1,000 firms spend 13% percent of their work time—the equivalent of seven weeks a year—mending employee relationships and otherwise dealing with the aftermath of incivility. And costs soar, of course, when consultants or attorneys must be brought in to help settle a situation.

What's a Leader to Do?

It can take constant vigilance to keep the workplace civil; otherwise, rudeness tends to creep into everyday interactions. Managers can use several strategies to keep their own behavior in check and to foster civility among others.

Managing yourself

Leaders set the tone, so you need to be aware of your actions and of how you come across to others.

Model good behavior. In one of our surveys, 25% of managers who admitted to having behaved badly said they were uncivil because their leaders—their own role models—were rude. If employees see that those who have climbed the corporate ladder tolerate or embrace uncivil behavior, they're likely to follow suit. So turn off your iPhone during meetings, pay attention to questions, and follow up on promises.

One way to help create a culture of respect and bring out your employees' best is to express your appreciation. Personal notes are particularly effective, especially if they emphasize being a role model, treating people well, and living the organization's values. Doug Conant, a former CEO of Campbell Soup, is well aware of the power of personal recognition. During his tenure as president and CEO, he sent more than 30,000 handwritten notes of thanks to employees.

Ask for feedback. You may need a reality check from the people who work for you. A manager at Hanover Insurance decided to ask his employees what they liked and didn't like about his leadership style. He learned that it really bothered them when he glanced at his phone or responded to e-mail during meetings. He now refrains from those activities, and his team appreciates the change.

Employees won't always be honest, but there are tools you can use on your own. For example, keep a journal in which you track instances of civility and incivility and note changes that you'd like to make.

Pay attention to your progress. As Josef, an IT professional, learned more about incivility, he became aware of his tendency to disparage a few nasty colleagues behind their backs. "I hadn't thought about it much until I considered the negative role modeling I was doing," he told us. "I criticized only people who were obnoxious to others and shared my criticisms only with people I trusted and in private, and somehow that made it seem OK. Then I started thinking about how I was just adding to the divide by spreading gossip and creating 'sides.' It was a real eye-opener, and I decided that I wanted to set a better example."

Within a short time Josef noticed that he was logging fewer occasions when he gossiped negatively and that he felt better about himself and his workplace. "I don't know whether anyone else would notice a difference—people already thought I was fair and supportive—but I know that I've changed," he said. "And there's another benefit for all of us: I'm seeing less incivility around me. I think that speaking up when colleagues or subordinates are rude can really make a difference. It puts them on alert that somebody is watching and cares how everyone is treated."

Managing the organization

Monitoring and adjusting your own behavior is an important piece of the puzzle, but you need to take action across the company as well.

Hire for civility. Avoid bringing incivility into the workplace to begin with. Some companies, including Southwest Airlines and Four Seasons, put civility at the fore when they interview applicants.

It's useful to give your team members a say about their prospective colleagues; they may pick up on behavior that would be suppressed in more-formal interviews. Rhapsody, an online subscription music service, conducts group interviews so that employees can evaluate potential teammates. It has been known to turn down applicants who are strong on paper but make the team uncomfortable in some way. In one case, a team considering two applicants felt that the apparently stronger one lacked emotional intelligence: She talked too much and seemed unwilling to listen. So the company hired the other candidate, who has worked out very well.

Only 11% of organizations report considering civility at all during the hiring process, and many of those investigate it in a cursory fashion. But incivility usually leaves a trail of some sort, which can be uncovered if someone's willing to look. One hospital had a near miss when bringing on a new radiologist. It offered the job to Dirk, a talented doctor who came highly recommended by his peers and had aced the interviews. But one assistant in the department had a hunch that something was off. Through a network of personal contacts, she learned that Dirk had left a number of badly treated subordinates in his wake—information that would never have surfaced from his CV. So the department head nixed the hire, telling Dirk that if he accepted the offer, the hospital would let him go right away, which would raise a flag for potential employers.

Teach civility. We're always amazed by how many managers and employees tell us that they don't understand what it means to be civil. One quarter of the offenders we surveyed said that they didn't recognize their behavior as uncivil.

People can learn civility on the job. Role-playing is one technique. At one hospital in Los Angeles, temperamental doctors have to attend "charm school" to decrease their brashness (and reduce the potential for lawsuits). Some organizations offer classes on managing the generation mix, in which they talk about differences in norms of civility and how to improve behavior across generations.

Video can be a good teaching tool, especially when paired with coaching. Film employees during various interactions so that they can observe their own facial expressions, posture, words, and tone of voice. It takes people a while to learn to ignore the camera, but eventually they resume their normal patterns of behavior.

After participating in such an exercise, the CEO of a medical firm told us, "I didn't realize what a jerk I sounded like." To his credit, he used the insight to fashion more-civil communication—and became less of a jerk. Another senior executive reported that he'd always thought he maintained a poker face, but the video revealed obvious "tells." For instance, if he lost interest in a discussion, he'd look away.

We recommend that after being taped, people watch the video in three modes: first, with both sound and image, to get an overall sense of their demeanor; second, without sound, to focus on non-verbal behaviors such as gestures, distancing, and facial expressions; and third, with only sound, to highlight tone of voice, volume and speed of speech, and word choice. People don't take issue just with words; tone can be equally or more potent.

Create group norms. Start a dialogue with your team about expectations. An insurance executive told us that he'd talked with his team about what behaviors worked and what didn't. By the end of the first meeting, the team had produced and taken ownership of concrete norms for civility, such as arriving on time and ignoring e-mail during meetings.

In one of our own workplaces, we've borrowed a practice from sports to take the edge off and to help one another avoid falling into occasional abrasiveness. In our world, incivility can flare up during presentations, because overly zealous professors may vigorously interrogate colleagues and visiting professors in an effort to demonstrate their own intellect. We warn colleagues who are engaging in this behavior by using hand signals to indicate the equivalent of soccer's yellow and red cards. The "yellow card" sign (a fist raised to the side of the head) conveys a warning, letting the interrogator know she needs to think about the phrasing, tone, and intensity of her comments and questions. The "red card" signal (two fingers held up, followed by the classic heave of the thumb) means she's finished for the session—she's been so offensive, repeatedly and after fair warning, that she needs to be "ejected from the game." Faculty members have learned that when they get the red card signal, they have to button it—no more today.

Ochsner Health System, a large Louisiana health care provider, has adopted what it calls "the 10/5 way": If you're within 10 feet of someone, make eye contact and smile. If you're within five feet, say hello. Ochsner has seen greater patient satisfaction and an increase in patient referrals as a result.

Reward good behavior. Collegiality should be a consideration in every performance review, but many companies think only about outcomes and tend to overlook damaging behaviors. What behavior does your review system motivate? All too often we see organizations badly miss the mark. They want collaboration, but you'd never know it from their evaluation forms, which focus entirely on individual assessment, without a single measure of teamwork.

Zappos implemented a "Wow" recognition program designed to capture people in the act of doing the right thing. Any employee at any level who sees a colleague doing something special can award a "Wow," which includes a cash bonus of up to $50. Recipients are automatically eligible for a "Hero" award. Heroes are chosen by top executives; they receive a covered parking spot for a month, a $150 Zappos gift card, and, with full symbolic flair, a hero's cape. Even lighthearted awards like these can be powerful symbols of the importance of civility.

Penalize bad behavior. Even the best companies occasionally make bad hires, and employees from an acquired firm may be accustomed to different norms. The trick is to identify and try to correct any troublesome behavior. Companies often avoid taking action, though, and most incidents go unreported, partly because employees know nothing will come of a report. If you want to foster respect, take complaints seriously and follow up.

Rather than confronting offenders, leaders often opt for an easier solution—moving them to a different location. The result is predictable: The behavior continues in a new setting. One manager told us that his department has been burned so often that it no longer considers internal candidates for managerial positions.

Sometimes the best path is to let someone go. Danny Meyer, the owner of many successful restaurants in Manhattan, will fire talent for uncivil behavior. Gifted but rude chefs don't last at his restaurants because they set off bad vibes. Meyer believes that customers can *taste* employee incivility, even when the behavior occurs in the kitchen.

Many top law firms, hospitals, and businesses we've dealt with have learned the hard way that it simply doesn't pay to harbor habitual offenders, even if they're rainmakers or protégés. Whether offenders have caused multimillion-dollar lawsuits or been responsible for the exit of throngs of employees, often the losses could have been mitigated by early, resolute action. A senior executive of a highly successful company told us recently, "Every mistake we've made in firing a questionable hire was in taking action too late, not too early."

Conduct postdeparture interviews. Organizational memory fades quickly. It's crucial, therefore, to gather information from and reflect on the experiences and reactions of employees who leave because of incivility. If you ask targets during their exit interviews why they're leaving, you'll usually get only vague responses. Interviews conducted six months or so later can yield a truer picture. Talking with former employees after they've distanced themselves from the organization and settled into their new work environments can give you insights about the violations of civility that prompted them to leave.

———————

Companies we've worked with calculate that the tab for incivility can run into the millions. Some years back Cisco put together a detailed estimate of what incivility was costing the company. It factored in its reputation as a consistently great place to work, assumed an extremely low probability of rudeness among its employees, and looked at only three potential costs. Even in this exemplary workplace, it was estimated that incivility cost $12 million a year. That realization led to the creation of Cisco's global workplace civility program.

We close with a warning to those who think consistent civility is an extravagance: Just one habitually offensive employee critically positioned in your organization can cost you dearly in lost employees, lost customers, and lost productivity.

Originally published in January–February 2013. Reprint R1301J

How Resilience Works

by Diane L. Coutu

WHEN I BEGAN MY CAREER IN JOURNALISM—I was a reporter at a national magazine in those days—there was a man I'll call Claus Schmidt. He was in his mid-fifties, and to my impressionable eyes, he was the quintessential newsman: cynical at times, but unrelentingly curious and full of life, and often hilariously funny in a sandpaper dry kind of way. He churned out hard-hitting cover stories and features with a speed and elegance I could only dream of. It always astounded me that he was never promoted to managing editor.

But people who knew Claus better than I did thought of him not just as a great newsman but as a quintessential survivor, someone who had endured in an environment often hostile to talent. He had lived through at least three major changes in the magazine's leadership, losing most of his best friends and colleagues on the way. At home, two of his children succumbed to incurable illnesses, and a third was killed in a traffic accident. Despite all this—or maybe because of it—he milled around the newsroom day after day, mentoring the cub reporters, talking about the novels he was writing—always looking forward to what the future held for him.

Why do some people suffer real hardships and not falter? Claus Schmidt could have reacted very differently. We've all seen that happen: One person cannot seem to get the confidence back after a layoff; another, persistently depressed, takes a few years off from life after her divorce. The question we would all like answered is, Why? What exactly is that quality of resilience that carries people through life?

It's a question that has fascinated me ever since I first learned of the Holocaust survivors in elementary school. In college, and later in my studies as an affiliate scholar at the Boston Psychoanalytic Society and Institute, I returned to the subject. For the past several months, however, I have looked on it with a new urgency, for it seems to me that the terrorism, war, and recession of recent months have made understanding resilience more important than ever. I have considered both the nature of individual resilience and what makes some organizations as a whole more resilient than others. Why do some people and some companies buckle under pressure? And what makes others bend and ultimately bounce back?

My exploration has taught me much about resilience, although it's a subject none of us will ever understand fully. Indeed, resilience is one of the great puzzles of human nature, like creativity or the religious instinct. But in sifting through psychological research and in reflecting on the many stories of resilience I've heard, I have seen a little more deeply into the hearts and minds of people like Claus Schmidt and, in doing so, looked more deeply into the human psyche as well.

The Buzz About Resilience

Resilience is a hot topic in business these days. Not long ago, I was talking to a senior partner at a respected consulting firm about how to land the very best MBAs—the name of the game in that particular industry. The partner, Daniel Savageau (not his real name), ticked off a long list of qualities his firm sought in its hires: intelligence, ambition, integrity, analytic ability, and so on. "What about resilience?" I asked. "Well, that's very popular right now," he said. "It's the new buzzword. Candidates even tell us they're resilient; they volunteer the information. But frankly, they're just too young to know that about themselves. Resilience is something you realize you have *after* the fact."

Idea in Brief

These are dark days: people are losing jobs, taking pay cuts, suffering foreclosure on their homes. Some of them are snapping—sinking into depression or suffering a permanent loss of confidence.

But others are snapping back; for example, taking advantage of a layoff to build a new career. What carries them through tough times? Resilience.

Resilient people possess three defining characteristics: They coolly accept the harsh realities facing them. They find meaning in terrible times. And they have an uncanny ability to improvise, making do with whatever's at hand.

In deep recessions, resilience becomes more important than ever. Fortunately, you can learn to be resilient.

"But if you could, would you test for it?" I asked. "Does it matter in business?"

Savageau paused. He's a man in his late forties and a success personally and professionally. Yet it hadn't been a smooth ride to the top. He'd started his life as a poor French Canadian in Woonsocket, Rhode Island, and had lost his father at six. He lucked into a football scholarship but was kicked out of Boston University twice for drinking. He turned his life around in his twenties, married, divorced, remarried, and raised five children. Along the way, he made and lost two fortunes before helping to found the consulting firm he now runs. "Yes, it does matter," he said at last. "In fact, it probably matters more than any of the usual things we look for." In the course of reporting this article, I heard the same assertion time and again. As Dean Becker, the president and CEO of Adaptiv Learning Systems, a four-year-old company in King of Prussia, Pennsylvania, that develops and delivers programs about resilience training, puts it: "More than education, more than experience, more than training, a person's level of resilience will determine who succeeds and who fails. That's true in the cancer ward, it's true in the Olympics, and it's true in the boardroom."

Academic research into resilience started about 40 years ago with pioneering studies by Norman Garmezy, now a professor emeritus at the University of Minnesota in Minneapolis. After studying why

Idea in Practice

Resilience can help you survive and recover from even the most brutal experiences. To cultivate resilience, apply these practices.

Face Down Reality

Instead of slipping into denial to cope with hardship, take a sober, down-to-earth view of the reality of your situation. You'll prepare yourself to act in ways that enable you to endure—training yourself to survive before the fact.

> *Example:* Admiral Jim Stockdale survived being held prisoner and tortured by the Vietcong in part by accepting he could be held for a long time. (He was held for eight years.) Those who didn't make it out of the camps kept optimistically assuming

they'd be released on shorter timetables—by Christmas, by Easter, by the Fourth of July. "I think they all died of broken hearts," Stockdale said.

Search for Meaning

When hard times strike, resist any impulse to view yourself as a victim and to cry, "Why me?" Rather, devise constructs about your suffering to create meaning for yourself and others. You'll build bridges from your present-day ordeal to a fuller, better future. Those bridges will make the present manageable, by removing the sense that the present is overwhelming.

> *Example:* Austrian psychiatrist and Auschwitz survivor Victor Frankl realized that

many children of schizophrenic parents did not suffer psychological illness as a result of growing up with them, he concluded that a certain quality of resilience played a greater role in mental health than anyone had previously suspected.

Today, theories abound about what makes resilience. Looking at Holocaust victims, Maurice Vanderpol, a former president of the Boston Psychoanalytic Society and Institute, found that many of the healthy survivors of concentration camps had what he calls a "plastic shield." The shield was comprised of several factors, including a sense of humor. Often the humor was black, but nonetheless it provided a critical sense of perspective. Other core characteristics that helped included the ability to form attachments to others and the possession of an inner psychological space that protected to survive the camp, he had to find some purpose. He did so by imagining himself giving a lecture after the war on the psychology of the concentration camp to help outsiders understand what he had been through. By creating concrete goals for himself, he rose above the sufferings of the moment.

Continually Improvise

When disaster hits, be inventive. Make the most of what you have, putting resources to unfamiliar uses and imagining possibilities others don't see.

Example: Mike founded a business with his friend Paul, selling educational materials to schools, businesses, and consulting firms. When a recession hit, they lost many core clients. Paul went through a bitter divorce, suffered a depression, and couldn't work. When Mike offered to buy him out, Paul slapped him with a lawsuit claiming Mike was trying to steal the business.

Mike kept the company going any way he could—going into joint ventures to sell English-language training materials to Russian and Chinese competitors, publishing newsletters for clients, and even writing video scripts for competitors. The lawsuit was eventually settled in his favor, and he had a new and much more solid business than the one he started out with.

the survivors from the intrusions of abusive others. Research about other groups uncovered different qualities associated with resilience. The Search Institute, a Minneapolis-based nonprofit organization that focuses on resilience and youth, found that the more resilient kids have an uncanny ability to get adults to help them out. Still other research showed that resilient inner-city youth often have talents such as athletic abilities that attract others to them.

Many of the early theories about resilience stressed the role of genetics. Some people are just born resilient, so the arguments went. There's some truth to that, of course, but an increasing body of empirical evidence shows that resilience—whether in children, survivors of concentration camps, or businesses back from the brink—can be learned. For example, George Vaillant, the director of the Study of Adult Development at Harvard Medical School in Boston, observes that within various groups studied during a 60-year period, some people became markedly more resilient over their lifetimes. Other psychologists claim that unresilient people more easily develop resiliency skills than those with head starts.

Most of the resilience theories I encountered in my research make good common sense. But I also observed that almost all the theories overlap in three ways. Resilient people, they posit, possess three characteristics: a staunch acceptance of reality; a deep belief, often buttressed by strongly held values, that life is meaningful; and an uncanny ability to improvise. You can bounce back from hardship with just one or two of these qualities, but you will only be truly resilient with all three. These three characteristics hold true for resilient organizations as well. Let's take a look at each of them in turn.

Facing Down Reality

A common belief about resilience is that it stems from an optimistic nature. That's true but only as long as such optimism doesn't distort your sense of reality. In extremely adverse situations, rose-colored thinking can actually spell disaster. This point was made poignantly to me by management researcher and writer Jim Collins, who happened upon this concept while researching *Good to Great*, his book on how companies transform themselves out of mediocrity. Collins had a hunch (an exactly wrong hunch) that resilient companies were filled with optimistic people. He tried out that idea on Admiral Jim Stockdale, who was held prisoner and tortured by the Vietcong for eight years.

Collins recalls: "I asked Stockdale: 'Who didn't make it out of the camps?' And he said, 'Oh, that's easy. It was the optimists. They were the ones who said we were going to be out by Christmas. And then they said we'd be out by Easter and then out by Fourth of July and out by Thanksgiving, and then it was Christmas again.' Then Stockdale turned to me and said, 'You know, I think they all died of broken hearts.'"

In the business world, Collins found the same unblinking attitude shared by executives at all the most successful companies he studied. Like Stockdale, resilient people have very sober and down-to-earth views of those parts of reality that matter for survival. That's not to say that optimism doesn't have its place: In turning around a demoralized sales force, for instance, conjuring a sense of possibility can be a very powerful tool. But for bigger challenges, a cool, almost pessimistic, sense of reality is far more important.

Perhaps you're asking yourself, "Do I truly understand—and accept—the reality of my situation? Does my organization?" Those are good questions, particularly because research suggests most people slip into denial as a coping mechanism. Facing reality, really facing it, is grueling work. Indeed, it can be unpleasant and often emotionally wrenching. Consider the following story of organizational resilience, and see what it means to confront reality.

Prior to September 11, 2001, Morgan Stanley, the famous investment bank, was the largest tenant in the World Trade Center. The company had some 2,700 employees working in the south tower on 22 floors between the 43rd and the 74th. On that horrible day, the first plane hit the north tower at 8:46 a.m., and Morgan Stanley started evacuating just one minute later, at 8:47 a.m. When the second plane crashed into the south tower 15 minutes after that, Morgan Stanley's offices were largely empty. All told, the company lost only seven employees despite receiving an almost direct hit.

Of course, the organization was just plain lucky to be in the second tower. Cantor Fitzgerald, whose offices were hit in the first attack, couldn't have done anything to save its employees. Still, it was Morgan Stanley's hard-nosed realism that enabled the company to benefit from its luck. Soon after the 1993 attack on the World Trade Center, senior management recognized that working in such a symbolic center of U.S. commercial power made the company vulnerable to attention from terrorists and possible attack.

With this grim realization, Morgan Stanley launched a program of preparedness at the micro level. Few companies take their fire drills seriously. Not so Morgan Stanley, whose VP of security for the Individual Investor Group, Rick Rescorla, brought a military discipline to the job. Rescorla, himself a highly resilient, decorated Vietnam vet, made sure that people were fully drilled about what to do in a catastrophe. When disaster struck on September 11, Rescorla was on a bullhorn telling Morgan Stanley employees to stay calm and follow their well-practiced drill, even though some building supervisors were telling occupants that all was well. Sadly, Rescorla himself, whose life story has been widely covered in recent months, was one of the seven who didn't make it out.

"When you're in financial services where so much depends on technology, contingency planning is a major part of your business," says President and COO Robert G. Scott. But Morgan Stanley was prepared for the very toughest reality. It had not just one, but three, recovery sites where employees could congregate and business could take place if work locales were ever disrupted. "Multiple backup sites seemed like an incredible extravagance on September 10," concedes Scott. "But on September 12, they seemed like genius."

Maybe it was genius; it was undoubtedly resilience at work. The fact is, when we truly stare down reality, we prepare ourselves to act in ways that allow us to endure and survive extraordinary hardship. We train ourselves how to survive before the fact.

The Search for Meaning

The ability to see reality is closely linked to the second building block of resilience, the propensity to make meaning of terrible times. We all know people who, under duress, throw up their hands and cry, "How can this be happening to me?" Such people see themselves as victims, and living through hardship carries no lessons for them. But resilient people devise constructs about their suffering to create some sort of meaning for themselves and others.

I have a friend I'll call Jackie Oiseaux who suffered repeated psychoses over a ten-year period due to an undiagnosed bipolar disorder. Today, she holds down a big job in one of the top publishing companies in the country, has a family, and is a prominent member of her church community. When people ask her how she bounced back from her crises, she runs her hands through her hair. "People sometimes say, 'Why me?' But I've always said, 'Why *not* me?' True, I lost many things during my illness," she says, "but I found many more—incredible friends who saw me through the bleakest times and who will give meaning to my life forever."

This dynamic of meaning making is, most researchers agree, the way resilient people build bridges from present-day hardships to a fuller, better constructed future. Those bridges make the present manageable, for lack of a better word, removing the sense that the present is overwhelming. This concept was beautifully articulated by Viktor E. Frankl, an Austrian psychiatrist and an Auschwitz survivor. In the midst of staggering suffering, Frankl invented "meaning therapy," a humanistic therapy technique that helps individuals make the kinds of decisions that will create significance in their lives.

In his book *Man's Search for Meaning*, Frankl described the pivotal moment in the camp when he developed meaning therapy. He was on his way to work one day, worrying whether he should trade his last cigarette for a bowl of soup. He wondered how he was going to work with a new foreman whom he knew to be particularly sadistic. Suddenly, he was disgusted by just how trivial and meaningless his life had become. He realized that to survive, he had to find some purpose. Frankl did so by imagining himself giving a lecture after the war on the psychology of the concentration camp, to help outsiders understand what he had been through. Although he wasn't even sure he would survive, Frankl created some concrete goals for himself. In doing so, he succeeded in rising above the sufferings of the moment. As he put it in his book: "We must never forget that we may also find meaning in life even when confronted with a hopeless situation, when facing a fate that cannot be changed."

Frankl's theory underlies most resilience coaching in business. Indeed, I was struck by how often businesspeople referred to his work. "Resilience training—what we call hardiness—is a way for us to help people construct meaning in their everyday lives," explains Salvatore R. Maddi, a University of California, Irvine psychology professor and the director of the Hardiness Institute in Newport Beach, California. "When people realize the power of resilience training, they often say, 'Doc, is this what psychotherapy is?' But psychotherapy is for people whose lives have fallen apart badly and need repair. We see our work as showing people life skills and attitudes. Maybe those things should be taught at home, maybe they should be taught in schools, but they're not. So we end up doing it in business."

Yet the challenge confronting resilience trainers is often more difficult than we might imagine. Meaning can be elusive, and just because you found it once doesn't mean you'll keep it or find it again. Consider Aleksandr Solzhenitsyn, who survived the war against the Nazis, imprisonment in the gulag, and cancer. Yet when he moved to a farm in peaceful, safe Vermont, he could not cope with the "infantile West." He was unable to discern any real meaning in what he felt to be the destructive and irresponsible freedom of the West. Upset by his critics, he withdrew into his farmhouse, behind a locked fence, seldom to be seen in public. In 1994, a bitter man, Solzhenitsyn moved back to Russia.

Since finding meaning in one's environment is such an important aspect of resilience, it should come as no surprise that the most successful organizations and people possess strong value systems. Strong values infuse an environment with meaning because they offer ways to interpret and shape events. While it's popular these days to ridicule values, it's surely no coincidence that the most resilient organization in the world has been the Catholic Church, which has survived wars, corruption, and schism for more than 2,000 years, thanks largely to its immutable set of values. Businesses that survive also have their creeds, which give them purposes beyond just making money. Strikingly, many companies describe their value systems in religious terms. Pharmaceutical giant Johnson & Johnson, for instance, calls its value system, set out in a document given to every new employee at orientation, the Credo. Parcel company UPS talks constantly about its Noble Purpose.

Value systems at resilient companies change very little over the years and are used as scaffolding in times of trouble. UPS Chairman and CEO Mike Eskew believes that the Noble Purpose helped the company to rally after the agonizing strike in 1997. Says Eskew: "It was a hugely difficult time, like a family feud. Everyone had close friends on both sides of the fence, and it was tough for us to pick sides. But what saved us was our Noble Purpose. Whatever side people were on, they all shared a common set of values. Those values are core to us and never change; they frame most of our important decisions. Our strategy and our mission may change, but our values never do."

The religious connotations of words like "credo," "values," and "noble purpose," however, should not be confused with the actual content of the values. Companies can hold ethically questionable values and still be very resilient. Consider Phillip Morris, which has demonstrated impressive resilience in the face of increasing unpopularity. As Jim Collins points out, Phillip Morris has very strong values, although we might not agree with them—for instance, the value of "adult choice." But there's no doubt that Phillip Morris executives believe strongly in its values, and the strength of their beliefs sets the company apart from most of the other tobacco companies. In this context, it is worth noting that resilience is neither ethically good nor bad. It is merely the skill and the capacity to be robust under conditions of enormous stress and change. As Viktor Frankl wrote: "On the average, only those prisoners could keep alive who, after years of trekking from camp to camp, had lost all scruples in their fight for existence; they were prepared to use every means, honest and otherwise, even brutal . . ., in order to save themselves. We who have come back . . . we know: The best of us did not return."

Values, positive or negative, are actually more important for organizational resilience than having resilient people on the payroll. If resilient employees are all interpreting reality in different ways, their decisions and actions may well conflict, calling into doubt the survival of their organization. And as the weakness of an organization becomes apparent, highly resilient individuals are more likely to jettison the organization than to imperil their own survival.

Ritualized Ingenuity

The third building block of resilience is the ability to make do with whatever is at hand. Psychologists follow the lead of French anthropologist Claude Levi-Strauss in calling this skill bricolage.[1] Intriguingly, the roots of that word are closely tied to the concept of resilience, which literally means "bouncing back." Says Levi-Strauss: "In its old sense, the verb *bricoler* . . . was always used with reference to some extraneous movement: a ball rebounding, a dog straying, or a horse swerving from its direct course to avoid an obstacle."

Bricolage in the modern sense can be defined as a kind of inventiveness, an ability to improvise a solution to a problem without proper or obvious tools or materials. *Bricoleurs* are always tinkering— building radios from household effects or fixing their own cars. They make the most of what they have, putting objects to unfamiliar uses. In the concentration camps, for example, resilient inmates knew to pocket pieces of string or wire whenever they found them. The string or wire might later become useful—to fix a pair of shoes, perhaps, which in freezing conditions might make the difference between life and death.

When situations unravel, bricoleurs muddle through, imagining possibilities where others are confounded. I have two friends, whom I'll call Paul Shields and Mike Andrews, who were roommates throughout their college years. To no one's surprise, when they graduated, they set up a business together, selling educational materials to schools, businesses, and consulting firms. At first, the company was a great success, making both founders paper millionaires. But the recession of the early 1990s hit the company hard, and many core clients fell away. At the same time, Paul experienced a bitter divorce and a depression that made it impossible for him to work. Mike offered to buy Paul out but was instead slapped with a lawsuit claiming that Mike was trying to steal the business. At this point, a less resilient person might have just walked away from the mess. Not Mike. As the case wound through the courts, he kept the company going any way he could—constantly morphing the business until he found a model that worked: going into joint ventures to sell English-language training materials to Russian and Chinese companies. Later, he branched off into publishing newsletters for clients. At one point, he was even writing video scripts for his competitors. Thanks to all this bricolage, by the time the lawsuit was settled in his favor, Mike had an entirely different, and much more solid, business than the one he had started with.

Bricolage can be practiced on a higher level as well. Richard Feynman, winner of the 1965 Nobel Prize in physics, exemplified what

I like to think of as intellectual bricolage. Out of pure curiosity, Feynman made himself an expert on cracking safes, not only looking at the mechanics of safecracking but also cobbling together psychological insights about people who used safes and set the locks. He cracked many of the safes at Los Alamos, for instance, because he guessed that theoretical physicists would not set the locks with random code numbers they might forget but would instead use a sequence with mathematical significance. It turned out that the three safes containing all the secrets to the atomic bomb were set to the same mathematical constant, e, whose first six digits are 2.71828.

Resilient organizations are stuffed with bricoleurs, though not all of them, of course, are Richard Feynmans. Indeed, companies that survive regard improvisation as a core skill. Consider UPS, which empowers its drivers to do whatever it takes to deliver packages on time. Says CEO Eskew: "We tell our employees to get the job done. If that means they need to improvise, they improvise. Otherwise we just couldn't do what we do every day. Just think what can go wrong: a busted traffic light, a flat tire, a bridge washed out. If a snowstorm hits Louisville tonight, a group of people will sit together and discuss how to handle the problem. Nobody tells them to do that. They come together because it's our tradition to do so."

That tradition meant that the company was delivering parcels in southeast Florida just one day after Hurricane Andrew devastated the region in 1992, causing billions of dollars in damage. Many people were living in their cars because their homes had been destroyed, yet UPS drivers and managers sorted packages at a diversion site and made deliveries even to those who were stranded in their cars. It was largely UPS's improvisational skills that enabled it to keep functioning after the catastrophic hit. And the fact that the company continued on gave others a sense of purpose or meaning amid the chaos.

Improvisation of the sort practiced by UPS, however, is a far cry from unbridled creativity. Indeed, much like the military, UPS lives on rules and regulations. As Eskew says: "Drivers always put their keys in the same place. They close the doors the same way. They wear their uniforms the same way. We are a company of precision." He believes that although they may seem stifling, UPS's rules were what allowed the company to bounce back immediately after Hurricane Andrew, for they enabled people to focus on the one or two fixes they needed to make in order to keep going.

Eskew's opinion is echoed by Karl E. Weick, a professor of organizational behavior at the University of Michigan Business School in Ann Arbor and one of the most respected thinkers on organizational psychology. "There is good evidence that when people are put under pressure, they regress to their most habituated ways of responding," Weick has written. "What we do not expect under life-threatening pressure is creativity." In other words, the rules and regulations that make some companies appear less creative may actually make them more resilient in times of real turbulence.

Claus Schmidt, the newsman I mentioned earlier, died about five years ago, but I'm not sure I could have interviewed him about his own resilience even if he were alive. It would have felt strange, I think, to ask him, "Claus, did you really face down reality? Did you make meaning out of your hardships? Did you improvise your recovery after each professional and personal disaster?" He may not have been able to answer. In my experience, resilient people don't often describe themselves that way. They shrug off their survival stories and very often assign them to luck.

Obviously, luck does have a lot to do with surviving. It was luck that Morgan Stanley was situated in the south tower and could put its preparedness training to work. But being lucky is not the same as being resilient. Resilience is a reflex, a way of facing and understanding the world, that is deeply etched into a person's mind and soul. Resilient people and companies face reality with staunchness, make meaning of hardship instead of crying out in despair, and improvise solutions from thin air. Others do not. This is the nature of resilience, and we will never completely understand it.

Originally published in May 2002. Reprint R0205B

Note

1. See, e.g., Karl E. Weick, "The Collapse of Sense-making in Organizations: The Mann Gulch Disaster," *Administrative Science Quarterly*, December 1993.

Emotional Agility

How Effective Leaders Manage Their Negative
Thoughts and Feelings. *by Susan David
and Christina Congleton*

SIXTEEN THOUSAND—that's how many words we speak, on average,
each day. So imagine how many unspoken ones course through our
minds. Most of them are not facts but evaluations and judgments
entwined with emotions—some positive and helpful (*I've worked
hard and I can ace this presentation; This issue is worth speaking up
about; The new VP seems approachable*), others negative and less so
(*He's purposely ignoring me; I'm going to make a fool of myself; I'm a
fake*).

The prevailing wisdom says that difficult thoughts and feelings
have no place at the office: Executives, and particularly leaders,
should be either stoic or cheerful; they must project confidence
and damp down any negativity bubbling up inside them. But that
goes against basic biology. All healthy human beings have an inner
stream of thoughts and feelings that include criticism, doubt, and
fear. That's just our minds doing the job they were designed to
do: trying to anticipate and solve problems and avoid potential
pitfalls.

In our people-strategy consulting practice advising companies
around the world, we see leaders stumble not because they *have*
undesirable thoughts and feelings—that's inevitable—but because
they get *hooked* by them, like fish caught on a line. This happens

in one of two ways. They buy into the thoughts, treating them like facts (*It was the same in my last job . . . I've been a failure my whole career*), and avoid situations that evoke them (*I'm not going to take on that new challenge*). Or, usually at the behest of their supporters, they challenge the existence of the thoughts and try to rationalize them away (*I shouldn't have thoughts like this . . . I know I'm not a total failure*), and perhaps force themselves into similar situations, even when those go against their core values and goals (*Take on that new assignment—you've got to get over this*). In either case, they are paying too much attention to their internal chatter and allowing it to sap important cognitive resources that could be put to better use.

This is a common problem, often perpetuated by popular self-management strategies. We regularly see executives with recurring emotional challenges at work—anxiety about priorities, jealousy of others' success, fear of rejection, distress over perceived slights—who have devised techniques to "fix" them: positive affirmations, prioritized to-do lists, immersion in certain tasks. But when we ask how long the challenges have persisted, the answer might be 10 years, 20 years, or since childhood.

Clearly, those techniques don't work—in fact, ample research shows that attempting to minimize or ignore thoughts and emotions serves only to amplify them. In a famous study led by the late Daniel Wegner, a Harvard professor, participants who were told to avoid thinking about white bears had trouble doing so; later, when the ban was lifted, they thought about white bears much more than the control group did. Anyone who has dreamed of chocolate cake and French fries while following a strict diet understands this phenomenon.

Effective leaders don't buy into *or* try to suppress their inner experiences. Instead they approach them in a mindful, values-driven, and productive way—developing what we call *emotional agility*. In our complex, fast-changing knowledge economy, this ability to manage one's thoughts and feelings is essential to business success. Numerous studies, from the University of London professor Frank Bond and others, show that emotional agility can help

Idea in Brief

The prevailing wisdom says that negative thoughts and feelings have no place at the office. But that goes against basic biology. All healthy human beings have an inner stream of thoughts and feelings that include criticism, doubt, and fear. David and Congleton have worked with leaders in various industries to build a critical skill they call emotional agility, which enables people to approach their inner experiences in a mindful, values-driven, and productive way rather than buying into or trying to suppress them. The authors offer four practices (adapted from Acceptance and Commitment Therapy, or ACT) designed to help readers do the same:

- **Recognize your patterns.** You have to realize that you're stuck before you can initiate change.

- **Label your thoughts and emotions.** Labeling allows you to see them as transient sources of data that may or may not prove helpful.

- **Accept them.** Respond to your ideas and emotions with an open attitude, paying attention and letting yourself experience them. They may be signaling that something important is at stake.

- **Act on your values.** Is your response going to serve your organization in the long term and take you toward being the leader you most want to be?

people alleviate stress, reduce errors, become more innovative, and improve job performance.

We've worked with leaders in various industries to build this critical skill, and here we offer four practices—adapted from Acceptance and Commitment Therapy (ACT), originally developed by the University of Nevada psychologist Steven C. Hayes—that are designed to help you do the same: Recognize your patterns; label your thoughts and emotions; accept them; and act on your values.

Fish on a Line

Let's start with two case studies. Cynthia is a senior corporate lawyer with two young children. She used to feel intense guilt about missed opportunities—both at the office, where her peers worked 80 hours a week while she worked 50, and at home, where she was often too

What Are Your Values?

THIS LIST IS DRAWN from the Personal Values Card Sort (2001), developed by W.R. Miller, J. C'de Baca, D.B. Matthews, and P.L. Wilbourne, of the University of New Mexico. You can use it to quickly identify the values you hold that might inform a challenging situation at work. When you next make a decision, ask yourself whether it is consistent with these values.

Accuracy	Friendship	Passion
Achievement	Fun	Popularity
Adventure	Generosity	Power
Authority	Genuineness	Purpose
Autonomy	Growth	Rationality
Caring	Health	Realism
Challenge	Helpfulness	Responsibility
Change	Honesty	Risk
Comfort	Humility	Safety
Compassion	Humor	Self-knowledge
Contribution	Justice	Service
Cooperation	Knowledge	Simplicity
Courtesy	Leisure	Stability
Creativity	Mastery	Tolerance
Dependability	Moderation	Tradition
Duty	Nonconformity	Wealth
Family	Openness	
Forgiveness	Order	

distracted or tired to fully engage with her husband and children. One nagging voice in her head told her she'd have to be a better employee or risk career failure; another told her to be a better mother or risk neglecting her family. Cynthia wished that at least one of the voices would shut up. But neither would, and in response she failed to put up her hand for exciting new prospects at the office and compulsively checked messages on her phone during family dinners.

Jeffrey, a rising-star executive at a leading consumer goods company, had a different problem. Intelligent, talented, and ambitious, he was often angry—at bosses who disregarded his views, subordinates who didn't follow orders, or colleagues who didn't pull their weight. He had lost his temper several times at work and been warned to get it under control. But when he tried, he felt that he was shutting off a core part of his personality, and he became even angrier and more upset.

These smart, successful leaders were hooked by their negative thoughts and emotions. Cynthia was absorbed by guilt; Jeffrey was exploding with anger. Cynthia told the voices to go away; Jeffrey bottled his frustration. Both were trying to avoid the discomfort they felt. They were being controlled by their inner experience, attempting to control it, or switching between the two.

Getting Unhooked

Fortunately, both Cynthia and Jeffrey realized that they couldn't go on—at least not successfully and happily—without more-effective inner strategies. We coached them to adopt the four practices.

Recognize your patterns

The first step in developing emotional agility is to notice when you've been hooked by your thoughts and feelings. That's hard to do, but there are certain telltale signs. One is that your thinking becomes rigid and repetitive. For example, Cynthia began to see that her self-recriminations played like a broken record, repeating the same messages over and over again. Another is that the story your mind is telling seems old, like a rerun of some past experience. Jeffrey noticed that his attitude toward certain colleagues (*He's incompetent; There's no way I'm letting anyone speak to me like that*) was quite familiar. In fact, he had experienced something similar in his previous job—and in the one before that. The source of trouble was not just Jeffrey's environment but his own patterns of thought and feeling. You have to realize that you're stuck before you can initiate change.

Label your thoughts and emotions

When you're hooked, the attention you give your thoughts and feelings crowds your mind; there's no room to examine them. One strategy that may help you consider your situation more objectively is the simple act of labeling. Just as you call a spade a spade, call a thought a thought and an emotion an emotion. *I'm not doing enough at work or at home* becomes *I'm having the thought that I'm not doing enough at work or at home.* Similarly, *My coworker is wrong—he makes me so angry* becomes *I'm having the thought that my coworker is wrong, and I'm feeling anger.* Labeling allows you to see your thoughts and feelings for what they are: transient sources of data that may or may not prove helpful. Humans are psychologically able to take this helicopter view of private experiences, and mounting scientific evidence shows that simple, straightforward mindfulness practice like this not only improves behavior and well-being but also promotes beneficial biological changes in the brain and at the cellular level. As Cynthia started to slow down and label her thoughts, the criticisms that had once pressed in on her like a dense fog became more like clouds passing through a blue sky.

Accept them
The opposite of control is acceptance—not acting on every thought or resigning yourself to negativity but responding to your ideas and emotions with an open attitude, paying attention to them and letting yourself experience them. Take 10 deep breaths and notice what's happening in the moment. This can bring relief, but it won't necessarily make you feel good. In fact, you may realize just how upset you really are. The important thing is to show yourself (and others) some compassion and examine the reality of the situation. What's going on—both internally and externally? When Jeffrey acknowledged and made room for his feelings of frustration and anger rather than rejecting them, quashing them, or taking them out on others, he began to notice their energetic quality. They were a signal that something important was at stake and that he needed to take productive action. Instead of yelling at people, he could make a clear request of a colleague or move swiftly on a pressing issue. The more Jeffrey accepted his anger and brought his curiosity to it, the more it seemed to support rather than undermine his leadership.

Evaluate Your Emotional Agility

Exercise

Choose a **challenging situation** in your work life—for example, "Receiving negative feedback from my boss" or "Asking my boss for a raise."

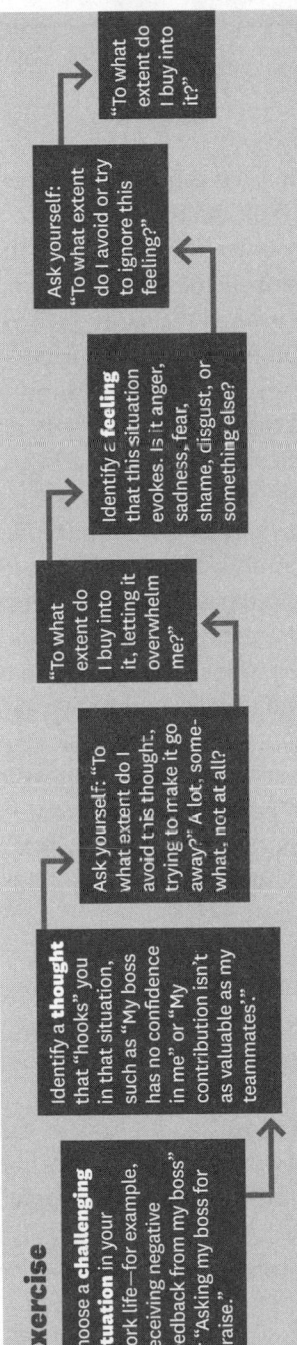

Identify a **thought** that "hooks" you in that situation, such as "My boss has no confidence in me" or "My contribution isn't as valuable as my teammates."

Ask yourself: "To what extent do I avoid t1is thought—, trying to make it go away?" A lot, somewhat, not at all?

"To what extent do I buy into it, letting it overwhelm me?"

Identify a **feeling** that this situation evokes. Is it anger, sadness, fear, shame, disgust, or something else?

Ask yourself: "To what extent do I avoid or try to ignore this feeling?"

"To what extent do I buy into it?"

Advice

If you primarily **avoid** your thoughts and feelings, try to acknowledge them instead. Notice thoughts as they arise and check your emotional state several times a day so that you can identify the useful information your mind is sending you.

If you primarily **buy into** your thoughts and feelings, find your ground. Take 10 deep breaths, notice your environment, and label—rather than being swept up in—them.

If you **alternate**, learn your patterns. Pay attention to which thoughts and feelings you avoid and which you buy into so that you can respond with one of the strategies we describe.

The next step is to take action that aligns with your **values.** (For examples, see the sidebar "What Are Your Values?") Identify which ones you want to apply in the context of the challenging situation you've described.

Act on your values

When you unhook yourself from your difficult thoughts and emotions, you expand your choices. You can decide to act in a way that aligns with your values. We encourage leaders to focus on the concept of *workability*: Is your response going to serve you and your organization in the long term as well as the short term? Will it help you steer others in a direction that furthers your collective purpose? Are you taking a step toward being the leader you most want to be and living the life you most want to live? The mind's thought stream flows endlessly, and emotions change like the weather, but values can be called on at any time, in any situation.

When Cynthia considered her values, she recognized how deeply committed she was to both her family and her work; she loved being with her children, but she also cared passionately about the pursuit of justice. Unhooked from her distracting and discouraging feelings of guilt, she resolved to be guided by her principles. She recognized how important it was to get home for dinner with her family every evening and to resist work interruptions during that time. But she also undertook to make a number of important business trips, some of which coincided with school events that she would have preferred to attend. Confident that her values, not solely her emotions, were guiding her, Cynthia finally found peace and fulfillment.

It's impossible to block out difficult thoughts and emotions. Effective leaders are mindful of their inner experiences but not caught in them. They know how to free up their internal resources and commit to actions that align with their values. Developing emotional agility is no quick fix—even those who, like Cynthia and Jeffrey, regularly practice the steps we've outlined here will often find themselves hooked. But over time, leaders who become increasingly adept at it are the ones most likely to thrive.

Originally published in November 2013. Reprint R1311L

Fear of Feedback

by Jay M. Jackman and Myra H. Strober

NOBODY LIKES PERFORMANCE REVIEWS. Subordinates are terrified they'll hear nothing but criticism. Bosses, for their part, think their direct reports will respond to even the mildest criticism with stonewalling, anger, or tears. The result? Everyone keeps quiet and says as little as possible. That's unfortunate, because most people need help figuring out how they can improve their performance and advance their careers.

This fear of feedback doesn't come into play just during annual reviews. At least half the executives with whom we've worked *never* ask for feedback. Many expect the worst: heated arguments, impossible demands, or even threats of dismissal. So rather than seek feedback, people avoid the truth and instead continue to try to guess what their bosses think.

Fears and assumptions about feedback often manifest themselves in psychologically maladaptive behaviors such as procrastination, denial, brooding, jealousy, and self-sabotage. But there's hope. Those who learn to adapt to feedback can free themselves from old patterns. They can learn to acknowledge negative emotions, constructively reframe fear and criticism, develop realistic goals, create support systems, and reward themselves for achievements along the way.

We'll look closely at a four-step process for doing just that. But before we turn to that process, let's explore why so many people are afraid to hear how they're doing.

Fear Itself

Obviously, some managers have excellent relationships with their bosses. They receive feedback on a regular basis and act on it in ways that improve their performance as well as their prospects for promotion. Sadly, however, such executives are in the minority. In most companies, feedback typically comes via cursory annual performance reviews, during which managers learn little beyond the amount of a forthcoming raise.

People avoid feedback because they hate being criticized, plain and simple. Psychologists have a lot of theories about why people are so sensitive to hearing about their own imperfections. One is that they associate feedback with the critical comments received in their younger years from parents and teachers. Whatever the cause of our discomfort, most of us have to train ourselves to seek feedback and listen carefully when we hear it. Absent that training, the very threat of critical feedback often leads us to practice destructive, maladaptive behaviors that negatively affect not only our work but the overall health of our organizations. The following are some examples of those behaviors.

Procrastination

We procrastinate—usually consciously—when we feel helpless about a situation and are anxious, embarrassed, or otherwise dissatisfied with it. Procrastination commonly contains an element of hostility or anger.

Consider how Joe, a highly accomplished computer scientist in a large technology company, responded to his frustration over not being promoted. (As with all the examples in this article, people's names have been changed.) Although everyone in the company respected his technical competence, he sensed something was wrong. Instead of seriously assessing his performance and asking for feedback, he became preoccupied with inessential details of his projects, played computer solitaire, and consistently failed to meet project deadlines. When Joe asked about his chances for advancement in his annual review, his boss singled out Joe's repeated failure

Idea in Brief

Nobody likes performance reviews. Subordinates are terrified they'll hear nothing but criticism. Bosses, for their part, think their direct reports will respond to even the mildest criticism with stonewalling, anger, or tears. The result? Everyone keeps quiet and says as little as possible. That's unfortunate, because most people need help figuring out how they can improve their performance and advance their careers. This fear of feedback doesn't come into play just during annual reviews. At least half the executives with whom the authors have worked never ask for feedback. People avoid the truth and instead try to guess what their bosses are thinking. Fears and assumptions about feedback often manifest themselves in psychologically maladaptive behaviors such as procrastination, denial, brooding, jealousy, and self-sabotage. But there's hope, say the authors. Those who learn adaptive techniques can free themselves from these destructive responses. They'll be able to deal with feedback better if they acknowledge negative emotions, reframe fear and criticism constructively, develop realistic goals, create support systems, and reward themselves for achievements along the way. The authors take you through four manageable steps for doing just that: self-assessment, external assessment, absorbing the feedback, and taking action toward change.

to finish projects on time or to seek formal extensions when he knew work would be late. In fact, Joe's continued procrastination became a serious performance issue that cost him a promotion.

Denial

We're in denial when we're unable or unwilling to face reality or fail to acknowledge the implications of our situations. Denial is most often an unconscious response.

Angela, a midlevel manager in a consulting firm, drifted into a state of denial when a hoped-for promotion never materialized. Her superiors told her that she hadn't performed as well as they'd expected. Specifically, they told her she'd requested too much time off to spend with her children, she hadn't sufficiently researched a certain industry, she hadn't met her yearly quota of bringing in ten new clients, and so on. Every time she tried to correct these problems, her male superiors put her off with a new series of excuses and challenges. The fact was, they had no intention of promoting her because they were deeply sexist. Accepting that fact would have required Angela to leave, but she chose instead to live in denial. Rather than recognize she was at a dead end, she did nothing about her situation and remained miserable in her job.

Brooding

Brooding is a powerful emotional response, taking the form of morbid preoccupation and a sense of foreboding. Faced with situations they feel they can't master, brooders lapse into passivity, paralysis, and isolation.

Adrian, a training manager, brooded when his boss set forth several stretch goals for him. Believing the goals to be unrealistic, Adrian concluded that he couldn't meet them. Rather than talk with his boss about this, he became desperately unhappy and withdrew from his colleagues. They in turn saw his withdrawal as a snub and began to ignore him. The more they avoided him, the more he brooded. By the end of six months, Adrian's brooding created a self-fulfilling prophecy; because he had met none of his goals, his new projects were assigned to someone else, and his job was in jeopardy.

Jealousy

Comparing ourselves with others is a normal behavior, but it becomes maladaptive when it is based on suspicion, rivalry, envy, or possessiveness. Jealous people may overidealize others whom they perceive to be more talented, competent, and intelligent; in so doing, they debilitate themselves.

Leslie, a talented vice president of a public relations firm, fell into the jealousy trap when her boss noted during a meeting that one of her colleagues had prepared a truly excellent report for a client. Leslie began comparing herself with her colleague, listening carefully to the boss's remarks during meetings and noting his smiles and nods as he spoke. Feeling that she could never rise to her colleague's level, Leslie lost all enthusiasm for her work. Instead of seeking a reality check with her boss, she allowed the green-eyed monster to consume her; ultimately, she quit her job.

Self-sabotage

Examples of self-sabotage, usually an unconscious behavior, are all too common. Even national leaders such as Bill Clinton and Trent Lott have hoisted themselves on their own petards.

Workplaces are full of people who unconsciously undercut themselves. Take, for example, the story of Nancy, a young associate who found herself unable to deal with more than two projects at once. During her review, Nancy resented her boss's feedback that she needed to improve her ability to multitask. But instead of initiating further discussion with him about the remark, she "accidentally" made a nasty comment about him one day within his earshot. As a result, he began looking for ways to get rid of her. When she was eventually fired, her innermost feelings of unworthiness were validated.

These and other maladaptive behaviors are part of a vicious cycle we have seen at play in too many organizations. Indeed, it's not uncommon for employees, faced with negative feedback, to rain private maledictions upon their supervisors. No wonder, then, that supervisors are reluctant to give feedback. But when employees' imagined and real fears go unchecked, the work environment becomes dysfunctional, if not downright poisonous.

Learning to Adapt

Adapting to feedback—which inevitably asks people to change, sometimes significantly—is critical for managers who find themselves in jobs, companies, and industries undergoing frequent transitions. Of course, adaptation is easier said than done, for resistance to change is endemic in human beings. But while most people feel they can't control the negative emotions that are aroused by change, this is not the case. It is possible—and necessary—to think positively about change. Using the following adaptive techniques, you can alter how you respond to feedback and to the changes it demands.

Recognize your emotions and responses

Understanding that you are experiencing fear ("I'm afraid my boss will fire me") and that you are exhibiting a maladaptive response to that fear ("I'll just stay out of his way and keep my mouth shut") are the critical initial steps toward adaptive change. They require ruthless self-honesty and a little detective work, both of which will go a long way toward helping you undo years of disguising your feelings. It's important to understand, too, that a particular maladaptive behavior does not necessarily tell you what emotion underlies it: You may be procrastinating out of anger, frustration, sadness, or other feelings. But persevering in the detective work is important, for the payoff is high. Having named the emotion and response, you can then act—just as someone who fears flying chooses to board a plane anyway. With practice, it gradually becomes easier to respond differently, even though the fear, anger, or sadness may remain.

Maria, a midlevel manager with whom we worked, is a good example of someone who learned to name her emotions and act despite them. Maria was several months overdue on performance reviews for the three people who reported to her. When we suggested that she was procrastinating, we asked her how she felt when she thought about doing the reviews. After some reflection, she said she was extremely resentful that her boss had not yet completed her own performance evaluation; she recognized that her procrastination was an expression of her anger toward him. We helped her realize that she could act despite her anger. Accordingly, Maria completed the performance evaluations for her subordinates and, in so doing, felt as if a huge weight had been lifted from her shoulders. Once she had completed the reviews, she noticed that her relationships with her three subordinates quickly improved, and her boss responded by finishing Maria's performance review.

We should note that Maria's procrastination was not an entrenched habit, so it was relatively easy to fix. Employees who start procrastinating in response to negative emotions early in their work lives won't change that habit quickly—but they can eventually.

Get support

Identifying your emotions is sometimes difficult, and feedback that requires change can leave you feeling inhibited and ashamed. For these reasons, it's critical to ask for help from trusted friends who will listen, encourage, and offer suggestions. Asking for support is often hard, because most corporate cultures expect managers to be self-reliant. Nevertheless, it's nearly impossible to make significant change without such encouragement. Support can come in many forms, but it should begin with at least two people—including, say, a spouse, a minister or spiritual counselor, a former mentor, an old high school classmate—with whom you feel emotionally safe. Ideally, one of these people should have some business experience. It may also help to enlist the assistance of an outside consultant or executive coach.

Reframe the feedback

Another adaptive technique, reframing, allows you to reconstruct the feedback process to your advantage. Specifically, this involves putting the prospect of asking for or reacting to feedback in a positive light so that negative emotions and responses lose their grip.

Take the example of Gary, a junior sales manager for a large manufacturing company. Gary's boss told him that he wasn't sociable enough with customers and prospects. The criticism stung, and Gary could have responded with denial or brooding. Indeed, his first response was to interpret the feedback as shallow. Eventually, though, Gary was able to reframe what he'd heard, first by grudgingly acknowledging it. ("He's right, I'm not very sociable. I tested as an introvert on the Myers-Briggs, and I've always been uncomfortable with small talk.") Then Gary reframed the feedback. Instead of seeing it as painful, he recognized that he could use it to help his career. Avoiding possible maladaptive responses, he was able to ask himself several important questions: "How critical is sociability to my position? How much do I want to keep this job? How much am I willing to change to become more sociable?" In responding, Gary realized two things: that sociability was indeed critical to success

Reframe Your Thinking

ALMOST EVERYONE DREADS performance reviews, which typically take place once a year. But how you respond to the boss's feedback—and how often you request it—will largely affect your performance and chances for career advancement. We've found that getting beyond that sense of dread involves recognizing and naming the emotions and behaviors that are preventing you from initiating feedback discussions. Once you determine those emotional and behavioral barriers, it's a matter of reframing your thoughts and moving toward more adaptive behavior. Below are some examples of how you might turn negative emotions into more positive, productive thoughts.

Possible negative emotion	Maladaptive response	Reframing statement
Anger (*I'm mad at my boss because he won't talk to me directly.*)	Acting out (*stomping around, complaining, being irritable, yelling at subordinates or family*)	It's up to me to get the feedback I need.
Anxiety (*I don't know what will happen.*)	Brooding (*withdrawal, nail biting*) Avoiding (*I'm too busy to ask for feedback.*)	Finding out can open up new opportunities for me.
Fear of confrontation (*I don't want to do this.*)	Denial, procrastination, self-sabotage (*canceling meetings with boss*)	Taking the initiative puts me in charge and gives me some power.

in sales and that he wasn't willing to learn to be more sociable. He requested a transfer and moved to a new position where he became much more successful.

Break up the task

Yet another adaptive technique is to divide up the large task of dealing with feedback into manageable, measurable chunks, and set realistic time frames for each one. Although more than two areas of behavior may need to be modified, it's our experience that most people can't change more than one or two at a time. Taking small

Possible negative emotion	Maladaptive response	Reframing statement
Fear of reprisal (If I speak up, will I get a pink slip?)	Denial (I don't need any feedback. I'm doing just fine.)	I really need to know honestly how I'm doing.
Hurt (Why did he say I wasn't trying hard enough?)	Irritability, jealousy of others (silence, plotting to get even)	I can still pay attention to what he said even though I feel hurt.
Defensiveness (I'm better than she says.)	Acting out by not supporting the boss (You can bet I'm not going to her stupid meeting.)	Being defensive keeps me from hearing what she has to say.
Sadness (I thought he liked me!)	Brooding, withdrawal (being quieter than usual, feeling demotivated)	How I'm doing in my job isn't about whether I'm liked.
Fear of change (How will I ever do all that he wants me to do?)	Denial (keep doing things the same way as before)	I must change to keep my job. I need to run the marathon one mile at a time.
Ambivalence (Should I stay or should I go?)	Procrastination, passivity (waiting for somebody else to solve the problem)	What really serves my interests best? Nobody is as interested in my well-being as I am. I need to take some action now.
Resignation (I have to leave!)	Resistance to change (It's just too hard to look for another job. It's not really so bad here.)	I'll be much happier working somewhere else.

steps and meeting discrete goals reduces your chances of being overwhelmed and makes change much more likely.

Jane, for example, received feedback indicating that the quality of her work was excellent but that her public presentations were boring. A quiet and reserved person, Jane could have felt overwhelmed by what she perceived as the subtext of this criticism: that she was a lousy public speaker and that she'd better transform herself from a wallflower into a writer and actress. Instead, she adapted by breaking down the challenge of "interesting presentations" into its constituent parts (solid and well-constructed content; a commanding delivery; an understanding of the audience; and so on). Then she undertook to teach herself to present more effectively by observing several effective speakers and taking an introductory course in public speaking.

It was important for Jane to start with the easiest task—in this case, observing good speakers. She noted their gestures, the organization of their speeches, their intonation, timing, use of humor, and so forth. Once she felt she understood what good speaking entailed, she was ready to take the introductory speaking course. These endeavors allowed her to improve her presentations. Though she didn't transform herself into a mesmerizing orator, she did learn to command the attention and respect of an audience.

Use incentives

Pat yourself on the back as you make adaptive changes. That may seem like unusual advice, given that feedback situations can rouse us to self-punishment and few of us are in the habit of congratulating ourselves. Nevertheless, nowhere is it written that the feedback process must be a wholly negative experience. Just as a salary raise or a bonus provides incentive to improve performance, rewarding yourself whenever you take an important step in the process will help you to persevere in your efforts. The incentive should be commensurate with the achievement. For example, an appropriate reward for completing a self-assessment might be an uninterrupted afternoon watching ESPN or, for a meeting with the boss, a fine dinner out.

Getting the Feedback You Need

Once you've begun to adapt your responses and behavior, it's time to start seeking regular feedback from your boss rather than wait for the annual performance review to come around. The proactive feedback process we recommend consists of four manageable steps: self-assessment, external feedback, absorbing the feedback, and taking action toward change. The story of Bob, a vice president of human resources, illustrates how one executive used the four-step process to take charge of his work life.

When we first met Bob, he had been on the job for three years and felt he was in a feedback vacuum. Once a year, toward the end of December, Harry—the gruff, evasive CEO to whom he reported—would call Bob in, tell him what a fine job he had been doing, announce his salary for the following year, and give him a small bonus. But this year, Bob had been dealing with thorny issues—including complaints from senior female executives about unfair compensation—and needed some real feedback. Bob wondered how Harry viewed his work. Were there aspects of Bob's performance that Harry wasn't happy with? Did Harry intend to retain Bob in his current position?

Self-assessment

We encouraged Bob to begin by assessing his own performance. Self-assessment can be a tough assignment, particularly if one has never received useful feedback to begin with. The first task in self-assessment was for Bob to determine which elements of his job were most important. The second was to recall informal feedback he had received from coworkers, subordinates, and customers—not only words, but facial expressions, body language, and silences.

Bob took several weeks to do his self-assessment. Once we helped him realize that he was procrastinating with the assessment, he enlisted a support system—his wife and an old college buddy—who encouraged him to finish his tally of recollections. At the end of the process, he recognized that he had received a good deal of positive informal feedback from many of the people with whom he interacted. But he also realized that he was too eager to please and needed to be more assertive in expressing his opinions. We helped him reframe these uncomfortable insights so that he could see them as areas for potential growth.

External feedback

The next phase of the proactive process—asking for feedback—is generally a two-part task: The first involves speaking to a few trusted colleagues to collect information that supports or revises your self-assessment. The second involves directly asking your boss for feedback. Gathering feedback from trusted colleagues shouldn't be confused with 360-degree feedback, which culls a wide variety of perspectives, including those from people who may not know you well. By speaking confidentially with people you genuinely trust, you can keep some of the fear associated with feedback at bay. Trusted colleagues can also help you identify your own emotional and possibly maladaptive responses to criticism, which is particularly beneficial prior to your meeting with your superior. Additionally, feedback conversations with colleagues can often serve as a form of dress rehearsal for the real thing. Sometimes, colleagues point out areas that warrant immediate attention; when they do, it's wise to make those changes before meeting with the boss. On the other hand, if you think you can't trust any of your colleagues, you should bypass such feedback conversations and move directly to setting up a meeting with your boss.

Bob asked for feedback from two trusted colleagues, Sheila and Paul, at meetings that he specifically scheduled for this purpose. He requested both positive and negative feedback and specific examples of areas in which he did well and in which he needed to improve. He listened intently to their comments, interrupting only for clarification. Both told him that he analyzed problems carefully and interacted well with employees. Yet Sheila noted that at particularly busy times of the year, Bob seemed to have difficulty setting his priorities, and Paul pointed out that Bob needed to be more assertive. Armed with his colleagues' feedback, Bob had a clearer notion of his strengths and weaknesses. He realized that some of his difficulties in setting priorities were owing to unclear direction from Harry, and he made a note to raise the matter with him.

The next step in external feedback—the actual meeting with your boss—requires delicate handling, particularly since the request may come as a surprise to him or her. In setting up the meeting, it's important to assure your boss that criticisms and suggestions will be heard, appreciated, and positively acted on. It's vital, too, to set the agenda for the meeting, letting your superior know that you have three or four questions based on your self-assessment and feedback from others. During the meeting, ask for specific examples and suggestions for change while remaining physically and emotionally neutral about the feedback you hear. Watch carefully not only for specific content but also for body language and tone, since feedback can be indirect as well as direct. When the meeting concludes, thank your boss and indicate that you will get back to her with a plan of action after you've had time to absorb what you've heard. Remember, too, that you can terminate the meeting if it becomes counterproductive (for example, if your boss responds to any of your questions with anger).

During his feedback meeting with Harry, Bob inquired about his work priorities. Harry told him that the company's financial situation looked precarious and that Bob should focus on locating and implementing a less costly health benefit plan. Harry warned Bob that a new plan would surely anger some employees, and because of that, Bob needed to develop a tougher skin to withstand the inevitable criticisms.

As Bob learned, feedback meetings can provide more than just a performance assessment; they can also offer some other important and unexpected insights. Bob had been so immersed in HR issues that he had never noted that Harry had been otherwise preoccupied with the company's financial problems.

Absorbing the feedback
Upon hearing critical feedback, you may well experience the negative emotions and maladaptive responses we described earlier. It's important to keep your reactions private until you can replace them with adaptive responses that lead to an appropriate plan of action.

Bob, for example, realized he felt irritated and vaguely hurt at the suggestion that he needed to toughen up. He brooded for a while but then reframed these feelings by recognizing that the negative feedback was as much a commentary on Harry's preoccupations as it was on Bob's performance. Bob didn't use the reframing to negate Harry's feedback; he accepted that he needed to be more assertive and hard-nosed in dealing with employees' issues.

Taking action
The last phase of the proactive feedback process involves coming to conclusions about, and acting on, the information you've received.

Bob, for example, chose to focus on two action strategies: implementing a less costly health care plan—which included preparing himself to tolerate employee complaints—and quietly looking for new employment, since he now understood that the company's future was uncertain. Both of these decisions made Bob uncomfortable, for they evoked his fear of change. But having developed his adaptive responses, he no longer felt trapped by fear. In the months following, he implemented the new health benefits plan without taking his employees' criticisms personally. He also kept an eye on the company's financials and reconnected with his professional network in case it became clear the organization was starting to founder.

The Rewards of Adaptation

Organizations profit when executives seek feedback and are able to deal well with criticism. As executives begin to ask how they are doing relative to management's priorities, their work becomes better aligned with organizational goals. Moreover, as an increasing number of executives in an organization learn to ask for feedback, they begin to transform a feedback-averse environment into a more honest and open one, in turn improving performance throughout the organization.

Equally important, using the adaptive techniques we've mentioned can have a positive effect on executives' private lives. When they free themselves from knee-jerk behaviors in response to emotions, they often find that relationships with family and friends improve. Indeed, they sometimes discover that rather than fear feedback, they look forward to leveraging it.

Originally published in April 2003. Reprint R0304H

The Young and the Clueless

by Kerry A. Bunker, Kathy E. Kram, and Sharon Ting

IN MANY WAYS, 36-year-old Charles Armstrong is a natural leader. He's brilliant, creative, energetic, aggressive—a strategic and financial genius. He's risen quickly through the ranks due to his keen business instincts and proven ability to deliver bottom-line results, at times jumping from one organization to another to leapfrog through the hierarchy. But now his current job is on the line. A division president at an international consumer products company, he's just uncovered a major production setback on a heavily promoted new product. Thousands of orders have been delayed, customers are furious, and the company's stock price has plummeted since the news went public.

Worse, the crisis was utterly preventable. Had Armstrong understood the value of building relationships with his peers and had his subordinates found him approachable, he might have been able to appreciate the cross-functional challenges of developing this particular product. He might have learned of the potential delay months earlier instead of at the eleventh hour. He could have postponed a national advertising campaign and set expectations with investors. He might have even found a way to solve the problems and launch the product on time. But despite his ability to dazzle his superiors with talent and intellect, Armstrong is widely viewed by his peers and subordinates as self-promoting, intolerant, and remote. Perhaps worse, he's only half aware of how others perceive him, and to the extent he does know, he's not terribly concerned. These relationships are not a priority for him. Like so many other talented young managers, Armstrong lacks the emotional competencies that would enable him to work more effectively as part of a team. And now his bosses seem to have unwittingly undermined his career, having promoted him too quickly, before he could develop the relationship skills he needs.

Break the Pattern

What happened with Charles Armstrong is an increasingly common phenomenon. In the past ten years, we've met dozens of managers who have fallen victim to a harmful mix of their own ambition and their bosses' willingness to overlook a lack of people skills. (As with all the examples in these pages, we've changed Armstrong's name and other identifying features to protect our clients' identities.) Indeed, most executives seek out smart, aggressive people, paying more attention to their accomplishments than to their emotional maturity. What's more, they know that their strongest performers have options—if they don't get the job they want at one company, they're bound to get it somewhere else. Why risk losing them to a competitor by delaying a promotion?

The answer is that promoting them can be just as risky. Putting these unseasoned managers into positions of authority too quickly robs them of the opportunity to develop the emotional competencies that come with time and experience—competencies like the ability to negotiate with peers, regulate their emotions in times of crisis, or win support for change. Bosses may be delighted with such managers' intelligence and passion—and may even see younger versions of themselves—but peers and subordinates are more likely to see them as arrogant and inconsiderate, or, at the very least, aloof. And therein lies the problem. At some point in a young manager's career, usually at the vice president level, raw talent and determined ambition become less important than the ability to influence

Idea in Brief

Hell-bent on sabotaging your company? Then promote your brightest young professionals into your most demanding roles—especially when they threaten to leave unless you fast-track them. Nonsense, you say? Hardly.

Promoting talented young managers too quickly prevents them from developing key **emotional competencies**—such as negotiating with peers, regulating negative emotions during crises, and building support for change—skills that come only with time and experience.

Worse, many "young and clueless" managers lack patience, openness, and empathy—qualities more vital than raw intellect at top leadership levels, where business issues grow more complex and stakes are notoriously high.

Aggressive and insensitive, fast-tracked managers may pooh-pooh relationships with peers and subordinates—not realizing they *need* those connections to conquer problems. Issues become crises, defeating managers. Your company, customers, and employees all pay the price.

The solution? **Delay promotions** so managers can mature emotionally. This isn't easy. You must balance confrontation and support, patience and urgency—and risk losing your finest. But premature promoting carries far greater risks.

and persuade. And unless senior executives appreciate this fact and make emotional competence a top priority, these high-potential managers will continue to fail, often at significant cost to the company.

Research has shown that the higher a manager rises in the ranks, the more important soft leadership skills are to his success.[1] Our colleagues at the Center for Creative Leadership have found that about a third of senior executives derail or plateau at some point, most often due to an emotional deficit such as the inability to build a team or regulate their own emotions in times of stress. And in our combined 55 years of coaching and teaching, we've seen firsthand how a young manager risks his career when he fails to develop emotional competencies. But the problem isn't youth per se. The problem is a lack of emotional maturity, which doesn't come easily or automatically and isn't something you learn from a book. It's one thing to understand the importance of relationships at an intellectual level

Idea in Practice

1. **Deepen 360-degree feedback.** Provide broad and deep feedback to help managers see themselves as others do—a must for building self-awareness. Give them verbatim written responses to open-ended questions from a wide variety of peers and subordinates, not just you. Managers may discount your views as biased or uninformed. Allow time for reflection and follow-up conversations.

   Example: Though his business acumen was unmatched in his company, a brilliant 42-year-old VP neglected peer relationships, earning a reputation as detached. Corporate wondered if he could inspire staff to support important new strategies. After an in-depth 360-degree review, he began strengthening interpersonal connections.

2. **Interrupt the ascent.** To help managers learn to move others' hearts and minds, give them special assignments outside their typical career path. They'll *have* to master negotiation and influence skills, rather than relying on rank for authority.

   Example: A quick-tempered regional sales director wasn't ready for promotion to VP. Her boss persuaded her to lead a year-long team investigating cross selling opportunities. She learned to use persuasion to win other division managers' support, building solid relationships. Now a VP, she's perceived as a well-connected manager who can negotiate on her team's behalf.

and to learn techniques like active listening; it's another matter entirely to develop a full range of interpersonal competencies like patience, openness, and empathy. Emotional maturity involves a fundamental shift in self-awareness and behavior, and that change requires practice, diligence, and time.

Armstrong's boss admits that he may have promoted the young manager too soon: "I was just like Charles when I was his age, but I was a director, not a division president. It's easier to make mistakes and learn when you aren't in such a big chair. I want him to succeed, and I think he could make a great CEO one day, but sometimes he puts me at risk. He's just too sure of himself to listen." And so, in many cases, executives do their employees and the company a service by delaying the promotion of a young manager and giving

3. **Act on your commitment.** If you've warned managers that promotion depends on emotional competencies, follow through. These competencies are *not* optional.

   Example: A conflict-averse senior VP managed his own group well but avoided collaborative situations, where the potential for conflict increased. Exploring external alliances, the firm considered collaboration vital. The CEO demoted him, temporarily pulling him from the succession plan. Assigned to a cross-functional team project, he learned to handle disputes and build consensus. He's back on track.

4. **Institutionalize personal development.** Make it clear that success at your company hinges on emotional competence.

   Example: One CEO articulated corporate values emphasizing continual learning, including asking for help. He created incentives encouraging such behaviors and built emotional-skills requirements into the firm's succession planning. Known for learning and growing, the firm attracts and retains talented young executives.

5. **Cultivate informal networks.** Encourage managers to forge mentoring relationships outside the usual hierarchy. They'll encounter diverse leadership styles and viewpoints, gain opportunities for reflection—and mature emotionally.

him the chance to develop his interpersonal skills. Interrupting the manager's ascent long enough to round out his experience will usually yield a much more effective and stable leader.

This article will look at five strategies for boosting emotional competencies and redirecting managers who are paying a price for damaged or nonexistent relationships. The strategies aren't terribly complicated, but implementing them and getting people to change their entrenched behaviors can be very difficult. Many of these managers are accustomed to receiving accolades, and it often isn't easy for them to hear—or act on—difficult messages. You may have to satisfy yourself with small victories and accept occasional slipups. But perhaps the greatest challenge is having the discipline to resist the charm of the young and the clueless—to refrain from promoting them before they are ready and to stay the course even if they threaten to quit.

Deepen 360-Degree Feedback

With its questionnaires and standardized rating scales, 360-degree feedback as it is traditionally implemented may not be sufficiently specific or detailed to get the attention of inexperienced managers who excel at bottom-line measures but struggle with more subtle relationship challenges. These managers will benefit from a deeper and more thorough process that includes time for reflection and follow-up conversations. That means, for example, interviewing a wider range of the manager's peers and subordinates and giving her the opportunity to read verbatim responses to open-ended questions. Such detailed and extensive feedback can help a person see herself more as others do, a must for the young manager lacking the self-awareness to understand where she's falling short.

We witnessed this lack of self-awareness in Bill Miller, a 42-year-old vice president at a software company—an environment where technical ability is highly prized. Miller had gone far on pure intellect, but he never fully appreciated his own strengths. So year after year, in assignment after assignment, he worked doubly hard at learning the complexities of the business, neglecting his relationships with his colleagues as an unintended consequence. His coworkers considered his smarts and business acumen among the finest in the company, but they found him unapproachable and detached. As a result, top management questioned his ability to lead the type of strategic change that would require motivating staff at all levels. Not until Miller went through an in-depth 360-degree developmental review was he able to accept that he no longer needed to prove his intelligence—that he could relax in that respect and instead work on strengthening his personal connections. After months of working hard to cultivate stronger relationships with his employees, Miller began to notice that he felt more included in chance social encounters like hallway conversations.

Art Grainger, a 35-year-old senior manager at a cement and con-crete company, was generally considered a champion by his direct reports. He was also known for becoming defensive whenever his peers or superiors questioned or even discussed his unit's perfor-mance. Through 360-degree reviews, he discovered that while every-one saw him as committed, results-oriented, and technically brilliant, they also saw him as overly protective, claiming he resisted any action or decision that might affect his department. Even his employees felt that he kept them isolated from the rest of the company, having said he reviewed all memos between departments, didn't invite people from other parts of the company to his department's meetings, and openly criticized other managers. Only when Grainger heard that his staff agreed with what his bosses had been telling him for years did he concede that he needed to change. Since then, he has come to see members of other departments as potential allies and has tried to redefine his team to include people from across the company.

It's worth noting that many of these smart young managers aren't used to hearing criticism. Consequently, they may discount nega-tive feedback, either because the comments don't mesh with what they've heard in previous conversations or because their egos are so strong. Or they may conclude that they can "fix" the problem right away—after all, they've been able to fix most problems they've encountered in the past. But developing emotional competen-cies requires practice and ongoing personal interactions. The good news is that if you succeed in convincing them that these issues are career threatening, they may apply the same zeal to their emotional development that they bring to their other projects. And that's why 360-degree feedback is so valuable: When it comes from multiple sources and is ongoing, it's difficult to ignore.

Interrupt the Ascent

When people are continually promoted within their areas of exper-tise, they don't have to stray far from their comfort zones, so they seldom need to ask for help, especially if they're good problem solvers. Accordingly, they may become overly independent and fail to cultivate relationships with people who could be useful to them in the future. What's more, they may rely on the authority that comes with rank rather than learning how to influence people. A command-and-control mentality may work in certain situations, particularly in lower to middle management, but it's usually insufficient in more senior positions, when peer relationships are critical and success depends more on the ability to move hearts and minds than on the ability to develop business solutions.

We sometimes counsel our clients to broaden young managers' skills by assigning them to cross-functional roles outside their expected career paths. This is distinct from traditional job rotation, which has employees spending time in different functional areas to enhance and broaden their knowledge of the business. Rather, the manager is assigned a role in which he doesn't have much direct authority. This will help him focus on developing other skills like negotiation and influencing peers.

Consider the case of Sheila McIntyre, a regional sales director at a technology company. McIntyre had been promoted quickly into the managerial ranks because she consistently outsold her colleagues month after month. In her early thirties, she began angling for another promotion–this time, to vice president—but her boss, Ron Meyer, didn't think she was ready. Meyer felt that McIntyre had a quick temper and little patience for people whom she perceived as less visionary. So he put the promotion on hold, despite McIntyre's stellar performance, and created a yearlong special assignment for her—heading a team investigating cross-selling opportunities. To persuade her to take the job, he not only explained that it would help McIntyre broaden her skills but promised a significant financial reward if she succeeded, also hinting that the hoped-for promotion would follow. It was a stretch for McIntyre. She had to use her underdeveloped powers of persuasion to win support from managers in other divisions. But in the end, her team presented a brilliant cross-selling strategy, which the company implemented over the following year. More important, she developed solid relationships with a number of influential people throughout the organization and learned a lot about the value of others' insights and experiences. McIntyre was eventually promoted to vice president, and to Meyer's satisfaction, her new reports now see her not just as a superstar salesperson but as a well-connected manager who can negotiate on their behalf.

Such cross-functional assignments—with no clear authority or obvious ties to a career path—can be a tough sell. It's not easy to convince young managers that these assignments are valuable, nor is it easy to help them extract relevant knowledge. If the managers feel marginalized, they may not stick around. Remember Bill Miller, the vice president who had neglected his emotional skills in his zeal to learn the business? While he was successful in some of his early informal attempts to build relationships, he was confused and demoralized when his boss, Jerry Schulman, gave him a special assignment to lead a task force reviewing internal processes. Miller had expected a promotion, and the new job didn't feel "real." Schulman made the mistake of not telling Miller that he saw the job as an ideal networking opportunity, so Miller began to question his future at the company. A few months into the new job, Miller gave his notice. He seized an opportunity—a step up—at an arch-rival, taking a tremendous amount of talent and institutional knowledge with him. Had Schulman shared his reasoning with Miller, he might have retained one of his most valuable players—one who had already seen the importance of developing his emotional competence and had begun to make progress.

Act On Your Commitment

One of the reasons employees get stuck in the pattern we've described is that their bosses point out deficits in emotional competencies but don't follow through. They either neglect to articulate the consequences of continuing the destructive behavior or make empty threats but proceed with a promotion anyway. The hard-charging young executive can only conclude that these competencies are optional.

A cautionary tale comes from Mitchell Geller who, at 29, was on the verge of being named partner at a law firm. He had alienated many of his peers and subordinates over the years through his arrogance, a shortcoming duly noted on his yearly performance reviews, yet his keen legal mind had won him promotion after promotion. With Geller's review approaching, his boss, Larry Snow, pointed to heavy attrition among the up-and-coming lawyers who worked for Geller and warned him that further advancement would be contingent on a change in personal style. Geller didn't take the feedback to heart—he was confident that he'd get by, as he always had, on sheer talent. And true to form, Snow didn't stick to his guns. The promotion came through even though Geller's behavior hadn't changed. Two weeks later, Geller, by then a partner responsible for managing client relationships, led meetings with two key accounts. Afterward, the first client approached Snow and asked him to sit in on future meetings. Then the second client withdrew his business altogether, complaining that Geller had refused to listen to alternative points of view.

Contrast Geller's experience with that of 39-year-old Barry Kessler, a senior vice president at an insurance company. For years, Kessler had been heir apparent to the CEO due to his strong financial skills and vast knowledge of the business—that is, until John Mason, his boss and the current CEO, began to question the wisdom of promoting him.

While Kessler managed his own group exceptionally well, he avoided collaboration with other units, which was particularly important as the company began looking for new growth opportunities, including potential alliances with other organizations. The problem wasn't that Kessler was hostile, it was that he was passively disengaged—a flaw that hadn't seemed as important when he was responsible only for his own group. In coaching Kessler, we learned that he was extremely averse to conflict and that he avoided situations where he couldn't be the decision maker. His aversions sharply limited his ability to work with peers.

Mason sent a strong signal, not only to Kessler but to others in the organization, when he essentially demoted Kessler by taking away some of his responsibilities and temporarily pulling him from the succession plan. To give Kessler an opportunity to develop the skills he lacked, Mason asked him to lead a cross-functional team dedicated to finding strategic opportunities for growth. Success would require Kessler to devote more time to developing his interpersonal skills. He had no authority over the other team members, so he had to work through disputes and help the team arrive at a consensus. Two years later, Kessler reports that he is more comfortable with conflict and feedback, and he's worked his way back into the succession plan.

By the way, it's counterproductive to hold managers to a certain standard of behavior without showing that the same standard applies to everyone, right up to top management. In many cases, that means acknowledging your own development goals, which isn't easy. One CEO we worked with, Joe Simons, came to realize during 360-degree feedback and peer coaching that his personal style was interfering with his subordinates' growth. Simons had declared innovation a corporate priority, yet his fear of failure led him to micromanage his employees, stifling their creativity. To stop this pattern and express his newfound commitment to improving his relationship skills, he revealed his personal goals—to seek advice more regularly and to communicate more openly—to his direct reports. He promised to change specific behaviors and asked for the team's feedback and support in this process. Going public with these goals was tough for Simons, a private person raised on traditional command-and-control leadership. Admitting that he needed to change some behaviors felt dangerously weak to him, especially given that the company was going through a difficult time and employees were looking to him for assurance, but his actions made his new priorities clear to employees.

Simons's candor won people's trust and respect, and over the course of many months, others in the company began to reflect more openly on their own emotional skills and engage in similar processes of personal development. Not only did his relationships with his direct reports improve, but Simons became a catalyst and model for others as well. He told us of an encounter with Gwen Marshall, the company's CFO and one of Simons's direct reports. Marshall was concerned about a new hire who wasn't coming up to speed as

Think Before Promoting

IT'S NOT UNUSUAL for a star performer to be promoted into higher management before he's ready. Yes, he may be exceptionally smart and talented, but he may also lack essential people skills. Rather than denying him the promotion altogether, his boss might do well to delay it—and use that time to help develop the candidate's emotional competencies. Here's how.

Deepen 360-Degree Feedback

Go beyond the usual set of questionnaires that make up the traditional 360-degree-feedback process. Interview a wide variety of the manager's peers and subordinates and let him read verbatim responses to open-ended performance questions.

Interrupt the Ascent

Help the inexperienced manager get beyond a command-and-control mentality by pushing him to develop his negotiation and persuasion skills. Instead of promoting him, give him cross-functional assignments where he can't rely on rank to influence people.

Act On Your Commitment

Don't give the inexperienced manager the impression that emotional competencies are optional. Hold him accountable for his interpersonal skills, in some cases taking a tough stance by demoting him or denying him a promotion, but with the promise that changed behaviors will ultimately be rewarded.

Institutionalize Personal Development

Weave interpersonal goals into the fabric of the organization and make emotional competence a performance measure. Also work to institute formal development programs that teach leadership skills and facilitate self-awareness, reflection, and opportunities to practice new emotional competencies.

Cultivate Informal Networks

Encourage the manager to develop informal learning partnerships with peers and mentors in order to expose him to different leadership styles and perspectives. This will provide him with honest and ongoing feedback and continual opportunities to learn.

quickly as she had hoped—he was asking lots of questions and, she felt, not taking enough initiative. She had just snapped at him at the close of a meeting, and he'd looked surprised and angry. In speaking to Simons about the incident, however, she acknowledged that her impatience was perhaps unfair. He was, after all, new to the job. What's more, the nature of finance demanded precise thinking and a thorough knowledge of the business. Marshall ended the conversation by saying she would apologize to the new employee. Simons was surprised at Marshall's comments—he was used to seeing her simply blow off steam and move on to the next task. But possibly due to Simons's example, she had become more attuned to the importance of her own emotional competence. Such reflection has become a habit among Simons's team—a change that has enhanced personal relationships and increased the team's overall performance.

Institutionalize Personal Development

One of the most effective ways to build managers' emotional competencies is to weave interpersonal goals into the fabric of the organization, where everyone is expected to demonstrate a specific set of emotional skills and where criteria for promotion include behaviors as well as technical ability. A built-in process will make it easier to uncover potential problems early and reduce the chances that people identified as needing personal development will feel singled out or unfairly held back. Employees will know exactly what's expected of them and what it takes to advance in their careers.

Here's a case in which institutionalizing personal development was extremely effective: Mark Jones is an executive who was tapped for the CEO job at a major manufacturing company on the condition that he engage a coach because of his reputation for being too blunt and aggressive. A yearlong coaching relationship helped Jones understand the pitfalls associated with his style, and he decided that others could benefit from arriving at such an understanding far earlier in their careers. To that end, he launched several major initiatives to shape the company culture in such a way that personal and professional learning were not only encouraged but expected.

First, he articulated a new set of corporate values and practices that were based on meeting business objectives and developing top-notch leadership skills. One of the values was "Dare to be transparent," which meant that all employees, especially those in senior leadership roles, were expected to be open about their weaknesses, ask for help, and offer honest, constructive feedback to their peers. Knowing that it would be necessary to create incentives and rewards for these new behaviors, Jones took an active role in the review and personal-development goals of the company's top 100 executives, and he mandated that all employees' performance plans incorporate specific actions related to developing their own emotional competencies. Jones also made emotional skills a key qualification in the search for a successor—a requirement that many organizations pay lip service to. Many of them often overvalue raw intellect and depth of knowledge, largely because of the war for talent, which has resulted in a singular focus on hiring and retaining the best and brightest regardless of their emotional competence. Finally, Jones created a new position, corporate learning officer; he and the CLO partnered with a nearby university to create a learning institute where corporate executives could teach in and attend leadership programs. Jones himself is a frequent lecturer and participant in the various courses.

Through all these actions, Jones has made it clear that employees need to make continual learning and emotional development a priority. He's also emphasized that everyone from the CEO on down is expected to set goals for improving personal skills. Since implementing the program, he is finding it easier to attract and retain talented young executives—indeed, his organization has evolved from a recruiter's nightmare to a magnet for young talent. It is becoming known as a place where emerging leaders can find real opportunities to learn and grow.

We worked with another company where the senior management team committed to developing the emotional competencies of the company's leaders. The team first provided extensive education on coaching to the HR department, which in turn supervised a program whereby top managers coached their younger and more inexperienced colleagues. The goal was to have both the experienced and inexperienced benefit: The junior managers provided feedback on the senior people's coaching skills, and the senior people helped foster emotional competencies in their less-experienced colleagues.

The results were encouraging. Wes Burke, an otherwise high-performing manager, had recently been struggling to meet his business targets. After spending time with Burke and conferring with his subordinates and peers, his coach (internal to the organization) came to believe that, in his zest to achieve his goals, Burke was unable to slow down and listen to other people's ideas. Burke wasn't a boor: He had taken courses in communication and knew how to fake listening behaviors such as nodding his head and giving verbal acknowledgments, but he was often distracted and not really paying attention. He never accepted this feedback until one day, while he was walking purposefully through the large operations plant he managed, a floor supervisor stopped him to discuss his ideas for solving an ongoing production problem. Burke flipped on his active-listening mode. After uttering a few acknowledgments and saying, "Thanks, let's talk more about that," he moved on, leaving the supervisor feeling frustrated and at a loss for how to capture his boss's interest. As it happened, Burke's coach was watching. He pulled the young manager aside and said, "You didn't hear a word Karl just said. You weren't really listening." Burke admitted as much to himself and his coach. He then apologized to Karl, much to the supervisor's surprise. Keeping this incident in mind helped Burke remember the importance of his working relationships. His coach had also helped him realize that he shouldn't have assumed his sheer will and drive would somehow motivate his employees. Burke had been wearing people down, physically and psychologically. A year later, Burke's operation was hitting its targets, an accomplishment he partially attributes to the one-on-one coaching he received.

Cultivate Informal Networks

While institutionalized programs to build emotional competencies are critical, some managers will benefit more from an informal network of relationships that fall outside the company hierarchy. Mentoring, for example, can help both junior and senior managers further their emotional development through a new type of relationship. And when the mentoring experience is a positive one, it often acts as a springboard to a rich variety of relationships with others throughout the organization. In particular, it gives junior managers a chance to experience different leadership styles and exposes them to diverse viewpoints.

Sonia Greene, a 32-year-old manager at a consulting firm, was hoping to be promoted to principal, but she hadn't raised the issue with her boss because she assumed he didn't think she was ready, and she didn't want to create tension. She was a talented consultant with strong client relationships, but her internal relationships were weak due to a combination of shyness, an independent nature, and a distaste for conflict, which inhibited her from asking for feedback. When her company launched a mentoring program, Greene signed up, and through a series of lengthy conversations with Jessica Burnham, a partner at the firm, she developed new insights about her strengths and weaknesses. The support of an established player such as Burnham helped Greene become more confident and honest in her development discussions with her boss, who hadn't been aware that Greene was willing to receive and act on feedback. Today, Greene is armed with a precise understanding of what she needs to work on and is well on her way to being promoted. What's more, her relationship with Burnham has prompted her to seek out other connections, including a peer group of up-and-coming managers who meet monthly to share experiences and offer advice to one another.

Peer networking is beneficial to even the most top-level executives. And the relationships needn't be confined within organizational boundaries. Joe Simons, a CEO we mentioned earlier, wanted to continue his own personal development, so he cultivated a relationship with another executive he'd met through our program. The two men have stayed in touch through regular e-mails and phone calls, keeping their discussions confidential so they can feel free to share even the most private concerns. They also get together periodically to discuss their goals for personal development.

Both have found these meetings invaluable, noting that their work relationships have continued to improve and that having a trustworthy confidant has helped each avoid relapsing into old habits during times of stress.

———————————

Delaying a promotion can be difficult given the steadfast ambitions of the young executive and the hectic pace of organizational life, which makes personal learning seem like an extravagance. It requires a delicate balance of honesty and support, of patience and goading. It means going against the norm of promoting people almost exclusively on smarts, talent, and business results. It also means contending with the disappointment of an esteemed subordinate.

But taking the time to build people's emotional competencies isn't an extravagance; it's critical to developing effective leaders. Give in to the temptation to promote your finest before they're ready, and you're left with executives who may thrive on change and demonstrate excellent coping and survival skills but who lack the self-awareness, empathy, and social abilities required to foster and nurture those strengths in others. MBA programs and management books can't teach young executives everything they need to know about people skills. Indeed, there's no substitute for experience, reflection, feedback, and, above all, practice.

Originally published in December 2002. Reprint R0212F

Note

1. In his HBR articles "What Makes a Leader?" (November–December 1998) and "Primal Leadership: The Hidden Driver of Great Performance" (with Richard Boyatzis and Annie McKee, December 2001), Daniel Goleman makes the case that emotional competence is the crucial driver of a leader's success.

About the Contributors

RICHARD BOYATZIS chairs the department of organizational behavior at the Weatherhead School of Management at Case Western Reserve University.

JOEL BROCKNER is the Phillip Hettleman Professor of Business at Columbia Business School.

KERRY A. BUNKER is a manager of the Awareness Program for Executive Excellence at the Center for Creative Leadership.

ANDREW CAMPBELL is a director of Ashridge Strategic Management Centre in London.

CHRISTINA CONGLETON, who was formerly a researcher on mindfulness and the brain at Massachusetts General Hospital, is an associate at Evidence Based Psychology and a certified coach.

DIANE L. COUTU is a former senior editor of *Harvard Business Review*.

SUSAN DAVID is the CEO of Evidence Based Psychology, a cofounder of the Institute of Coaching, and an instructor in psychology at Harvard University.

SYDNEY FINKELSTEIN is the Steven Roth Professor of Management at the Tuck School of Business at Dartmouth College.

DANIEL GOLEMAN cochairs the Consortium for Research on Emotional Intelligence in Organizations at Rutgers University.

JAY M. JACKMAN is a psychiatrist and human resources consultant in Stanford, California.

KATHY E. KRAM is a professor of organizational behavior at the Boston University School of Management.

ANNIE McKEE is on the faculty of the University of Pennsylvania's Graduate School of Education.

CHRISTINE PEARSON is a professor of global leadership at Thunderbird School of Global Management.

CHRISTINE PORATH is an associate professor at Georgetown University's McDonough School of Business.

MYRA H. STROBER is a labor economist and professor at Stanford University's School of Education, and by courtesy at the Stanford Graduate School of Business. She is also a human resources consultant.

SHARON TING is a manager of the Awareness Program for Executive Excellence at the Center for Creative Leadership.

VANESSA URCH DRUSKAT is an assistant professor of organizational behavior at the Weatherhead School of Management at Case Western Reserve University.

JO WHITEHEAD is a director of Ashridge Strategic Management Centre in London.

STEVEN B. WOLFF is an assistant professor of management at the School of Management at Marist College.

HBR Guide to
Emotional
Intelligence

HARVARD BUSINESS REVIEW PRESS
Boston, Massachusetts

What Is Emotional Intelligence?

## CHAPTER 1

Leading by Feel

LIKE IT OR NOT, leaders need to manage the mood of their organizations. The most gifted leaders accomplish that by using a mysterious blend of psychological abilities known as *emotional intelligence.* They're self-aware and empathetic. They can read and regulate their own emotions while intuitively grasping how others feel and gauging their organization's emotional state.

But where does emotional intelligence come from? And how do leaders learn to use it? The management literature (and even common sense) suggests that both nature and nurture feed emotional intelligence. Part genetic predisposition, part life experience, and part old-fashioned training, emotional intelligence emerges in varying degrees from one leader to the next, and managers apply it with varying skill. Wisely and compassionately deployed, emotional intelligence spurs leaders, their people, and their organizations to superior performance; naively or maliciously applied, it can paralyze leaders or allow them to manipulate followers for personal gain.

We invited 18 leaders and scholars (including business executives, leadership researchers, psychologists, a neurologist, a cult expert, and a symphony conductor) to explore the nature and management of emotional intelligence—its sources, uses, and abuses. Their responses differed dramatically, but there were some common themes: the importance of consciously and conscientiously

Excerpted from *Harvard Business Review*, January 2004 (product #R0401B)

honing one's skills, the double-edged nature of self-awareness, and the danger of letting any one emotional intelligence skill dominate. Here are some of their perspectives.

Be Realistic

John D. Mayer *is a professor of psychology at the University of New Hampshire. He and Yale psychology professor Peter Salovey are credited with first defining the concept of emotional intelligence in the early 1990s.*

This is a time of growing realism about emotional intelligence— especially concerning what it is and what it isn't. The books and articles that have helped popularize the concept have defined it as a loose collection of personality traits, such as self-awareness, optimism, and tolerance. These popular definitions have been accompanied by exaggerated claims about the importance of emotional intelligence. But diverse personality traits, however admirable, don't necessarily add up to a single definition of emotional intelligence. In fact, such traits are difficult to collectively evaluate in a way that reveals their relationship to success in business and in life.

Even when they're viewed in isolation, the characteristics commonly associated with emotional intelligence and success may be more complicated than they seem. For example, the scientific jury is out on how important self-awareness is to successful leadership. In fact, too much self-awareness can reduce self-esteem, which is often a crucial component of great leadership.

From a scientific standpoint, emotional intelligence is the ability to accurately perceive your own and others' emotions; to understand the signals that emotions send about relationships; and to manage your own and others' emotions. It doesn't necessarily include the qualities (like optimism, initiative, and self-confidence) that some popular definitions ascribe to it.

Researchers have used performance tests to measure people's accuracy at identifying and understanding emotions; for example, asking them to identify the emotions conveyed by a face or which among several situations is most likely to bring about happiness. People who get high scores on these tests are indeed different from others. In the business world, they appear better able to deal with customers' complaints or to mediate disputes, and they may excel at making strong and positive personal connections with subordinates and customers over the long term. Of course, emotional intelligence isn't the only way to attain success as a leader: A brilliant strategist who can maximize profits may be able to hire and keep talented employees even if he or she doesn't have strong personal connections with them.

Is there value in scales that, based on popular conceptions, measure qualities like optimism and self-confidence but label them "emotional intelligence"? Certainly, these personality traits are important in business, so measuring and (sometimes) enhancing them can be useful. But recent research makes it clear that these characteristics are distinct from emotional intelligence as it is scientifically defined. A person high in emotional intelligence may be realistic rather than optimistic and insecure rather than confident. Conversely, a person may be highly self-confident and optimistic but lack emotional intelligence. The danger lies in assuming that because a person is optimistic or confident, they are also emotionally intelligent, when, in fact, the presence of those traits will tell you nothing of the sort.

Never Stop Learning

Daniel Goleman is the cochair of the Consortium for Research on Emotional Intelligence in Organizations based at Rutgers University's Graduate School of Applied and Professional Psychology in Piscataway, New Jersey.

You can be a successful leader without much emotional intelligence if you're extremely lucky and you've got everything else going for you: booming markets, bumbling competitors, and clueless higher-ups. If you're incredibly smart, you can cover for an absence of emotional intelligence until things get tough for the business. But at that point, you won't have built up the social capital needed to

5 Components of Emotional Intelligence

IN 1998, IN WHAT HAS become one of HBR's most enduring articles, "What Makes a Leader?" Daniel Goleman introduced a framework of five components of emotional intelligence that allow individuals to recognize, connect with, and learn from their own and other people's mental states, as well as their hallmarks. While there are many frameworks offering varying sets of EI competencies (and other models that conceive of emotional intelligence not as a set of competencies but rather as the ability to abstract and problem solve in the emotional domain), Goleman's approach, outlined in exhibit 1, can be a helpful way to start building an understanding of emotional intelligence:

EXHIBIT 1

EI Component	Definition	Hallmarks	Example
Self-awareness	Knowing one's emotions, strengths, weaknesses, drives, values, and goals—and their impacts on others	• Self-confidence • Realistic self-assessment • Self-deprecating sense of humor • Thirst for constructive criticism	A manager knows tight deadlines bring out the worst in him. So he plans his time to get work done well in advance.
Self-regulation	Controlling or redirecting disruptive emotions and impulses	• Trustworthiness • Integrity • Comfort with ambiguity and change	When a team botches a presentation, its leader resists the urge to scream. Instead, she considers possible reasons for the failure, explains the consequences to her team, and explores solutions with them.
Motivation	Being driven to achieve for the sake of achievement	• A passion for the work itself and for new challenges • Unflagging energy to improve	A portfolio manager at an investment company sees his fund tumble for three consecutive quarters. Major clients defect.

El Component	Definition	Hallmarks	Example
		• Optimism in the face of failure	Instead of blaming external circumstances, she decides to learn from the experience— and engineers a turnaround.
Empathy	Considering others' feelings, especially when making decisions	• Expertise in attracting and retaining talent • Ability to develop others • Sensitivity to cross-cultural differences	An American consultant and her team pitch a project to a potential client in Japan. Her team interprets the client's silence as disapproval and prepares to leave. The consultant reads the client's body language and senses interest. She continues the meeting, and her team gets the job.
Social skill	Managing relationships to move in desired directions	• Effectiveness in leading change • Persuasiveness • Extensive networking • Expertise in building and leading teams	A manager wants his company to adopt a better internet strategy. He finds kindred spirits and assembles a de facto team to create a prototype website. He persuades allies in other divisions to fund the company's participation in a relevant convention. His company forms an internet division—and puts him in charge of it.

Adapted from "What Makes a Leader?" by Daniel Goleman, originally published in *Harvard Business Review*, June 2006.

pull the best out of people under tremendous pressure. The art of sustained leadership is getting others to produce superior work, and high IQ alone is insufficient to that task.

The good news is that emotional intelligence can be learned and improved at any age. In fact, data shows that, on average, people's emotional intelligence tends to increase as they age. But the specific leadership competencies that are based on emotional intelligence don't necessarily come through life experience. For example, one of the most common complaints I hear about leaders, particularly newly promoted ones, is that they lack empathy. The problem is that they were promoted because they were outstanding individual performers—and being a solo achiever doesn't teach you the skills necessary to understand other people's concerns.

Leaders who are motivated to improve their emotional intelligence can do so if they're given the right *information, guidance, and support*. The information they need is a candid assessment of their strengths and limitations from people who know them well and whose opinions they trust. The guidance they need is a specific developmental plan that uses naturally occurring workplace encounters as the laboratory for learning. The support they need is someone to talk to as they practice how to handle different situations, what to do when they've blown it, and how to learn from those setbacks. If leaders cultivate these resources and practice continually, they can develop specific emotional intelligence skills—skills that will last for years.

Get Motivated

Richard Boyatzis *is a professor and the chair of the department of organizational behavior at Case Western Reserve University's Weatherhead School of Management in Cleveland.*

People can develop their emotional intelligence if they really want to. But many managers jump to the conclusion that their complement of emotional intelligence is predetermined. They think, "I could never be good at this, so why bother?" The central issue isn't a lack of *ability* to change; it's the lack of *motivation* to change.

Leadership development is not all that different from other areas in which people are trying to change their behaviors. Just look at the treatments for alcoholism, drug addiction, and weight loss: They all require the desire to change. More subtly, they all require a positive, rather than a negative, motivation. You have to *want* to change. If you think you'll lose your job because you're not adequately tuned in to your employees, you might become determinedly empathetic or compassionate for a time. But change driven by fear or avoidance probably isn't going to last. Change driven by hopes and aspirations, change that's pursued because it's desired, will be more enduring.

There's no such thing as having too much emotional intelligence. But there is a danger in being preoccupied with, or overusing, one aspect of it. For example, if you overemphasize the emotional intelligence competencies of initiative or achievement, you'll always be changing things at your company. Nobody would know what you were going to do next, which would be quite destabilizing for the organization. If you overuse empathy, you might never fire anybody. If you overuse teamwork, you might never build diversity or listen to a lone voice. Balance is essential.

Train the Gifted

Elkhonon Goldberg *is a clinical professor of neurology at New York University School of Medicine and the director of the Institute of Neuropsychology and Cognitive Performance in New York.*

In the past, neuropsychologists were mostly concerned with cognitive impairment. Today, they are increasingly interested in the biological underpinnings of cognitive differences in people without impairments—including differences in people's emotional intelligence.

Emotional intelligence can be learned, to a degree. It's like mathematical or musical ability. Can you become a musician if you lack natural aptitude? Yes, you can, if you take lessons and practice enough. But will you ever be a Mozart? Probably not. In the same way, emotional intelligence develops through a combination of biological endowment and training. And people who don't have that endowment probably won't become deeply emotionally intelligent just through training. Trying to drum emotional intelligence into someone with no aptitude for it is an exercise in futility. I believe the best way to get emotionally intelligent leaders is to select for people who already show the basic qualities you want. Think about it: That's how athletic coaches operate. They don't just work with anyone who wants to play a sport; they train the naturally gifted. Business managers should do the same.

How do you identify the naturally gifted? I'd say you have to look for those with a genuine, instinctive interest in other people's experiences and mental worlds. It's an absolute prerequisite for developing emotional intelligence. If a manager lacks this interest, maybe your training resources are better directed elsewhere.

Seek Frank Feedback

Andrea Jung *is the chair and CEO of Avon Products, which is based in New York.*

Emotional intelligence is in our DNA here at Avon because relationships are critical at every stage of our business. It starts with the relationships our 4.5 million independent sales reps have with their customers and goes right up through senior management to my office. So the emphasis on emotional intelligence is much greater here than it was at other companies in which I've worked. We incorporate emotional intelligence education into our development training for senior managers, and we factor in emotional intelligence competencies when we evaluate employees' performance.

Of all a leader's competencies, emotional and otherwise, self-awareness is the most important. Without it, you can't identify the impact you have on others. Self-awareness is very important for me as CEO. At my level, few people are willing to tell me the things that are hardest to hear. We have a CEO advisory counsel—ten people chosen each year from Avon offices throughout the world—and they tell me the good, the bad, and the ugly about the company. Anything can be said. It helps keep me connected to what people really think and how my actions affect them. I also rely on my children for honest appraisals. You can get a huge dose of reality by seeing yourself through your children's eyes, noticing the ways they react to and reflect what you say and do. My kids are part of my 360-degree feedback. They're the most honest of all.

I grew up in a very traditional Chinese family. My parents were concerned that the way I'd been raised—submissive, caring, and averse to conflict—would hinder my ability to succeed in the *Fortune* 500 environment. They were afraid I couldn't make the tough decisions. But I've learned how to be empathetic and still make hard decisions that are right for the company. These are not incompatible abilities. When Avon has had to close plants, for example, I've tried to act with compassion for the people involved. And I've gotten letters from some of the associates who were affected, expressing sadness but also saying thanks for the fair treatment. Leaders' use of emotional intelligence when making tough decisions is important to their success—and to the success of their organizations.

Engage Your Demons

David Gergen *directs the Center for Public Leadership at Harvard University's John F. Kennedy School of Government in Cambridge, Massachusetts. He served as an adviser to presidents Nixon, Ford, Reagan, and Clinton.*

American history suggests not only that emotional intelligence is an indispensable ingredient of political leadership but also that it can be enhanced through sustained effort. George Washington had to work hard to control his fiery temper before he became a role model for the republic, and Abraham Lincoln had to overcome deep melancholia to display the brave and warm countenance that made him a magnet for others. Franklin Delano Roosevelt provides an even more graphic example: In his early adult years, FDR seemed carefree and condescending. Then, at 39, he was stricken with polio. By most accounts, he transformed himself over the next seven years of struggle into a leader of empathy, patience, and keen self-awareness.

Richard Nixon thought he might transform himself through his own years in the wilderness, and he did make progress. But he could never fully control his demons, and they eventually brought him down. Bill Clinton, too, struggled for self-mastery and made progress, but he could not fully close the cracks in his character, and he paid a stiff price. Not all people succeed, then, in achieving self-awareness and self-control. What we have been told since the time of the Greeks is that every leader must try to control his own passions before he can hope to command the passions of others.

Best-selling author Rabbi Harold Kushner argues persuasively that the elements of selfishness and aggression that are in most of us—and our struggles to overcome them—are exactly what make for better leadership. In *Living a Life That Matters,* Kushner writes of the personal torments of leaders from Jacob, who wrestled all night with an angel, to Martin Luther King Jr., who tried to cleanse himself of weakness even as he cleansed the nation's soul. "Good people do bad things," Kushner concludes, "If they weren't mightily tempted by their *yetzer ha'ra* [will to do evil], they might not be capable of the mightily good things they do."

Find Your Voice

William George *is the former chairman and CEO of Medtronic, a medical technology company in Minneapolis.*

Authentic leadership begins with self-awareness, or knowing yourself deeply. Self-awareness is not a trait you are born with but a capacity you develop throughout your lifetime. It's your understanding of your strengths and weaknesses, your purpose in life, your values and motivations, and how and why you respond to situations in a particular way. It requires a great deal of introspection and the ability to internalize feedback from others.

No one is born a leader; we have to consciously develop into the leader we want to become. It takes many years of hard work and the ability to learn from extreme difficulties and disappointments. But in their scramble to get ahead, many would-be leaders attempt to skip this crucial developmental stage. Some of these people do get to the top of companies through sheer determination and aggressiveness. However, when they finally reach the leader's chair, they can be very destructive because they haven't focused on the hard work of personal development.

To mask their inadequacies, these leaders tend to close themselves off, cultivating an image or persona rather than opening up to others. They often adopt the styles of other leaders they have observed.

Leaders who are driven to achieve by shortcomings in their character, for example, or a desire for self-aggrandizement, may take inordinate risks on behalf of the organization. They may even come to believe they are so important that they place their interests above those of the organization.

Self-awareness and other emotional intelligence skills come naturally to some, less so to others—but these skills can be learned. One of the techniques I have found most useful in gaining deeper self-awareness is meditation. In 1975, my wife dragged me, kicking and screaming, to a weekend course in Transcendental Meditation. I have meditated 20 minutes, twice a day, ever since. Meditation makes me calmer, more focused, and better able to discern what's really important. Leaders, by the very nature of their positions, are under extreme pressure to keep up with the many voices clamoring for their attention. Indeed, many leaders lose their way. It is only through a deep self-awareness that you can find your inner voice and listen to it.

Know the Score

Michael Tilson Thomas *is the music director of the San Francisco Symphony.*

A conductor's authority rests on two things: the orchestra's confidence in the conductor's insightful knowledge of the whole score; and the orchestra's faith in the conductor's good heart, which seeks to inspire everyone to make music that is excellent, generous, and sincere.

Old-school conductors liked to hold the lead in their hands at all times. I do not. Sometimes I lead. Other times I'll say, "Violas, I'm giving you the lead. Listen to one another; and find your way with this phrase." I'm not trying to drill people, military style, to play music exactly together. I'm trying to encourage them to play as one, which is a different thing. I'm guiding the performance, but I'm aware that they're executing it. It's their sinews, their heartstrings. I'm there to help them do it in a way that is convincing and natural for them but also a part of the larger design.

My approach is to be in tune with the people with whom I'm working. If I'm conducting an ensemble for the first time, I will relate what I want them to do to the great things they've already done. If I'm conducting my own orchestra, I can see in the musicians' bodies and faces how they're feeling that day, and it becomes very clear who may need encouragement and who may need cautioning.

The objectivity and perspective I have as the only person who is just listening is a powerful thing. I try to use this perspective to help the ensemble reach its goals.

Keep It Honest

Carol Bartz *is the chairman, president, and CEO of Autodesk, a design software and digital content company in San Rafael, California.*

A friend needed to take a six-month assignment in a different part of the country. She had an ancient, ill, balding but beloved dog that she could not take with her. Her choices boiled down to boarding the poor animal, at enormous expense, or putting it out of its obvious misery. Friends said, "Board the dog," though behind my friend's back, they ridiculed that option. She asked me what I thought, and I told her, kindly but clearly, that I thought she should have the dog put to sleep rather than spend her money keeping it in an environment where it would be miserable and perhaps die anyway. My friend was furious with me for saying this. She boarded the dog and went away on her assignment. When she returned, the dog was at death's door and had to be put to sleep. Not long after that, my friend came around to say thanks. "You were the only person who told me the truth," she said. She came to appreciate that I had cared enough to tell her what I thought was best, even if what I said hurt at the time.

That event validated a hunch that has stood me in good stead as I've led my company. Empathy and compassion have to be balanced with honesty. I have pulled people into my office and told them to deal with certain issues for the sake of themselves and their teams. If they are willing to learn, they will say, "Gee, no one ever told me." If they are unwilling, they're not right for this organization. And I must let them go for the sake of the greater good.

Go for the Gemba

Hirotaka Takeuchi *is the dean of Hitotsubashi University's Graduate School of International Corporate Strategy in Tokyo.*

Self-awareness, self-control, empathy, humility, and other such emotional intelligence traits are particularly important in Asia. They are part of our Confucian emphasis on *wah*, or social harmony. When books on emotional intelligence were first translated into Japanese, people said, "We already know that. We're actually trying to get beyond that." We've been so focused on wah that we've built up a supersensitive structure of social niceties, where everyone seeks consensus. In the Japanese hierarchy, everyone knows his or her place, so no one is ever humiliated. This social supersensitivity—itself a form of emotional intelligence—can lead people to shy away from conflict. But conflict is often the only way to get to the *gemba*—the front line, where the action really is, where the truth lies.

Thus, effective management often depends not on coolly and expertly resolving conflict—or simply avoiding it—but on embracing it at the gemba. Japan's most effective leaders do both. The best example is Nissan's Carlos Ghosn. He not only had the social skills to listen to people and win them over to his ideas, but he also dared to lift the lid on the corporate hierarchy and encourage people at all levels of the organization to offer suggestions to operational, organizational, and even interpersonal problems—even if that created conflict. People were no longer suppressed, so solutions to the company's problems bubbled up.

Balance the Load

Linda Stone *is the former vice president of corporate and industry initiatives at Microsoft in Redmond, Washington.*

Emotional intelligence is powerful—which is precisely why it can be dangerous. For example, empathy is an extraordinary relationship-building tool, but it must be used skillfully or it can do serious damage to the person doing the empathizing. In my case, overdoing empathy took a physical toll. In May 2000, Steve Ballmer charged me with rebuilding Microsoft's industry relationships, a position that I sometimes referred to as "chief listening officer." The job was part ombudsperson, part new initiatives developer, part pattern recognizer, and part rapid-response person. In the first few months of the job—when criticism of the company was at an all-time high—it became clear that this position was a lightning rod. I threw myself into listening and repairing wherever I could.

Within a few months, I was exhausted from the effort. I gained a significant amount of weight, which, tests finally revealed, was probably caused by a hormone imbalance partially brought on by stress and lack of sleep. In absorbing everyone's complaints, perhaps to the extreme, I had compromised my health. This was a wake-up call: I needed to reframe the job.

I focused on connecting the people who needed to work together to resolve problems rather than taking on each repair myself. I persuaded key people inside the company to listen and work directly with important people outside the company, even in cases where the internal folks were skeptical at first about the need for this direct connection. In a sense, I tempered my empathy and ratcheted up relationship building. Ultimately, with a wiser and more balanced use of empathy, I became more effective and less stressed in my role.

Question Authority

Ronald Heifetz *is a cofounder of the Center for Public Leadership at Harvard University's John F. Kennedy School of Government in Cambridge, Massachusetts, and a partner at Cambridge Leadership Associates, a consultancy in Cambridge.*

Emotional intelligence is necessary for leadership but not suf-ficient. Many people have some degree of emotional intelligence and can indeed empathize with and rouse followers; a few of them can even generate great charismatic authority. But I would argue that if they are using emotional intelligence solely to gain formal or informal authority, that's not leadership at all. They are using their emotional intelligence to grasp what people want, only to pan-der to those desires in order to gain authority and influence. Easy answers sell.

Leadership couples emotional intelligence with the courage to raise the tough questions, challenge people's assumptions about strategy and operations—and risk losing their goodwill. It demands a commitment to serving others; skill at diagnostic, strategic, and tactical reasoning; the guts to get beneath the surface of tough reali-ties; and the heart to take heat and grief.

For example, David Duke did an extraordinary job of convincing Ku Klux Klan members to get out of their backyards and into hotel conference rooms. He brought his considerable emotional intelli-gence to bear, his capacity to empathize with his followers, to pluck their heartstrings in a powerful way that mobilized them. But he avoided asking his people the tough questions: Does our program actually solve our problem? How will creating a social structure of white supremacy give us the self-esteem we lack? How will it solve the problems of poverty, alcoholism, and family violence that cor-rode our sense of self-worth?

Like Duke, many people with high emotional intelligence and charismatic authority aren't interested in asking the deeper ques-tions, because they get so much emotional gain from the adoring crowd. For them, that's the end in itself. They're satisfying their own hungers and vulnerabilities: their need to be liked; their need for power and control; or their need to be needed, to feel important, which renders them vulnerable to grandiosity. But that's not primal leadership. It's primal hunger for authority.

Maintaining one's primacy or position is not in and of itself lead-ership, however inspiring it may seem to be. Gaining primal author-ity is relatively easy.

## CHAPTER 2

Do You Lead with Emotional Intelligence?

by Annie McKee

GREAT LEADERS MOVE US—they inspire, motivate, and energize us. How? They do it through emotional intelligence. Dan Goleman woke us all up when he published his groundbreaking book on the topic (in 1995). Since then we've learned a lot about EI competencies, such as self-awareness and empathy, and about what people can do to develop them. To gain a deeper understanding of your own emotional intelligence, respond to the statements in this questionnaire as honestly as possible, checking one of the columns from "Always" to "Never."

To calculate your score, as you finish each section count the checkmarks in each column and record the number in the "Total per column" line. Multiply your total score for each column by the number in the row below it, and record it in the row below that. Add this row together to get your total score for how you perceive yourself along each of the dimensions of EI.

Adapted from content posted on hbr.org on June 5, 2015, as "Quiz Yourself: Do You Lead with Emotional Intelligence?"

Reflecting on your strengths and where you can improve is important, but don't stop there. Other people's perspectives matter too. After reviewing your scores, ask one or two trusted friends to evaluate you using the same statements, to learn what others see in you.

Annie McKee is a senior fellow at the University of Pennsylvania and the director of the PennCLO Executive Doctoral Program. She is the author of *Primal Leadership* (with Daniel Goleman and Richard Boyatzis), as well as *Resonant Leadership* and *Becoming a Resonant Leader*. Her new book, *How to Be Happy at Work*, is forthcoming from Harvard Business Review Press in September 2017.

How would you describe yourself?

	ALWAYS	MOST OF THE TIME	FREQUENTLY	SOMETIMES	RARELY	NEVER
EMOTIONAL SELF-AWARENESS						
1 I can describe my emotions in the moment I experience them.						
2 I can describe my feelings in detail, beyond just "happy," "sad," "angry," and so on.						
3 I understand the reasons for my feelings.						
4 I understand how stress affects my mood and behavior.						
5 I understand my leadership strengths and weaknesses.						
Total per column						
Points per answer	x 5	x 4	x 3	x 2	x 1	x 0
Multiply the two rows above						
TOTAL SELF-AWARENESS SCORE (sum of the row above)						
POSITIVE OUTLOOK						
6 I'm optimistic in the face of challenging circumstances.						
7 I focus on opportunities rather than obstacles.						
8 I see people as good and well-intentioned.						
9 I look forward to the future.						
10 I feel hopeful.						
Total per column						
Points per answer	x 5	x 4	x 3	x 2	x 1	x 0
Multiply the two rows above						
TOTAL POSITIVE OUTLOOK SCORE (sum of the row above)						

(continued)

How would you describe yourself?

EMOTIONAL SELF-CONTROL

	ALWAYS	MOST OF THE TIME	FREQUENTLY	SOMETIMES	RARELY	NEVER
11 I manage stress well.						
12 I'm calm in the face of pressure or emotional turmoil.						
13 I control my impulses.						
14 I use strong emotions, such as anger, fear, and joy, appropriately and for the good of others.						
15 I'm patient.						
Total per column						
Points per answer	x 5	x 4	x 3	x 2	x 1	x 0
Multiply the two rows above						
TOTAL EMOTIONAL SELF-CONTROL SCORE (sum of the row above)						

ADAPTABILITY

	ALWAYS	MOST OF THE TIME	FREQUENTLY	SOMETIMES	RARELY	NEVER
16 I'm flexible when situations change unexpectedly.						
17 I'm adept at managing multiple, conflicting demands.						
18 I can easily adjust goals when circumstances change.						
19 I can shift my priorities quickly.						
20 I adapt easily when a situation is uncertain or ever-changing.						
Total per column						
Points per answer	x 5	x 4	x 3	x 2	x 1	x 0
Multiply the two rows above						
TOTAL ADAPTABILITY SCORE (sum of the row above)						

EMPATHY						
21	I strive to understand people's underlying feelings.					
22	My curiosity about others drives me to listen attentively to them.					
23	I try to understand why people behave the way they do.					
24	I readily understand others' viewpoints even when they are different from my own.					
25	I understand how other people's experiences affect their feelings, thoughts, and behavior.					
Total per column						
Points per answer		x 5	x 4	x 3	x 2	x 1	x 0
Multiply the two rows above						
TOTAL EMPATHY SCORE (sum of the row above)						

Self-Awareness: Understand Your Emotions, Know Your Behaviors

## CHAPTER 3

You Can't Manage Emotions Without Knowing What They Really Are

by Art Markman

AT THIS POINT, everybody knows emotional intelligence matters in the workplace. Yet there are two aspects of emotions that make it hard for people to exercise their emotional intelligence. First, most people are still not completely clear about what emotions actually are. Second, even when we understand emotions conceptually, it can still be hard to deal with our own emotional states.

To tackle the first problem: While in everyday speech, *emotion* and *feeling* are often used interchangeably, psychologists distinguish between them. Emotions are interpretations of feelings.

The feelings you have (what psychologists call *affect*) emerge from your motivational system. You generally feel good when you're succeeding at your goals and bad when you're not. The more deeply your motivational system is engaged with a situation, the stronger your feelings.

Adapted from content posted on hbr.org on December 23, 2015 (product #H02KOK)

The motivational system, however, is not that well connected to the brain regions that help you to tell stories about the world. In order to make sense of what you're feeling, you use information about what's going on around you to help you translate those feelings into emotions—emotions help to guide your actions by giving you explicit feedback on how well you are currently achieving the goals the motivational system has engaged.

Often, that interpretation is easy. If you are crossing the street and suddenly have to leap out of the way of an oncoming car, it is clear that the strong negative feeling you are having is fear from nearly getting hit by the car. If a colleague compliments you on a job well done, it is obvious that the positive feeling you are having is pride.

But things are not always so clear. You might have a bad interaction with a family member before getting to work. As the day wears on, you may interpret your negative feelings as frustration with the project you're working on rather than lingering negative affect from the events of the morning.

Many people try to power through their negative feelings rather than attempting to understand them. But this is a lost opportunity. Emotions provide valuable information about the state of your motivational system. Ignoring them is like driving around lost, not only refusing to ask for directions but refusing to consult the map or the GPS—or even to look through the windshield. You will still be moving forward, but who knows where you will end up? Conversely, paying too much attention to your feelings is also bad. That's like staring at your road atlas without ever turning on the car: You can't get anywhere that way.

When you have negative feelings, slow down and pay some attention to *what* you are feeling and *why* you are feeling the way you are.

When you find yourself stressed, anxious, or angry, take five or 10 minutes for yourself during the day. Sit alone and breathe deeply. The deep breaths help to take some of the energy or arousal out of the feelings you are having. That can help you to think more clearly.

Then start to think about some of the events of your day. Pay attention to how those thoughts influence what you are feeling.

Are there particular events that increase or decrease the intensity of those feelings?

You may not completely understand the source of your feelings the first time you do this. Over time, you will become more adept at paying attention to when and where you start to feel bad.

Of course, once you have figured out what's bothering you, it's time to plan a course of action. If you keep thinking about things that bother you, you run the risk of solving nothing while getting yourself more upset. Instead, use your knowledge about the source of the bad feeling to figure out how to deal with it.

Finally, if you're really upset about something, hold off on actually executing your plan until you have given yourself a chance to calm down. Responses that seemed like a good idea in the moment may seem less ideal to a cooler head.

Being willing to understand your feelings will have two benefits in the long term. First, it will help you to discover some of the aspects of your life that trigger negative feelings. That is useful, because you don't want to misinterpret your negative feelings and attribute them to something else. For example, you would like to be able to recognize when events in your personal life are spilling over into work and are causing you to feel badly about the work you do. Second, by understanding the sources of your own emotions, you will become more expert in understanding the people around you as well. We often ignore our own feelings—and then also ignore those of our colleagues.

Once you can better understand what emotions are and where your own emotions come from, you'll have a much better ability to practice emotional intelligence.

———————

Art Markman, PhD, is the Annabel Irion Worsham Centennial Professor of Psychology and Marketing at the University of Texas at Austin and founding director of the program in the Human Dimensions of Organizations. He has written over 150 scholarly papers on topics including reasoning, decision making, and motivation. He is the author of several books including *Smart Thinking, Smart Change,* and *Habits of Leadership.*

## CHAPTER 4

A Vocabulary for Your Emotions

by Susan David

DEALING EFFECTIVELY WITH EMOTIONS is a key leadership skill. And naming our emotions—what psychologists call *labeling*—is an important first step in dealing with them effectively. But it's harder than it sounds: Many of us struggle to identify what exactly we are feeling, and oftentimes the most obvious label isn't actually the most accurate.

There are a variety of reasons why this is so difficult: We've been trained to believe that strong emotions should be suppressed. We have certain (sometimes unspoken) societal and organizational rules against expressing them. Or we've never learned a language to accurately describe our emotions. Consider these two examples:

> Neena is in a meeting with Jared, and the whole time he has been saying things that make her want to explode. In addition to interrupting her at every turn, he's reminded everyone *again* about that one project she worked on that failed. She's so angry.

Adapted from content posted on hbr.org on November 10, 2016, as "3 Ways to Better Understand Your Emotions" (product #H038KF)

Mikhail gets home after a long day and sighs as he hangs up his coat. His wife asks if anything's wrong. "I'm just stressed," he says, pulling out his laptop to finish a report.

Anger and stress are two of the emotions we see most in the workplace—or at least, those are the terms we use for them most frequently. Yet they are often masks for deeper feelings that we could and should describe in more nuanced and precise ways, so that we develop greater levels of *emotional agility*, a critical capability that enables us to interact more successfully with ourselves and the world.

Yes, Neena may be mad, but what if she is also sad—sad that her project failed, and maybe also anxious that that failure is going to haunt her and her career? With Jared interrupting her so frequently, that anxiety feels increasingly justified. Why didn't the project work? And what's going to become of her job now? All of these emotions feed into her anger, but they are also separate feelings that she should identify and address.

And what if what's behind Mikhail's stress is the fact that he's just not sure he's in the right career? Long days used to be fun—why aren't they any more? He's surely stressed, but what's going on under that?

These questions open up a world of potential inquiry and answers for Neena and Mikhail. Like them, we need a more nuanced vocabulary for emotions, not just for the sake of being more precise, but because incorrectly diagnosing our emotions makes us respond incorrectly. If we think we need to attend to anger, we'll take a different approach than if we're handling disappointment or anxiety—or we might not address them at all. It's been shown that when people don't acknowledge and address their emotions, they display a lowered sense of well-being and more physical symptoms of stress, like headaches.[1] There is a high cost to avoiding our feelings.[2] On the flip side, having the right vocabulary allows us to see the real issue at hand—to take a messy experience, understand it more clearly, and build a roadmap to address the problem.[3]

Here are three ways to get a more accurate and precise sense of your emotions:

Broaden Your Emotional Vocabulary

Words matter. If you're experiencing a strong emotion, take a moment to consider what to call it. But don't stop there: Once you've identified it, try to come up with two more words that describe how you are feeling. You might be surprised at the breadth of your emotions—or that you've unearthed a deeper emotion buried beneath the more obvious one.

Exhibit 2 shows a vocabulary list of emotion terms; you can find much more by searching Google for any one of these.

It's equally important to do this with "positive" emotions as well as "negative" ones. Being able to say that you are *excited* about a new job (not just "I'm nervous") or *trusting* of a colleague (not just "He's nice"), for example, will help you set your intentions for the role or the relationship in a way that is more likely to lead to success down the road.

Consider the Intensity of the Emotion

We're apt to leap to basic descriptors like "angry" or "stressed" even when our feelings are far less extreme. I had a client, Ed (not his real name), who was struggling in his marriage; he frequently

EXHIBIT 2

List of emotion terms

Angry	Sad	Anxious	Hurt	Embarrassed	Happy
Grumpy	Disappointed	Afraid	Jealous	Isolated	Thankful
Frustrated	Mournful	Stressed	Betrayed	Self-conscious	Trusting
Annoyed	Regretful	Vulnerable	Isolated	Lonely	Comfortable
Defensive	Depressed	Confused	Shocked	Inferior	Content
Spiteful	Paralyzed	Bewildered	Deprived	Guilty	Excited
Impatient	Pessimistic	Skeptical	Victimized	Ashamed	Relaxed
Disgusted	Tearful	Worried	Aggrieved	Repugnant	Relieved
Offended	Dismayed	Cautious	Tormented	Pathetic	Elated
Irritated	Disillusioned	Nervous	Abandoned	Confused	Confident

described his wife as "angry" and often got angry in return. But as the vocabulary chart suggests, every emotion comes in a variety of flavors. When we talked about other words for his wife's emotions, Ed saw that there were times that she was perhaps just annoyed or impatient. This insight completely changed their relationship, because he could suddenly see that she wasn't just angry all the time—and so could actually respond to her specific emotion and concern without getting angry himself. Similarly, it matters in your own self-assessment whether you are angry or just grumpy, mournful or just dismayed, elated or just pleased.

As you label your emotions, also rate them on a scale of 1–10. How deeply are you feeling the emotion? How urgent is it, or how strong? Does that make you choose a different set of words?

Write It Out

James Pennebaker has done 40 years of research into the links between writing and emotional processing. His experiments revealed that people who write about emotionally charged episodes experience a marked increase in their physical and mental well-being. Moreover, in a study of recently laid-off workers, he found that those who delved into their feelings of humiliation, anger, anxiety, and relationship difficulties were three times more likely to have been reemployed than those in control groups.

These experiments also revealed that over time those who wrote about their feelings began to develop insights into what those feelings meant (or didn't mean!), using phrases such as "I have learned . . ."; "It struck me that . . ."; "The reason that . . ."; "I now realize . . ."; and "I understand . . . ." The process of writing allowed them to gain a new perspective on their emotions and to understand them and their implications more clearly.

Here's an exercise you can use to reflect through writing. You could do this every day, but it's particularly important when you're going through a tough time or a big transition, or if you're feeling emotional turmoil.

- Set a timer for 20 minutes.

- Using either a notebook or computer, write about your emotional experiences from the past week, month, or year.

- Don't worry about making it perfect or readable; go where your mind takes you.

- At the end, you don't have to save the document; the point is that those thoughts are now out of you and on the page.

You can also use these three approaches—broadening your vocabulary, noting the intensity of an emotion, and writing it out—when trying to better understand *another person's* emotions. As we saw with the example of Ed and his wife, we are just as likely to mislabel someone else's emotions as our own, with similarly complicating consequences. By understanding what they are feeling more precisely, you will be better equipped to respond in a constructive way.

Once you understand *what* you are feeling, then you can better address and learn from those more accurately described emotions. If Neena addresses the sadness and regret she feels in the wake of her failed project—as well as the anxiety about what it means for her career—that is more productive than trying to figure out how to deal with her anger at Jared. And if Mikhail can recognize his own career anxiety, he can start to craft a plan to build his future more deliberately—rather than simply miring himself in more of the same work when he gets home each night.

Susan David is a founder of the Harvard/McLean Institute of Coaching and is on faculty at Harvard University. She is author of *Emotional Agility* (Avery, 2016), based on the concept named by HBR as a Management Idea of the Year. As a speaker and adviser, David has worked with the senior leadership of hundreds of major organizations, including the United Nations, Ernst & Young, and the World Economic Forum. For more information, go to www.susandavid.com or follow her on Twitter @SusanDavid_PhD.

Notes

1. Todd B. Kashdan, "Unpacking Emotion Differentiation: Transforming Unpleasant Experience by Perceiving Distinctions in Negativity," *Current Directions in Psychological Science* 24, no. 1 (2015).

2. Tori Rodriguez, "Negative Emotions Are Key to Well-Being," *Scientific American Mind*, May 1, 2013, https://www.scientific american.com/article/negative-emotions-key-well-being/.

3. Lisa Feldman Barrett et al., "Knowing What You're Feeling and Knowing What to Do About It: Mapping the Difference Between Emotion Differentiation and Emotion Regulation," *Cognition and Emotion* 15, no. 6 (2001): 713–724.

CHAPTER 5

Are You Sure You Show Respect?

by Christine Porath

FOR THE LAST 20 YEARS, I've studied the costs of incivility, as well as the benefits of civility. Across the board, I've found that civility pays. It enhances your influence and performance—and is positively associated with being perceived as a leader.[1]

Being respectful doesn't just benefit you, though; it benefits everyone around you. In a study of nearly 20,000 employees around the world (conducted with HBR), I found that when it comes to garnering commitment and engagement from employees, there's one thing that leaders need to demonstrate: respect. No other leadership behavior had a bigger effect on employees across the outcomes we measured. Being treated with respect was more important to employees than recognition and appreciation, communicating an inspiring vision, providing useful feedback—or even opportunities for learning, growth, and development.

Originally published on hbr.org on May 11, 2015, as "The Leadership Behavior That's Most Important to Employees" (product #H022CI)

However, even when leaders know that showing respect is critical, many struggle to demonstrate it. If you're one of those leaders, consider the following steps:

Ask for focused feedback on your best behaviors

This technique, originated by researcher Laura Roberts and colleagues, will help you see your most respectful self.[2] Collect feedback via email from about 10 people (coworkers, friends, family). Ask each for positive examples of your best behavior. When and how have they seen you treat people well? After compiling the feedback, try to organize the data by summarizing and categorizing it into themes. For example, create a table with columns for commonality, examples (of the behavior), and your thoughts. You might also use Wordle.net to identify themes (you'll also get a colorful picture that can serve as a reminder of you at your best, most civil self). Then look for patterns: When, where, how, with whom are you at your best? Use your insights to reinforce what you're doing well. Be mindful of additional opportunities to be your best civil self. Leverage your interpersonal strengths.

Discover your shortcomings

Gather candid feedback from your colleagues and friends not only on what you're doing that conveys respect, but also on how you can improve. Specifically, what are your shortcomings? Identify a couple of trusted colleagues who have the best intentions for you and your organization. These are folks who you believe will provide direct and honest feedback. Ask for their views about how you treat other people. What do you do well? What could you do better? Listen carefully.

Consider the actions of Lieutenant Christopher Manning, a naval intelligence officer at the Pentagon, who has systematized ways to get continuous feedback from his direct reports. He expanded the scope of anonymous feedback surveys to include not only how he could improve the organization and himself as a leader, but also his team members' personal happiness (e.g., including how supported people felt by him), and work-life balance. He also instituted an anonymous comment box and encouraged an open-door policy. He even provides incentives for the most insightful critiques, such as the chance to attend a course or conference of interest, extra time off, and public recognition. And he meets one-on-one with his direct reports frequently. The regular feedback from these sources has helped him hone his skills. The bonus: He's found that those who report to him are more engaged and respect him more.

If you don't feel comfortable soliciting the feedback of your entire team, you can also ask a trusted direct report to gather feedback within the organization about whether you (the leader) consistently demonstrate civility, and what situations may trigger uncivil behavior.

Work with a coach

Coaches can uncover potential weaknesses through surveying and interviewing those with whom you work; they can also shadow you at meetings and events to pick up on subtleties including nonverbal behavior. A skilled coach may unearth some of the underlying assumptions, experiences, and personal qualities that make one prone to uncivil behavior.

Ask, specifically, how you can improve

Once you have clarity on which behaviors you want to improve, gather information from others about *how* best to go about this. This "feedforward" method, originated by author Marshall Goldsmith, is a terrific way to gather specific ideas for improving your behavior. The process consists of five steps:

1. Describe your goal clearly and simply to anyone you know.

2. Ask for two suggestions. Encourage creative ideas.

3. Listen carefully. Write the suggestions down.

4. Respond with "thank you." Nothing more. No excuses or defensiveness.

5. Repeat by asking additional people.

Enlist your team in keeping you accountable

Choose one change that could improve your behavior and then experiment, asking your team to help you by letting you know when they see improvement. For example, after a meeting, ask your team if they saw an improvement in the behavior that you're working on. What was the impact?

Here's an example: A woman I know of—let's call her Karen—enlisted her team to help her change a specific behavior. The team had grown increasingly frustrated by her inability to listen and empower them. While she was highly intelligent, she was constantly interrupting people in meetings and taking over initial ideas before they could even be presented. Karen worked with a coach to develop a technique to avoid this pattern—in this case, tapping her toe instead of interrupting someone. (Other coaches have developed similar techniques, such as counting to 10.) She informed her team that she was working on the behavior, and after a couple of days of meetings, she checked in with them on her progress. This helped establish a norm for more open dialogue—and a shared sense that the team members could count on each other to support their own development.

Make time for reflection

Keep a journal to provide insight into when/where/why you are your best and when you are uncivil. Identify situations that cause you to lose your temper. A leader I worked with named Monica noticed that she was far more curt in the late afternoon. She began her days before 5:00 a.m. By the time late afternoon hit, she was tired and was less emotionally attuned. She was brusque in conversations and less civil in email. Before she started journaling and reflecting on her day, Monica was unaware of the effect of time of day—and her energy management—on her demeanor. Now she is much more mindful of her behavior. For challenging situations such as conflict, people who trigger her, and communication that requires tact, she waits until the following morning to respond.

Consider tracking your own energy through the day via an energy audit tool, such as "Energy Audit—Awareness and Action," which is available from the University of Michigan.[3] Reflection helps you identify strategies to maintain composure and be your best, most civil self. After adopting some of the improvement strategies, do you see a decrease in incivility, or an increase in civility? Track yourself and review progress on a regular basis (e.g., weekly or monthly).

The path toward building greater self-awareness and treating people more respectfully at work doesn't have to be walked alone. While you're working to improve your own behavior, encourage your team members to do the same. Have an open discussion with your team about what you and your teammates do or say that conveys respect. How or when are you and your teammates less than civil to each other? What could you do or say better? Discuss what the team will gain by being more respectful of each other. As the entire team develops norms, hold one another accountable for them. Consider yourselves coaches that are helping to improve both individual and team performance.

The key to mastering civility begins with improving your self-awareness. Armed with this information, you can begin tweaking your behavior to enhance your influence and effectiveness. Small acts can have big returns. Your civility will cascade throughout your organization, with benefits to you—and your organization.

Christine Porath is an associate professor of management at Georgetown University, the author of *Mastering Civility: A Manifesto for the Workplace* (Grand Central Publishing, forthcoming), and a coauthor of *The Cost of Bad Behavior* (Portfolio, 2009).

Notes

1. Christine L. Porath et al., "The Effects of Civility on Advice, Leadership, and Performance," *Journal of Applied Psychology* 100 no. 5, (September 2015): 1527–1541.

2. Center for Positive Organizations, "Reflected Best Self Exercise," http://positiveorgs.bus.umich.edu/cpo-tools/reflected-best-self-exercise-2nd-edition/.

3. The energy audit is available at http://positiveorgs.bus.umich.edu/wp-content/uploads/GrantSpreitzer-EnergyAudit.pdf.

Manage Your Emotions

## CHAPTER 6

Make Your Emotions Work for You

by Susan David

WE OFTEN HEAR TIPS and tricks for helping us to "control" our emotions, but that's the wrong idea. Strong emotions aren't bad; they don't need to be pushed down or controlled; they are, in fact, data. Our emotions evolved as a signaling system, a way to help us communicate with each other and to better understand ourselves. What we need to do is learn to develop *emotional agility*, the capacity to mine even the most difficult emotions for data that can help us make better decisions.

What's the Function of the Emotion?

To make the most of that data, ask yourself what the *function* of your emotion is. What is it telling you? What is it trying to signal?

Consider the example of Mikhail, who found himself in a perpetual cycle of stress because of the never-ending onslaught of tasks at work. As he more precisely defined his emotions, he realized what he was feeling wasn't just stress: he felt a more general dissatisfaction with his work, disappointment in some of his career choices, and anxiety

---

Adapted from content posted on hbr.org on November 28, 2016, as "How to Manage Your Emotions Without Fighting Them" (product #H038NO)

about what the future held for him. Once Mikhail recognized and accepted these emotions, he was able to see what they were signaling to him: He had started to question whether he was on the right career path.

This revelation meant that instead of tackling a productivity problem by becoming more disciplined about prioritizing his tasks or saying no to extra work, Mikhail was able to do something much more appropriate and constructive. He began working with a career coach. By examining what his emotions were telling him, rather than pushing them away or focusing on the wrong problem, he learned something new about himself and was eventually able to find a new career path where he was just as busy—but felt much less stressed.

Our emotions can teach us valuable lessons. Let them shine a light on what you want to change, how you want to act in the future, or what is valuable to you.

Is Your Reaction Aligned with Your Values?

Our emotions can also help us understand our deepest values. They can often signal what is more important to us: You feel love for your family. You feel ambition at work and appreciate achievement and self-worth. You feel fulfilled when you've been able to help a direct report achieve their goals. You feel peace and satisfaction on a mountain summit. It's far better to focus on these deeper values rather than your immediate emotions, which can spur poor decisions.

Let's say that you need to give some difficult feedback to one of your direct reports. You're anxious about the conversation and you've been putting it off (which just makes you more anxious). In examining your emotions, you realize that one of the values behind your procrastination is fairness. She's a strong employee, and you just don't want to be unfair to her. So, you ask yourself: How does having or not having the conversation either bring you toward or move you away from your value of fairness? Looking at the situation in this light, you can see that giving her the feedback and helping her to succeed is actually *more* fair to her—and to your whole team—than caving to your anxieties. You've been able to unhook yourself from the thrall of your immediate emotions and make a better choice that is true to the values that underlie them.

This kind of thinking can help you avoid situations in which you do something that makes you feel good in the short term but doesn't align with your values in the long term. Avoiding a conversation is a typical example, but there are many others: brashly telling someone off for getting on your nerves when you value compassion; sticking with a comfortable job that doesn't align with your dream of starting a business when you value growth; criticizing yourself for the smallest things when you really value self-affirmation.

Managing emotions isn't just doing away with them; it's putting strategies in place that let you use them effectively rather than letting them govern your behaviors and actions. Your emotions are your natural guidance system—and they are more effective when you don't try to fight them.

Susan David is a founder of the Harvard/McLean Institute of Coaching and is on faculty at Harvard University. She is author of *Emotional Agility* (Avery, 2016), based on the concept named by HBR as a Management Idea of the Year. As a speaker and adviser, David has worked with the senior leadership of hundreds of major organizations, including the United Nations, Ernst & Young, and the World Economic Forum. For more information, go to www.susandavid.com or follow her on Twitter @SusanDavid_PhD.

## CHAPTER 7

Defuse a Challenging Interaction

CONFLICTS STIR UP MANY EMOTIONS, especially negative thoughts and feelings. To successfully manage these disagreements in the moment, you need to address your own emotions as well as those of the other person.

Reframe Negative Thoughts

During difficult interactions, you may begin to question your perceptions about yourself. For example, suppose a direct report says, "I didn't attend the meeting because I didn't think you valued my ideas." In response, you wonder to yourself, "Maybe I'm not a competent manager after all."

For many people, the sense that their self-image is being challenged creates intense emotions. These feelings can become overwhelming, making it virtually impossible to converse productively about any subject. To experience—and then let go of—difficult feelings:

- **Focus on the other person's intentions and on the facts.** If you discover that your employee had legitimate reasons for

---

Adapted from "Address Emotions" in the Harvard ManageMentor topic "Difficult Interactions" (Harvard Business Publishing, 2016, electronic) not showing up at a weekly meeting, your annoyance may fade away.

- **Examine your contributions to the problem.** If you realize that you've accidentally advised an employee to focus on an unnecessary task, your frustration may dissipate.

- **Question your assumptions.** If you find your belief that a colleague doesn't value product quality is mistaken, you may feel less anger over her tendency to take shortcuts.

Your goal in reframing negative thoughts is to be able to express your complete range of emotions without judging or blaming the other person.

Neutralize Unproductive Behaviors

Although you can work to manage your own reactions, you can't control those of the other person in the conflict. Try the techniques in exhibit 3 for dealing with unproductive behaviors:

EXHIBIT 3

Tackling unproductive behaviors

If the other person . . .	Try to . . .
Is aggressive and disrespectful	• Command respect by remaining calm. • Interrupt verbal attacks by repeating the person's name. • Communicate your bottom line: "When you're ready to speak to me with respect, I will take all the time you want to discuss this."
Doesn't listen to your side	• Go into the conversation prepared to support your own perceptions and ideas. • Redirect the person to your idea or information with phrases such as "I was just wondering . . . " "Bear with me a minute," or "What do you suppose . . . ?" • Acknowledge that the person possesses valuable knowledge, too.

Has an explosive outburst	• Take a break and then continue the conversation. • Get the person's attention by waving your arms and calling their name loudly enough to be heard. • Express genuine concern for the person: "Joe, nobody should have to feel this way! I want to help."
Is uncommunicative	• Schedule plenty of time for the person to respond to your ideas and questions. • Ask open-ended questions: "What are you thinking?" "How do you want to proceed?" "Where should we go from here?" • Gaze expectantly at the person for a longer-than-usual period of time after making a comment or asking a question.
Assumes that the situation can't get better	• Give the person time to consider your plan and get back to you. • Bring up and address the negative aspects of an idea before the other person does.

## CHAPTER 8

Stay Grounded in Stressful Moments

by Leah Weiss

MINDFULNESS SHOULD BE AS MUCH a physical practice as it is a mental one. Given its name, you might think mindfulness is something you do only with your mind. In fact, lots of research, including my own, has shown that paying attention to our bodies is often an easy way into mindfulness and helps us reduce stress while it's happening.

This may seem counterintuitive because when our mind is overwhelmed, our body is often the last thing we're thinking about. If we notice our bodies at all in moments of stress, most likely it is as they interrupt our normal activities: carpal tunnel syndrome, back pain, breast pumping, dental appointments, sore feet, sick days, or simply the routine hunger that forces us to stop what we're doing multiple times a day and eat. Yet if we focus our attention on our bodies, they can be our anchor in what's happening right now, even if the sensations are unpleasant.

This is how anchoring works: We bring our attention into our bodies, noticing—rather than avoiding—the tension, circulation, pain, pleasure, or just neutral physical experience of, say, our right

---

Adapted from content posted on hbr.org on November 18, 2016, as "A Simple Way to Stay Grounded in Stressful Moments" (product #H039WF)

shoulder or the arch of our left foot. This practice helps us snap back to reality. In fact, our bodies are the quickest, surest way back to the present moment when our minds are lost in rehashing the past or rehearsing the future.

We cause ourselves a lot of unnecessary suffering when our minds aren't paying attention. The amygdala, located in the brain's medial temporal lobe, is the part of the brain that detects and processes fear. When our amygdala is activated by a situation that is interpreted as a potential threat, even if we are just reading an unpleasant email, it initiates physiological changes such as increased muscle tension and accelerated breathing. This association becomes so strong that we take the body's reaction as evidence of danger, just as Pavlov's dogs took the sound of the bell as evidence of dinner. As a result, a vicious cycle can develop wherein the increased muscle tension and rapid breathing caused by an activated amygdala further activates the amygdala. Thankfully, we can use anchoring to break out of it.

One of my students who was working on a startup business used to panic before meeting with potential venture capitalists. His mind would spin with fears of the worst outcomes: his pitch rejected, his business idea exposed as worthless. Once he learned to tune in to his body, to use a brief minute to anchor by taking a few breaths and feeling his feet on the ground, he calmed down and became poised to have much better conversations. Here are some simple, effective anchoring practices you can use:

- **Take a single breath.** It takes just one intentional breath to change our perspective. A single breath gives you a break from the mind's chatter and a chance for your body to regulate after amping up in response to a perceived threat. Most of the time, when you're in distress, you're in the middle of telling yourself a story and you fully believe it. A breath can take you out of the story, making you less gullible. You can follow the breath into your body, where you gain just enough distance to judge whether your head is with you (in line with your current intentions and greater purpose) or against you, and then consciously choose which way you want to go.

- **Pay attention to emotions.** Another reason to anchor in your body is that it's where you feel your emotions, which are important to acknowledge even if they may seem like a liability, especially at work. I've studied the downsides of emotional suppression and I can assure you—it's not beneficial.[1]

  It's paradoxical, but nonjudgmentally engaging with negative emotions *negatively* correlates with negative emotions and mood disorder. In other words, if you acknowledge and recognize unpleasant emotions, they have less power to cause you distress. In one study, participants wrote every day for four days about either a traumatic experience or a neutral event.[2] Those who wrote about trauma made fewer health center visits in the following six months than those who wrote about a neutral event. When you pay attention to your body, you can catch emotional information upstream, before it hijacks your whole system—once it does, it's too late to use it to your advantage.

- **Remember that your colleagues have bodies too.** Annoyed with your boss? Think you can't last another day with an impossible colleague? If you let it, your body can connect you to other people—even difficult ones—since the body is a major part of what we have in common. This sounds obvious, but the implications are profound. Our bodies and the pleasure and pain that come with them—their attendant aches and illnesses, their needs and indignities, the impossibility of choosing the one we want, the fear of losing it someday, and the ways we fight our bodies or pretend they don't exist—are shared experiences. When you ignore your body (or try to), you miss out on a fundamental part of what we have in common. The empathy gained from this awareness helps you to have productive professional relationships, rather than suffering from ongoing frustration and pain.

- **Magnify little pleasures.** Don't underestimate the joy of taking that first sip of afternoon coffee. It's human nature to notice pain more than pleasure, but with reminders and practice you can experience joy throughout the day in the simple, reliable pleasures of having a body. It might be from sitting when you've been standing for too long, or standing up and stretching when you've been sitting; holding a new pen with a particularly cushy, ergonomic grip; laughing hard when something's funny; eating when you're hungry; the relative quiet of the office after a morning with screaming kids; slipping out of uncomfortable shoes under your desk. Every day, no matter how lousy, affords countless opportunities like these to feel good. Recently, I had a meeting at the VA hospital in Palo Alto and came across two veterans as I was walking. They were sitting in front of the building, both in wheelchairs. One man leaned over to his companion and said, "Well, it's great that we can move our hands." The other responded, "Yes, you are right. That is great!" Their perspective provides a powerful reminder that most of us can, if we choose, find within our daily routine a small joy worthy of being celebrated.

Stress is an inevitable aspect of our lives at work, but you don't need elaborate practices or escape mechanisms to engage with it. You simply need to have the wherewithal to ground yourself in a physical sensation, to anchor and come back to reality. You need only a brief moment to tap your feet on the ground and be reminded that you have a reliable and ever-present instrument to mitigate your stress. And, it just so happens, you were born with it.

Leah Weiss is a teacher, writer, and researcher at Stanford Graduate School of Business, the Director of Education at HopeLab, and the author of the forthcoming book *Heart at Work*.

Notes

1. Debora Cutuli, "Cognitive Reappraisal and Expressive Suppression Strategies Role in the Emotion Regulation: An Overview on Their Modulatory Effects and Neural Correlates," *Frontiers in Systems Neuroscience*, September 19, 2014; Andrea Hermann et al., "Brain Structural Basis of Cognitive Reappraisal and

Expressive Suppression," *Social Cognitive and Effective Neuroscience* 9, no. 9 (September 2014): 1435–1442.; and Sally Moore et al., "Are Expressive Suppression and Cognitive Reappraisal Associated with Stress-Related Symptoms?" *Behaviour Research and Therapy* 46, no. 9 (September 2008): 993–1000.

2. James J. Gross, ed., *Handbook of Emotion Regulation*, 2nd edition. New York: The Guilford Press, 2014.

CHAPTER 9

Recovering from an Emotional Outburst

by Susan David

IT HAPPENS—WE ALL GET emotional at work. You might scream, or cry, or pound the table and stamp your feet. This is not ideal office behavior, of course, and there are ramifications to these outbursts, but they don't have to be career-killers either. If you take a close look at what happened, why you acted the way you did, and take steps to remedy the situation, you can turn an outburst into an opportunity.

If you tend to suppress your emotions, you're likely to just ignore your tantrum and move on. If you are prone to ruminating over your mistakes, you'll overthink your outburst and beat yourself up about it.

Neither of these strategies is productive; they don't help you solve the problem *or* promote your own well-being. Instead, treat your outburst for what it is: data. A key emotional intelligence skill is being able to manage your emotion, but you can't manage what you can't recognize and understand. So first, be open to emotions. What was I feeling here? Emotions are signals, beacons that show you that you care about something.

Adapted from content posted on hbr.org on May 8, 2015, as "Recovering from an Emotional Outburst at Work" (product #H022A3)

To *recognize* your emotions, you have to be able to differentiate between feelings—sadness, anger, frustration (see chapter 4 in this guide). In many work environments, people suffer from what psychologists call *alexithymia*—a dispositional difficulty in accurately labeling and expressing what they're feeling. These people tend to be vague about their emotions. So a manager will say to herself, for example, "Gee, I yelled because I was really stressed out." But that gives her no information about what was really going on.

Once you've recognized the emotion—fear, disappointment, anger—your next step is to *understand* what, exactly, caused it: "Why is it that I reacted in this particular way?" "What was happening in this situation that I found upsetting?" "What values of mine may have been transgressed or challenged?" For example, maybe you lost it and screamed at a colleague when you found out that your project was cut. If you dig deeper, you may find that it wasn't exactly about the project but rather how the decision was made—that you didn't feel it was made fairly.

The research on emotions shows that there are general triggers that you should be aware of.[1] When your outburst is anger—yelling, stomping your feet—it's typically because you're frustrated or feel thwarted. You've been stopped from doing something that's important to you. When you feel sadness or cry, it's usually because of a loss. Acting out on anxiety is prompted by a sense of threat. It's helpful to think about these universal triggers, and then ask, "What is it specifically that was important to me in this situation?"

Once you've recognized how you feel, and why you feel it, you can focus on what to do to make things better—to *manage* the situation. It goes without saying that you should apologize if you yelled or lost your cool, but that's not enough. Your goal isn't just to repair the relationship, but to strengthen it.

After you've calmed down and you return to your team the following day or week, instead of saying, "Gee, I'm so sorry about what I did; now let's move on," address what really happened for you. You might say something like, "I got really mad and I'm not proud of my behavior. I've been thinking long and hard about what it was that I found so upsetting and I've realized that my sense of fairness was challenged because of how the defunding decisions were made."

There's research that shows that when you appropriately disclose your emotions in this way, people are more likely to treat you with compassion and forgiveness than if you had just offered an apology.[2] From there you start a shared conversation about what's important to each of you and how you can work better together.

No one wants to earn a reputation as a crier or a screamer at work. Instead of running and hiding or wallowing in self-pity when you've lost it, bring a good dose of compassion and curiosity to the situation. To be kind and compassionate toward yourself—especially in the moments you are least proud of—is not the same as letting yourself off the hook. In fact, studies show that people who are self-compassionate are much more likely to hold themselves to high standards and work to make things right.[3] And treating yourself that way is more likely to inspire others to do the same.

Susan David is a founder of the Harvard/McLean Institute of Coaching and is on faculty at Harvard University. She is author of *Emotional Agility* (Avery, 2016), based on the concept named by HBR as a Management Idea of the Year. As a speaker and adviser, David has worked with the senior leadership of hundreds of major organizations, including the United Nations, Ernst & Young, and the World Economic Forum. For more information, go to www.susandavid.com or follow her on Twitter @SusanDavid_PhD.

Notes

1. R. S. Lazarus, "From Psychological Stress to Emotions: A History of Changing Outlooks," *Annual Review of Psychology* 44 (1993): 1–22.

2. James J. Gross, "Emotion Regulation: Affective, Cognitive, and Social Consequences," *Psychophysiology* 39 (2002): 281–291.

3. Kristin D. Neff, "Self-Compassion, Self-Esteem, and Well-Being," *Social and Personality Psychology Compass* 5, no. 1 (2011): 1–12.

Everyday Emotional Intelligence

## CHAPTER 10

Writing Resonant Emails

by Andrew Brodsky

IMAGINE SENDING A DETAILED QUESTION to your boss and getting a one-word response: "No." Is she angry? Offended by your email? Or just very busy? When I conduct research with organizations on the topic of communication, one of the most common themes raised by both employees and managers is the challenge of trying to communicate emotional or sensitive issues over email. Email, of course, lacks most normal cues for relaying emotion, such as tone of voice and facial expressions.

But in many cases, using email is simply unavoidable. So how can you balance the need to communicate with avoiding the potential pitfalls of using emotion in email? Here are three concrete, research-based recommendations:

Understand what drives how emails are interpreted

It is clear that people often misinterpret emotion in email, but what drives the direction of the misinterpretation? For one, people infuse their emotional expectations into how they read messages, regardless

Adapted from content posted on hbr.org on April 23, 2013, as "The Do's and Don'ts of Work Email" (product #H020WK)

of the sender's actual intent.[1] Consider the email, *"Good job on the current draft, but I think we can continue to improve it."* Coming from a peer, this email will seem very collaborative; coming from a supervisor, it may seem critical.

In addition to relative position (emails from people high in power tend to be perceived as more negative), there are other contextual factors to consider: the length of a relationship (emails from people we know well tend to be perceived as less negative), the emotional history of the relationship, and the individual's personality (negative people tend to perceive messages as more negative).

The first step in avoiding miscommunication is to try to stand in the recipient's shoes, and imagine how they are likely to interpret your message. Doing so can help you to prevent misunderstandings before they ever occur.

Mimic behaviors

What is the best way to convey emotions via email? Emoticons? Word choice? Exclamation points? There is no single correct answer; the proper cues will vary based on the context. For instance, you likely wouldn't want to send a smiley face emoticon to a client organization that is known for having a very formal culture. Alternatively, you wouldn't want to send an overly formal email to a very close colleague.

One strategy that has been found to be very effective across settings is to engage in behavioral mimicry—using emoticons, word-choice, and slang/jargon in a similar manner to the person with whom you are communicating. In a set of studies of American, Dutch, and Thai negotiators, using behavioral mimicry in the early stages of text-based chat negotiations increased individual outcomes by 30%. This process of mimicry increases trust because people tend to feel an affinity toward those who act similarly to them.[2]

State your emotions

While mimicking behaviors can be effective, it is still a rather subtle strategy that leaves the potential for emotional ambiguity. The simplest solution to avoid any confusion is to just explicitly state the emotion that you want to relay in your email.

One excellent example of how this works comes from a media organization I recently worked with. I asked employees for an email that they felt was written very poorly, and one employee provided me with the following message from a manager:

The intro of the commercial needs to be redone. I'm sure that's the client's doing and you will handle it :). Warm Regards, [Manager's Name].

To me as an outsider (and I'm guessing to the manager as well), this email seemed well crafted to avoid offending the employee. However, the employee felt differently and explained: "She knows perfectly well that I made the terrible intro, and she was saying, 'Well, I'm sure the client made that segment and that you will tackle it,' and then she put a little smiley face at the end. So overall, a condescendingly nasty tone."

If the manager had avoided subtlety and stated her meaning directly, there might have been less room for interpretation. For example, what if she had written:

I am very happy with your work so far. I think the intro could be improved, though; would you mind giving it another shot?

The employee would have had far less ambiguity to fill in with her own emotional expectations.

Yet people rarely state their intended emotions, even when the stakes are high. Research from NYU has shown that many people are overconfident in their ability to accurately relay emotions when it comes to email.[3] It may seem obvious to the message sender that a coworker who never takes sick days will realize a comment about them leaving early is humorous rather than serious. However, that coworker might be particularly concerned about being seen as lazy and will feel hurt or offended.

Given the constantly evolving nature of organizational communication, there is still a lot to learn about effective email use. However, there are some clear areas where we can improve. In reality, we all have the same flaw: We tend to be overly focused on ourselves and our own goals, while failing to amply account for other people's perspectives. Using these methods for bridging your and your email recipient's perspectives, by both increasing message clarity and building trust, will help you to ensure effective communication.

_____

Andrew Brodsky is a PhD candidate in organizational behavior at Harvard Business School.

Notes

1. Kristin Byron, "Carrying Too Heavy a Load? The Communication and Miscommunication of Emotion by Email," *Academy of Management Review* 33, no. 2 (April 2008): 309–327.

2. William W. Maddux et al., "Chameleons Bake Bigger Pies and Take Bigger Pieces: Strategy Behavioral Mimicry Facilitates Negotiation Outcomes," *Journal of Experimental Social Psychology* 44, no. 2 (March 2008): 461–468; and Roderick I. Swaab et al., "Early Words That Work: When and How Virtual Linguistic Mimicry Facilitates Negotiation Outcomes," *Journal of Experimental Psychology* 47, no. 3 (May 2011): 616–621.

3. Justin Kruger et al., "Egocentrism Over E-mail: Can We Communicate as Well as We Think?" *Journal of Personality and Social Psychology* 89, no. 6 (December 2005): 925–936.

## CHAPTER 11

Running Powerful Meetings

by Annie McKee

YES, WE ALL HATE MEETINGS. Yes, they are usually a waste of time. And yes, they're here to stay. So it's your responsibility as a leader to make them better. This doesn't mean just making them shorter, more efficient, and more organized. People need to enjoy them and—dare I say it—have fun.

So how do we fix meetings so they are more enjoyable and produce more positive feelings? Sure, invite the right people, create better agendas, and be better prepared. Those are baseline fixes. But if you really want to improve how people work together at meetings, you'll need to rely on—and maybe develop—a couple of key emotional intelligence competencies: empathy and emotional self-management.

Why empathy? Empathy is a competency that allows you to read people. Who is supporting whom? Who is pissed off, and who is coasting? Where is the resistance? This isn't as easy as it seems. Sometimes, the smartest resisters often look like supporters, but they're not supportive at all. They're smart, sneaky idea killers.

Adapted from content posted on hbr.org on March 23, 2015, as "Empathy Is Key to a Great Meeting" (product #H01YDY)

Carefully reading people will also help you understand the major and often hidden conflicts in the group. Hint: These conflicts probably have nothing to do with the topics discussed or decisions being made at the meeting. They are far more likely to be linked to very human dynamics like who is allowed to influence whom (headquarters versus the field, expats versus local nationals) and power dynamics between genders and among people of various races.

Empathy lets you see and manage these power dynamics. Many of us would like to think that these sorts of concerns—and office politics in general—are beneath us, unimportant, or just for those Machiavellian folks we all dislike. Realistically, though, power is hugely important in groups because it is the real currency in most organizations. And it plays out in meetings. Learning to read how the flow of power is moving and shifting can help you lead the meeting—and everything else.

Keep in mind that employing empathy will help you understand how people are responding to *you*. As a leader you may be the most powerful person at the meeting. Some people, the dependent types, will defer at every turn. That feels good, for a minute. Carry on that way, and you're likely to create a dependent group—or one that is polarized between those who will do anything you want and those who will not.

This is where emotional self-management comes in, for a couple of reasons. First, take a look at the dependent folks in your meetings. Again, it can feel really good to have people admire you and agree with your every word. In fact, this can be a huge relief in our conflict-ridden organizations. But again, if you don't manage your response, you will make group dynamics worse. You will also look like a fool. Others are reading the group, too, and they will rightly read that you like it when people go along with you. They will see that you are falling prey to your own ego or to those who want to please or manipulate you.

Second, strong emotions set the tone for the entire group. We take our cue from one another about how to feel about what's going on around us. Are we in danger? Is there cause for celebration? Should we be fed up and cynical or hopeful and committed? Here's why this matters in meetings: If you, as a leader, effectively project out your more positive emotions, such as hope and enthusiasm, others will "mirror" these feelings and the general tone of the group will be marked by optimism and a sense of "we're in this together, and we can do it."[1] And there is a strong neurological link between feelings and cognition. We think more clearly and more creatively when our feelings are largely positive and when we are appropriately challenged, as Mihaly Csikszentmihalyi wrote in his classic *Creativity: Flow and the Psychology of Discovery and Invention*.

The other side of the coin is obvious. Your negative emotions are also contagious, and they are almost always destructive if unchecked and unmanaged. Express anger, contempt, or disrespect, and you will definitely push people into fight mode—individually and collectively. Express disdain, and you'll alienate people far beyond the end of the meeting. And it doesn't matter who you feel this way about. All it takes is for people to see it, and they will catch it—and worry that next time your target will be them.

This is not to say that all positive emotions are good all the time or that you should never express negative emotions. The point is that the leader's emotions are highly infectious. Know this and manage your feelings accordingly to create the kind of environment where people can work together to make decisions and get things done.

It may go without saying, but you can't do any of this with your phone on. As Daniel Goleman shares in his book *Focus: The Hidden Driver of Excellence*, we are not nearly as good at multitasking as we think we are. Actually we stink at it. So turn it off and pay attention to the people you are with today.

In the end, it's your job to make sure people leave your meeting feeling pretty good about what's happened, their contributions, and you as the leader. Empathy allows you to read what's going on, and self-management helps you move the group to a mood that supports getting things done—and happiness.

Annie McKee is a senior fellow at the University of Pennsylvania and the director of the PennCLO Executive Doctoral Program. She is the author of *Primal Leadership* (with Daniel Goleman and Richard Boyatzis), as well as *Resonant Leadership* and *Becoming a Resonant Leader.* Her new book, *How to Be Happy at Work,* is forthcoming from Harvard Business Review Press in September 2017.

Note

1. V. Ramachandran, "The Neurons That Shaped Civilization," TED talk, November 2009, https://www.ted.com/talks/vs_rama chandran_the_neurons_ that_shaped_civilization?language=en.

## CHAPTER 12

Giving Difficult Feedback

by Monique Valcour

OVER THE YEARS, I'VE ASKED hundreds of executive students what skills they believe are essential for leaders. "The ability to give tough feedback" comes up frequently. But what exactly is "tough feedback"? The phrase connotes bad news, like when you have to tell a team member that they've screwed up on something important. "Tough" also signifies the way we think we need to be when giving negative feedback: firm, resolute, and unyielding.

But "tough" also points to the discomfort some of us experience when giving negative feedback, and to the challenge of doing so in a way that motivates change instead of making the other person feel defensive. Managers fall into a number of common traps when offering feedback. We might be angry at an employee and use the conversation to blow off steam rather than to coach. Or we may delay giving needed feedback because we anticipate that the employee will become argumentative and refuse to accept responsibility. We might try surrounding negative feedback with positive feedback, like disguising a bitter-tasting pill in a spoonful of honey. But this

Adapted from content posted on hbr.org on August 11, 2015, as "How to Give Tough Feedback That Helps People Grow" (product #H029QB)

approach is misguided, because we don't want the negative feedback to slip by unnoticed in the honey. Instead, it's essential to create conditions in which the receiver can take in feedback, reflect on it, and learn from it.

To get a feel for what this looks like in practice, I juxtapose two feedback conversations that occurred following a workplace conflict. MJ Paulitz, a physical therapist in the Pacific Northwest, was treating a hospital patient one day when a fellow staff member paged her. Following procedure, she excused herself and stepped out of the treatment room to respond to the page. The colleague who sent it didn't answer her phone when MJ called, nor had she left a message describing the situation that warranted the page. This happened two more times during the same treatment session. The third time she left her patient to respond to the page, MJ lost her cool and left an angry voicemail message for her colleague. Upset upon hearing the message, the staff member reported it to their supervisor as abusive.

MJ's first feedback session took place in her supervisor's office. She recalls, "When I went into his office, he had already decided that I was the person at fault, he had all the information he needed, and he wasn't interested in hearing my side of the story. He did not address the three times she pulled me out of patient care. He did not acknowledge that that might have been the fuse that set me off." Her supervisor referred MJ to the human resources department for corrective action. She left seething with a sense of injustice.

MJ describes the subsequent feedback conversation with human resources as transformative. "The woman in HR could see that I had a lot of just-under-the-surface feelings, and she acknowledged them. The way she did it was genius: She eased into it. She didn't make me go first. Instead, she said, 'I can only imagine what you're feeling right now. Here you are in my office, in corrective action. If it were me, I might be feeling angry, frustrated, embarrassed... Are any of these true for you?' That made a huge difference."

With trust established, MJ was ready to take responsibility for her behavior and commit to changing it. Next the HR person said, "Now let's talk about how you reacted to those feelings in the moment." She created a space that opened up a genuine dialogue.

The subsequent conversation created powerful learning that has stuck with MJ to this day:

Oftentimes, when we're feeling a strong emotion, we go down what the HR person called a "cowpath," because it's well worn, very narrow, and always leads to the same place. Let's say you're angry. What do you do? You blow up. It's okay that you feel those things; it's just not okay to blow up. She asked me to think about what I could do to get on a different path.

The feedback from the HR person helped me learn to find the space between what I'm feeling and the next thing that slides out of my mouth. She gave me the opportunity to grow internally. What made it work was establishing a safe space, trust, and rapport, and then getting down to "you need to change"— rather than starting with "you need to change," which is what my supervisor did. I did need to change; that was the whole point of the corrective action. But she couldn't start there, because I would have become defensive, shut down and not taken responsibility. I still to this day think that my coworker should have been reprimanded. But I also own my part in it. I see that I went down that cowpath, and I know that I won't do it a second time.

The difference in the two feedback sessions illustrated above boils down to coaching, which deepens self-awareness and catalyzes growth, versus reprimanding, which sparks self-protection and avoidance of responsibility. To summarize, powerful, high-impact feedback conversations share the following elements:

1. An intention to help the employee grow, rather than to show him he was wrong. The feedback should increase, not drain, the employee's motivation and resources for change. When preparing for a feedback conversation as a manager, reflect on what you hope to achieve and on what impact you'd like to have on the employee, perhaps by doing a short meditation just before the meeting.

2. Openness on the part of the feedback giver, which is essential to creating a high-quality connection that facilitates change. If you start off feeling uncomfortable and self-protective, your employee will match that energy, and you'll each leave the conversation frustrated with the other person.

3. Inviting the employee into the problem-solving process. You can ask questions such as: What ideas do you have? What are you taking away from this conversation? What steps will you take, by when, and how will I know?

Giving developmental feedback that sparks growth is a critical challenge to master, because it can make the difference between an employee who contributes powerfully and positively to the organization and one who feels diminished by the organization and contributes far less. A single conversation can switch an employee on—or shut her down. A true developmental leader sees the raw material for brilliance in every employee and creates the conditions to let it shine, even when the challenge is tough.

Monique Valcour is a management academic, coach, and consultant.

## CHAPTER 13

Making Smart Decisions

A summary of the full-length HBR article "Why Good Leaders Make Bad Decisions" by Andrew Campbell, Jo Whitehead, and Sydney Finkelstein, highlighting key ideas and company examples, and a checklist for putting the idea into action.

Idea in Brief

- Leaders make decisions largely through unconscious processes that neuroscientists call pattern recognition and emotional tagging. These processes usually make for quick, effective decisions, but they can be distorted by bias.

- Managers need to find systematic ways to recognize the sources of bias—what the authors call "red flag conditions"— and then design safeguards that introduce more analysis, greater debate, or stronger governance. The authors identify three of these red flag conditions as the presence of:

  - Inappropriate self-interest, which, according to research, can bias even well-intentioned professionals such as doctors and auditors.

  - Distorting attachments to people, places, and things— for example, an executive's reluctance to sell a business unit they've worked in.

  - Misleading memories, which may seem relevant and comparable to the current situation but lead our thinking down the wrong path by obscuring important differentiating factors.

- By using the approach described in this article, companies will avoid many flawed decisions that are caused by the way our brains operate.

Adapted from *Harvard Business Review*, February 2009 (product #R0902D)

Idea in Practice

Leaders make quick decisions by recognizing patterns in the situations they encounter, and then responding to the emotional associations attached to those patterns. Most of the time, the process works well, but it can result in serious mistakes when those emotional associations are biased.

Example: When Wang Laboratories launched its own personal computer, founder An Wang chose to create a proprietary operating system even though the IBM PC was clearly becoming the standard. This blunder was influenced by his belief that IBM had cheated him early in his career, which made him reluctant to consider using a system linked to an IBM product.

To guard against distorted decision making and strengthen the decision process, get the help of an independent person to identify which decision makers are likely to be affected by self-interest, emotional attachments, or misleading memories.

Example: The about-to-be-promoted head of the cosmetics business at one Indian company was consid-

ering whether to appoint her number-two as her successor. She recognized that her judgment might be distorted by her attachment to her colleague and by her vested interest in keeping her workload down during the transition. The executive asked a headhunter to evaluate her colleague and to determine whether better candidates could be found externally.

If the risk of distorted decision making is high, build safeguards into the decision process. Expose decision makers to additional experience and analysis, design in more debate and opportunities for challenge, add more oversight, and monitor whether the decision is generating the expected results.

Example: In helping the CEO make an important strategic decision, the chairman of one global chemical company encouraged the chief executive to seek advice from investment bankers, set up a project team to analyze options, and create a steering committee that included the chairman and the CFO to review the CEO's proposal.

Identifying Red Flags

RED FLAGS ARE USEFUL ONLY if they can be spotted before a decision is made. How can you recognize them in complex situations? We have developed the following seven-step process:

1. **Lay out the range of options.** It's never possible to list them all. But it's normally helpful to note the extremes. These provide boundaries for the decision.

2. **List the main decision makers.** Who is going to be influential in making the judgment calls and the final choice? There may be only one or two people involved. But there could also be 10 or more.

3. **Choose one decision maker to focus on.** It's usually best to start with the most influential person. Then identify red flag conditions that might distort that individual's thinking. Discuss with the individual if needed.

4. **Check for inappropriate self-interest or distorting attachments.** Is any option likely to be particularly attractive or unattractive to the decision maker because of personal interests or attachments to people, places, or things? Do any of these interests or attachments conflict with the objectives of the decision?

5. **Check for misleading memories.** What are the uncertainties in this decision? For each area of uncertainty, consider whether the decision maker might draw on potentially misleading memories. Think about past experiences that could mislead, especially ones with strong emotional associations. Think also about previous judgments that could now be unsound, given the current situation.

6. **Repeat the analysis with the next-most-influential person.** In a complex case, it may be necessary to consider many more people, and the process may bring to light a long list of possible red flags.

7. **Review the list of red flags you have identified for bias.** Determine whether the balance of red flags is likely to bias the decision in favor of or against some options. If so, put one or more safeguards in place. Biases can cancel each other out, so it is necessary to assess the balance taking account of the likely influence of each person involved in the decision.

———————

Andrew Campbell is a director of the Ashridge Strategic Management Centre in England. **Jo Whitehead** (jo.whitehead@ashridge.org.uk) is a director of the Ashridge Strategic Management Centre in London. **Sydney Finkelstein** is the Steven Roth Professor of Management and Director of the Leadership Center at the Tuck School of Business at Dartmouth College. His new book is *Superbosses: How Exceptional Leaders Manage the Flow of Talent* (Portfolio/Penguin, 2016). Campbell, Whitehead, and Finkelstein are the coauthors of *Think Again: Why Good Leaders Make Bad Decisions and How to Keep It from Happening to You* (Harvard Business Review Press, 2008).

CHAPTER 14

An Emotional Strategy for Negotiations

by Alison Wood Brooks

IT IS, WITHOUT QUESTION, my favorite day of the semester—the day when I teach my MBA students a negotiation exercise called "Honoring the Contract."

I assign students to partners, and each reads a different account of a (fictitious) troubled relationship between a supplier (a manufacturer of computer components) and a client (a search engine startup). They learn that the two parties signed a detailed contract eight months earlier, but now they're at odds over several of the terms (sales volume, pricing, product reliability, and energy efficiency specs). Each student assumes the role of either client or supplier and receives confidential information about company finances and politics. Then each pair is tasked with renegotiating—a process that could lead to an amended deal, termination of the contract, or expensive litigation.

What makes this simulation interesting, however, lies not in the details of the case but in the top-secret instructions given to one side of each pairing before the exercise begins: "Please start the

Reprinted from "Emotion and the Art of Negotiation" in *Harvard Business Review*, December 2015 (product #R1512C)

negotiation with a display of anger. You must display anger for a minimum of 10 minutes at the beginning." The instructions go on to give specific tips for showing anger: Interrupt the other party. Call them "unfair" or "unreasonable." Blame them personally for the disagreement. Raise your voice.

Before the negotiations begin, I spread the pairs all over the building so that the students can't see how others are behaving. Then, as the pairs negotiate, I walk around and observe. Although some students struggle, many are spectacularly good at feigning anger. They wag a finger in their partner's face. They pace around. I've never seen the exercise result in a physical confrontation—but it has come close. Some of the negotiators who did not get the secret instructions react by trying to defuse the other person's anger. But some react angrily themselves—and it's amazing how quickly the emotional responses escalate. When I bring everyone back into the classroom after 30 minutes, there are always students still yelling at each other or shaking their heads in disbelief.

During the debriefing, we survey the pairs to see how angry they felt and how they fared in resolving the problem. Often, the more anger the parties showed, the more likely it was that the negotiation ended poorly—for example, in litigation or an impasse (no deal). Once I've clued the entire class in on the setup, discussion invariably makes its way to this key insight: Bringing anger to a negotiation is like throwing a bomb into the process, and it's apt to have a profound effect on the outcome.

Until 20 years ago, few researchers paid much attention to the role of emotions in negotiating—how feelings can influence the way people overcome conflict, reach agreement, and create value when dealing with another party. Instead, negotiation scholars focused primarily on strategy and tactics—particularly the ways in which parties can identify and consider alternatives, use leverage, and execute the choreography of offers and counteroffers. Scientific understanding of negotiation also tended to home in on the transactional nature of working out a deal: how to get the most money or profit from the process. Even when experts started looking at psychological influences on negotiations, they focused on diffuse and nonspecific moods—such as whether negotiators felt generally positive or negative, and how that affected their behavior.

Over the past decade, however, researchers have begun examining how specific emotions—anger, sadness, disappointment, anxiety, envy, excitement, and regret—can affect the behavior of negotiators. They've studied the differences between what happens when people simply feel these emotions and what happens when they also express them to the other party through words or actions. In negotiations that are less transactional and involve parties in long-term relationships, understanding the role of emotions is even more important than it is in transactional deal making.

This new branch of research is proving extremely useful. We all have the ability to regulate how we experience emotions, and specific strategies can help us improve tremendously in that regard. We also have some control over the extent to which we express our feelings—and again, there are specific ways to cloak (or emphasize) an expression of emotion when doing so may be advantageous. For instance, research shows that feeling or looking anxious results in suboptimal negotiation outcomes. So individuals who are prone to anxiety when brokering a deal can take certain steps both to limit their nervousness and to make it less obvious to their negotiation opponent. The same is true for other emotions.

In the pages that follow, I discuss—and share coping strategies for—many of the emotions people typically feel over the course of a negotiation. Anxiety is most likely to crop up before the process begins or during its early stages. We're prone to experience anger or excitement in the heat of the discussions. And we're most likely to feel disappointment, sadness, or regret in the aftermath.

Avoiding Anxiety

Anxiety is a state of distress in reaction to threatening stimuli—in particular, novel situations that have the potential for undesirable outcomes. In contrast to anger, which motivates people to escalate conflict (the "fight" part of the fight-or-flight response), anxiety trips the "flight" switch and makes people want to exit the scene.

Because patience and persistence are often desirable when negotiating, the urge to exit quickly is counterproductive. But the negative effects of feeling anxious while negotiating may go further. In
my recent research, I wondered if anxious negotiators also develop
low aspirations and expectations, which could lead them to make
timid first offers—a behavior that directly predicts poor negotiating
outcomes.

In work with Maurice Schweitzer in 2011, I explored how anxiety influences negotiations. First we surveyed 185 professionals
about the emotions they expected to feel before negotiating with a
stranger, negotiating to buy a car, and negotiating to increase their
salary. When dealing with a stranger or asking for a higher salary,
anxiety was the dominant emotional expectation; when negotiating
for the car, anxiety was second only to excitement.

To understand how anxiety can affect negotiators, we then asked
a separate group of 136 participants to negotiate a cell phone contract that required agreeing on a purchase price, a warranty period,
and the length of the contract. We induced anxiety in half the participants by having them listen to continuous three-minute clips of
the menacing theme music from the film *Psycho*, while the other
half listened to pleasant music by Handel. (Researchers call this *inci-
dental* emotional manipulation, and it's quite powerful. Listening
to the *Psycho* music is genuinely uncomfortable: People's palms get
sweaty, and some listeners become jumpy.)

In this experiment and three others, we found that anxiety had
a significant effect on how people negotiated. People experiencing
anxiety made weaker first offers, responded more quickly to each
move the counterpart made, and were more likely to exit negotiations early (even though their instructions clearly warned that
exiting early would reduce the value they received from the negotiation). Anxious negotiators made deals that were 12% less financially
attractive than those made by negotiators in the neutral group. We
did discover one caveat, however: People who gave themselves high
ratings in a survey on negotiating aptitude were less affected by anxiety than others.

Those experiments examined what happens when people feel anxious. But what happens when they express that anxiety, making it clear to their counterparts that they're nervous (and perhaps vulnerable)? In 2012, with Francesca Gino and Maurice Schweitzer, I conducted eight experiments to explore how anxious people behaved in situations in which they could seek advice from others. We found that relative to people who did not feel anxious, they were less confident, more likely to consult others when making decisions, and less able to discriminate between good and bad advice. In the most relevant of these experiments, we found that anxious participants did not discount advice from someone with a stated conflict of interest, whereas subjects feeling neutral emotions looked upon that advice skeptically. Although this research didn't directly address how the subjects would negotiate, it suggests that people who express anxiety are more likely to be taken advantage of in a negotiation, especially if the other party senses their distress.

Excellent negotiators often make their counterparts feel anxious on purpose. For example, on the TV show *Shark Tank*, six wealthy investors ("sharks") negotiate with entrepreneurs hoping for funding. The entrepreneurs must pitch their ideas in front of a huge television audience and face questions from the investors that are often aggressive and unnerving. As this is going on, stress-inducing music fills the TV studio. This setup does more than create drama and entertainment for viewers; it also intentionally puts pressure on the entrepreneurs. The sharks are professional negotiators who want to knock the entrepreneurs off balance so that it will be easier to take ownership of their good ideas at the lowest price possible. (When multiple sharks want to invest, they often drop comments that are intended to make opposing investors anxious too.) If you watch the show closely, you'll probably notice a pattern: The entrepreneurs who seem least rattled by the environmental stressors tend to negotiate the most carefully and deliberately—and often strike the best deals.

The takeaway from both research and practice is clear: Try your utmost to avoid feeling anxious while negotiating. How can you manage that? Train, practice, rehearse, and keep sharpening your negotiating skills. Anxiety is often a response to novel stimuli, so the more familiar the stimuli, the more comfortable and the less anxious you will feel. (That's why clinicians who treat anxiety disorders often rely on exposure therapy: People who are nervous about flying on airplanes, for instance, are progressively exposed to the experience, first getting used to the sights and sounds, then sitting in airliner seats, and ultimately taking flights.) Indeed, although many people enroll in negotiation classes to learn strategies and increase skills, one of the primary benefits is the comfort that comes from repeatedly practicing deal making in simulations and exercises. Negotiation eventually feels more routine, so it's not such an anxiety-inducing experience.

Another useful strategy for reducing anxiety is to bring in an outside expert to handle the bargaining. Third-party negotiators will be less anxious because their skills are better honed, the process is routine for them, and they have a lower personal stake in the outcome. Outsourcing your negotiation may sound like a cop-out, but it's a frequent practice in many industries. Home buyers and sellers use real estate brokers partly for their negotiating experience; athletes, authors, actors, and even some business executives rely on agents to hammer out contracts. Although there are costs to this approach, they are often more than offset by the more favorable terms that can be achieved. And although anxious negotiators may have the most to gain from involving a third party (because anxiety can be a particularly difficult emotion to regulate in an uncomfortable setting), this strategy can also be useful when other negative emotions surface.

Managing Anger

Like anxiety, anger is a negative emotion, but instead of being self-focused, it's usually directed toward someone else. In most circumstances, we try to keep our tempers in check. When it comes to negotiating, however, many people believe that anger can be a productive emotion—one that will help them win a larger share of the pie.

This view stems from a tendency to view negotiations in competitive terms rather than collaborative ones. Researchers call this the *fixed-pie bias*: People, particularly those with limited experience making deals, assume that a negotiation is a zero-sum game in which their own interests conflict directly with a counterpart's. (More experienced negotiators, in contrast, look for ways to expand the pie through collaboration, rather than nakedly trying to snatch a bigger slice.) Anger, the thinking goes, makes one seem stronger, more powerful, and better able to succeed in this grab for value.

In fact, there's a body of research—much of it by Keith Allred, a former faculty member at Harvard's Kennedy School of Government—that documents the consequences of feeling angry while negotiating. This research shows that anger often harms the process by escalating conflict, biasing perceptions, and making impasses more likely. It also reduces joint gains, decreases cooperation, intensifies competitive behavior, and increases the rate at which offers are rejected. Angry negotiators are less accurate than neutral negotiators both in recalling their own interests and in judging other parties' interests. And angry negotiators may seek to harm or retaliate against their counterparts, even though a more cooperative approach might increase the value that both sides can claim from the negotiation.

Despite these findings, many people continue to see advantages to feeling or appearing angry. Some even attempt to turn up the volume on their anger, because they think it will make them more effective in a negotiation. In my own research, I have found that given a choice between feeling angry and feeling happy while negotiating, more than half the participants want to be in an angry state and view it as significantly advantageous.

There *are* cases when feeling angry can lead to better outcomes. Research by Gerben van Kleef at the University of Amsterdam demonstrates that in a one-time, transactional negotiation with few opportunities to collaborate to create value, an angry negotiator can wind up with a better deal. There may even be situations in which a negotiator decides to feign anger, because the counterpart, in an attempt to defuse that anger, is likely to give ground on terms. This might work well if you are haggling with a stranger to buy a car, for example.

But negotiators who play this card must be aware of the costs. Showing anger in a negotiation damages the long-term relationship between the parties. It reduces liking and trust. Research by Rachel Campagna at the University of New Hampshire shows that false representations of anger may generate small tactical benefits but also lead to considerable and persistent blowback. That is, faking anger can create authentic feelings of anger, which in turn diminish trust for both parties. Along the same lines, research by Jeremy Yip and Martin Schweinsberg demonstrates that people who encounter an angry negotiator are more likely to walk away, preferring to let the process end in a stalemate.

In many contexts, then, feeling or expressing anger as a negotiating tactic can backfire. So in most cases, tamping down any anger you feel—and limiting the anger you express—is a smarter strategy. This may be hard to do, but there are tactics that can help.

Building rapport before, during, and after a negotiation can reduce the odds that the other party will become angry. If you seek to frame the negotiation cooperatively—to make it clear that you're seeking a win-win solution instead of trying to get the lion's share of a fixed pie—you may limit the other party's perception that an angry grab for value will work well. If the other party does become angry, apologize. Seek to soothe. Even if you feel that his anger is unwarranted, recognize that you're almost certainly better positioned tactically if you can reduce the hostility.

Perhaps the most effective way to deal with anger in negotiations is to recognize that many negotiations don't unfold all at once but take place over multiple meetings. So if tensions are flaring, ask for a break, cool off, and regroup. This isn't easy when you're angry, because your fight-or-flight response urges you to escalate, not pull back. Resist that urge and give the anger time to dissipate. In heated negotiations, hitting the pause button can be the smartest play.

Finally, you might consider reframing anger as sadness. Though reframing one negative emotion as another sounds illogical, shared feelings of sadness can lead to cooperative concession making, whereas oppositional anger often leads to an impasse.

Preparing Your Emotional Strategy

PREPARATION IS KEY TO SUCCESS IN NEGOTIATIONS. It's vital to give advance thought to the objective factors involved (Who are the parties? What are the issues? What is my best outside option if we don't reach a deal?), but it is perhaps even more important to prepare your emotional strategy. Use the following questions and tips to plan ahead for each stage of the negotiation.

	Ask yourself:	Remember:
The buildup	• How do I feel? • Should I express my emotions? • How might the people across the table feel? • Are they likely to hide or express their emotions? • Should I recruit a third party to negotiate on my behalf?	• It's normal to feel anxious and excited. • Try to avoid expressing anxiety. • Expressing forward-looking excitement may help build rapport. • In emotionally charged situations (such as a divorce), consider having a third party (such as a lawyer) negotiate on your behalf.
The main event	• What things could happen that would make me feel angry? • What things might I do that would trigger my counterparts to feel angry? • What might they do or ask that would make me feel anxious?	• Be careful about expressing anger; it may extract concessions but harm the long-term relationship. • Avoid angering your counterparts; they are likely to walk away. • Preparing answers to tough questions is critical for staying calm in the moment.
The finale	• What are the possible outcomes of the negotiation? What do I hope to achieve? What do I expect to achieve? • How would those outcomes make me feel? • Should I express those feelings? To whom? • How are my counterparts likely to feel about the possible outcomes?	• To reduce disappointment, outline clear aspirations and expectations and adjust them throughout the negotiation. • When you feel pleased about an outcome, it may be wise to keep it to yourself. • The best negotiators create value for everyone, claiming the lion's share for themselves but making their counterparts feel that they, too, won.

Handling Disappointment and Regret

It can be tempting to see negotiations in binary terms—you either win or lose. Of course, that is generally too simplistic: Most complex negotiations will end with each side having achieved some of its goals and not others—a mix of wins and losses. Still, as a negotiation winds down, it's natural to look at the nascent agreement and feel, on balance, more positive or negative about it.

Disappointment can be a powerful force when it's expressed to the other party near the end of the negotiation. There's a relationship between anger and disappointment—both typically arise when an individual feels wronged—and it's useful to understand how one can be used more constructively than the other. (Think back to how you reacted as a child if your parents said "I'm very disappointed in you" instead of "I'm very angry with you.") Although expressing anger may create defensiveness or increase the odds of a standoff, expressing disappointment can serve a more tactical purpose by encouraging the other party to look critically at her own actions and consider whether she wants to change her position to reduce the negative feelings she's caused you.

Research shows that one cause of disappointment in a negotiation is the speed of the process. When a negotiation unfolds or concludes too quickly, participants tend to feel dissatisfied. They wonder if they could or should have done more or pushed harder. Negotiation teachers see this in class exercises: Often the first students to finish up are the most disappointed by the outcome. The obvious way to lessen the likelihood of disappointment is to proceed slowly and deliberately.

Regret is slightly different from disappointment. While the latter tends to involve sadness about an outcome, someone feeling regret is looking a little more upstream, at the course of actions that led to this unhappy outcome, and thinking about the missteps or mistakes that created the disappointment.

Studies show that people are most likely to regret actions they didn't take—the missed opportunities and errors of omission, rather than errors of commission. That can be a powerful insight for negotiators, whose primary actions should be asking questions, listening, proposing solutions, and brainstorming new alternatives if the parties can't agree. Ironically, people often don't ask questions while negotiating: They may forget to raise important matters or feel reluctant to probe too deeply, deeming it invasive or rude. Those fears are often misplaced. In fact, people who ask a lot of questions tend to be better liked, and they learn more things.

In negotiations, information is king and learning should be a central goal. One way to reduce the potential for regret is to ask questions without hesitation. Aim to come away from the negotiation with the sense that every avenue was explored.

Skilled negotiators use another technique to minimize the odds of regret: the *post-settlement settlement*. This strategy recognizes that tension often dissipates when there's a deal on the table that makes everyone happy, and sometimes the best negotiating happens after that tension is released. So instead of shaking hands and ending the deal making, one party might say, "We're good. We have terms we can all live with. But now that we know we've reached an agreement, let's spend a few more minutes chatting to see if we can find anything that sweetens it for both sides." Done ineptly, this might seem as if one party is trying to renege or renegotiate. However, when handled deftly, a post-settlement settlement can open a pathway for both sides to become even more satisfied with the outcome and stave off regrets.

Tempering Happiness and Excitement

There isn't much research on how happiness and excitement affect negotiations, but intuition and experience suggest that expressing these emotions can have significant consequences. The National Football League prohibits and penalizes "excessive celebrations" after a touchdown or big play because such conduct can generate ill will. For the same reason, the "winner" in a deal should not gloat as the negotiations wrap up. Nonetheless, this happens all the time. In workshops, I routinely see students unabashedly boast and brag (sometimes to the entire class) about how they really stuck it to their opponents in a negotiation exercise. Not only do these students risk looking like jerks, but in a real-world setting, they might suffer more dire consequences: the other party might invoke a right of rescission,

Managing Your Counterpart's Emotions

NEGOTIATING IS AN INTERPERSONAL PROCESS. There will always be at least one other party (and often many more) involved. In the adjoining article, I discuss how to manage your own emotions during a negotiation. But what about the other people at the table? Can you manage their emotions as well? I suggest two strategies for doing so:

1. *Be observant.* Perceiving how other people are feeling is a critical component of emotional intelligence, and it's particularly key in negotiations (as Adam Galinsky and his colleagues have found). So tune in to your counterpart's body language, tone of voice, and choice of words. When her verbal and nonverbal cues don't match up, ask questions. For example, "You are telling me you like this outcome, but you seem uneasy. Is something making you uncomfortable?" Or "You say you're angry, but you seem somewhat pleased. Are you truly upset about something? Or are you trying to intimidate me?"

Asking specific questions based on your perceptions of the other party's emotional expressions will make it easier for you to understand her perspective (a task people are shockingly bad at, according to research by Nicholas

---

seek to renegotiate, or take punitive action the next time the parties need to strike a deal.

Although it's unpleasant to feel disappointed after a negotiation, it can be even worse to make your counterparts feel that way. And in certain situations, showing happiness or excitement triggers disappointment in others. The best negotiators achieve great deals for themselves but leave their opponents believing that they, too, did fabulously, even if the truth is different. In deals that involve a significant degree of future collaboration—say, when two companies agree to merge, or when an actor signs a contract with a producer to star in an upcoming movie—it can be appropriate to show excitement, but it's important to focus on the opportunities ahead rather than the favorable terms one party just gained.

Another danger of excitement is that it may increase your commitment to strategies or courses of action that you'd be better off abandoning. In my negotiation class, we do an exercise in which students must decide whether or not to send a race car driver into an important race with a faulty engine. Despite the risks, most students

Epley). It will also make it difficult for a counterpart to lie to you; evidence suggests that people prefer to tell lies of omission about facts rather than lies of commission about feelings.

2. **Don't be afraid to exert direct influence on your counterpart's emotions.** This may sound manipulative or even unscrupulous, but you can use this influence for good. For example, if your counterpart seems anxious or angry, injecting humor or empathetic reassurance can dramatically change the tone of the interaction. By the same token, if your counterpart seems overconfident or pushy, expressing well-placed anger can inspire a healthy dose of fear.

In recent research with Elizabeth Baily Wolf, I have found that it's possible to go even further in managing others' emotions: You display an emotion, your counterpart sees it, and then you shape his interpretation of it. For example, imagine that you start crying at work. (Crying is a difficult-to-control and often embarrassing behavior.) Saying "I'm in tears because I'm passionate" rather than "I'm sorry I'm so emotional" can completely change the way others react and the way they view your self-control and competence.

opt to go ahead with the race because they are excited and want to maximize their winnings. The exercise has parallels to a real-life example: the launch of the *Challenger* space shuttle. Though the engineers who designed the *Challenger*'s faulty O-ring had qualms about it, NASA managers were overly excited and determined to proceed with the launch. Their decision ultimately led to the craft's explosion and the loss of its seven crew members.

There are two lessons for negotiators here. First, be considerate: Do not let your excitement make your counterparts feel that they lost. Second, be skeptical: Do not let your excitement lead to overconfidence or an escalation of commitment with insufficient data.

Negotiating requires some of the same skills that playing poker does—a strategic focus, the imagination to see alternatives, and a knack for assessing odds, reading people, understanding others' positions, and bluffing when necessary. However, whereas the parties in a negotiation must strive for agreement, poker players make decisions unilaterally. Poker also lacks win-win outcomes or pie-sharing strategies: Any given hand is generally a zero-sum game, with one player's gains coming directly from the other players' pots.

Nonetheless, negotiators can learn a crucial lesson from the card table: the value of controlling the emotions we feel and especially those we reveal. In other words, good negotiators need to develop a poker face—not one that remains expressionless, always hiding true feelings, but one that displays the right emotions at the right times.

And although all human beings experience emotions, the frequency and intensity with which we do so differs from person to person. To be a better deal maker, conduct a thorough assessment of which emotions you are particularly prone to feel before, during, and after negotiations, and use techniques to minimize (or maximize) the experience and suppress (or emphasize) the expression of emotions as needed.

In one of my favorite scenes from the TV show *30 Rock*, hard-driving CEO Jack Donaghy (Alec Baldwin), who fancies himself an expert negotiator, explains to a colleague why he struck a poor deal: "I lost because of emotion, which I always thought was a weakness, but now I have learned can also be a weapon." Borrowing Jack's insightful metaphor, I urge you to wield your emotions thoughtfully. Think carefully about when to draw these weapons, when to shoot, and when to keep them safely tucked away in a hidden holster. Try to avoid feeling anxious, be careful about expressing anger, ask questions to circumvent disappointment and regret, and remember that happiness and excitement can have adverse consequences.

Just as you prepare your tactical and strategic moves before a negotiation, you should invest effort in preparing your emotional approach. It will be time well spent.

Alison Wood Brooks is an assistant professor at Harvard Business School. She teaches negotiation in the MBA and executive education curricula and is affiliated with the Behavioral Insights Group.

CHAPTER 15

Working Across Cultures

by Andy Molinsky

ONE OF THE GREATEST ASSETS we have as natives of a culture is our ability to quickly "read" another person's emotions. Over time, we learn how to understand whether our colleagues are truly interested in a project or just giving it lip service by noticing the expression on their faces. We can tell when someone really likes something we've proposed by the way they react. And we can often detect motivation as well—whether someone is truly willing to put in the extra time and effort to make something happen—just by seeing the fire in their eyes or the passion in their voice.

The problem, of course, comes when we cross cultures and venture into a completely different world of emotional expression. Emotions vary tremendously across cultures—both in terms of their expression and their meaning. Without a detailed understanding of these emotional landscapes, crossing cultures can become a communication minefield.

Take, for example, the expression of enthusiasm. In the United States, it's culturally acceptable, even admirable, to show enthusiasm

Originally published on hbr.org on April 20, 2015, as "Emotional Intelligence Doesn't Translate Across Borders" (product #H020D6)

in a business setting, assuming it's appropriate for the situation. When arguing for a point in a meeting, for example, it is quite appropriate to express your opinions passionately; it can help to convince those around you. Or when speaking with a potential employer at a networking event, it is often encouraged to express your interest quite enthusiastically; the employer may interpret how invested you are in a job based on your expressed eagerness.

In many other cultures, however, enthusiasm means something quite different. In Japan, for example, there are strict boundaries about when and where people are allowed to display emotion.[1] During the regular workday, Japanese individuals are not typically emotionally expressive. Even if they feel excited about their work, they will rarely show it explicitly. This often changes outside of the workplace setting, though, where Japanese people can show a great deal of emotion—for example, when drinking, having dinner with work colleagues, or singing karaoke. In China, self-control and modesty are the coin of the realm, not one's ability to outwardly express emotion.[2] In fact, expressing too much outward enthusiasm, especially in front of a boss, could be seen as showing off, which is not typically condoned in Chinese culture.

Given these differences and the importance of getting it right when communicating across cultures, what are thoughtful managers to do?

A first tip is to treat emotions like another language. If you're traveling or moving to France, you're bound to learn French, or at least some key phrases. Treat emotions in the same way. Try your best to learn the language of emotions in whatever culture you're working in. Observe whether people tend to express emotions readily or keep them to themselves, and if, as in the Japan example above, there are differences in when and where people freely express emotion. Diagnose any gaps between how you'd express emotions in your culture and how people you'll be interacting with express emotion in theirs.

In addition to learning the language of emotions, make sure you also learn how to respond constructively when you do encounter emotions different from your own. For example, if you're expecting a smile from your boss after suggesting a new idea but instead get a blank stare, don't necessarily assume she hates you or your idea. Instead, gather more information to fully understand her point of view. You might ask a follow-up question to get a better sense of her opinion: Ask if your proposal was clear or if she felt your idea addressed the concerns she had. Keep in mind that cultural norms differ in terms of how appropriate it might be to ask questions like these to your boss, but the general idea is to do what you can to collect data to help you decipher emotional expressions, rather than relying solely on your initial, knee-jerk reaction or presumption.

Andy Molinsky is a professor of international management and organizational behavior at the Brandeis International Business School. He is the author of *Global Dexterity* (Harvard Business Review Press, 2013) and the new book *Reach: A New Strategy to Help You Step Outside Your Comfort Zone, Rise to the Challenge, and Build Confidence* (Penguin Random House, 2017). Follow Andy on Twitter @andymolinsky.

Notes

1. Fumiyo Araki and Richard L. Wiseman, "Emotional Expressions in the United States and Japan," *International Communication Studies* 6, no. 2 (1996).

2. Ibid.

Dealing with Difficult People

## CHAPTER 16

Make Your Enemies Your Allies

by Brian Uzzi and Shannon Dunlap

JOHN CLENDENIN WAS FRESH OUT of business school in 1984 when he took on his first managerial position, in Xerox's parts and supply division. He was an obvious outsider: young, African American, and a former Marine, whose pink shirts and brown suits stood out amid the traditional gray and black attire of his new colleagues. "I was strikingly different," he recalls. And yet his new role required him to lead a team including employees who had been with Xerox for decades.

One of his direct reports was Tom Gunning, a 20-year company veteran who believed Clendenin's job should have gone to him, not to a younger, nontechnical newcomer. Gunning also had a cadre of pals on the team. As a result, Clendenin's first days were filled with strained smiles and behind-the-back murmurs. Though he wasn't looking for adversaries, "I knew these guys were discontented about me coming in," Clendenin remembers.

He was right to be wary. Anyone who has faced a rival at work— a colleague threatened by your skills, a superior unwilling to acknowledge your good ideas, or a subordinate who undermines

Reprinted from *Harvard Business Review*, May 2012 (product #R1205K)

you—knows such dynamics can prove catastrophic for your career, and for your group or organization. When those with formal or informal power are fighting you, you may find it impossible to accomplish— or get credit for—any meaningful work.

And even if you have the upper hand, an antagonistic relationship inevitably casts a cloud over you and your team, sapping energy, stymieing progress, and distracting group members from their goals.

Because rivalries can be so destructive, it's not enough to simply ignore, sidestep, or attempt to contain them. Instead, effective leaders turn rivals into collaborators—strengthening their positions, their networks, and their careers in the process. Think of these relationships not as chronic illnesses you have to endure but as wounds that must be treated in order for you to lead a healthy work life.

Here we share a method, called the 3Rs (using *redirection, reciprocity,* and *rationality*), for efficiently and effectively turning your adversaries into your allies. If you execute each step correctly, you will develop new "connective tissue" within your organization, boosting your ability to broker knowledge and drive fresh thinking. The method is drawn from our own inductive case studies— including interviews with business leaders such as John Clendenin, who agreed to let us tell his story in this article—and from empirical research conducted by Brian and others investigating the physiology of the brain, the sociology of relationships, and the psychology of influence.

Emotions and Trust

Many well-intentioned efforts to reverse rivalries fail in large part because of the complex way trust operates in these relationships. Research shows that trust is based on both reason and emotion. If the emotional orientation toward a person is negative—typically because of a perceived threat—then reason will be twisted to align with those negative feelings. This is why feuds can stalemate trust: New facts and arguments, no matter how credible and logical, may be seen as ploys to dupe the other side. This effect is not just psychological; it is physiological. When we experience negative emotions, blood recedes from the thinking part of the brain, the cerebral cortex, and rushes to its oldest and most involuntary part, the "reptilian" stem, crippling the intake of new information.

Most executives who decide they want to reverse a rivalry will, quite understandably, turn to reason, presenting incentives for trustworthy collaboration. But in these situations, the "emotional brain" must be managed before adversaries can understand evidence and be persuaded.

When John Clendenin looked at Tom Gunning at Xerox, he immediately saw grounds for a strong partnership beyond a perfunctory subordinate-superior relationship. Gunning had 20 years' worth of organizational and technical knowledge, and contacts around the company, but he lacked the leadership skills and vision that Clendenin possessed. Conversely, Clendenin understood management but needed Gunning's expertise and connections to successfully navigate his new company. Unfortunately, Gunning's emotions were getting in the way. Clendenin needed to employ the 3Rs.

Redirection

Step 1 is to redirect your rival's negative emotions so that they are channeled away from you. Clendenin decided to have a one-on-one meeting with Gunning, but not in his office, because that would only remind Gunning of the promotion he'd lost. Instead, he found out where Gunning liked to eat and took him there for lunch. "I was letting him know that I understood his worth," Clendenin says of this contextual redirection.

He followed this with a plain statement of redirection, telling Gunning that a third entity beyond the control of both men was the root cause of their situation. "I didn't put you in this position," Clendenin said. "Xerox put us both in this position."

Many executives scoff when they first hear this story, believing Clendenin's actions to be too transparent. But redirection doesn't have to be hidden. With stage magic, for example, audience members understand that redirection is happening, but that doesn't lessen their acceptance or spoil the payoff of the technique. Other personal interactions work similarly. For instance, we accept flattery even if we recognize it as such.

Another common redirection tactic is to introduce a discussion of things you and your rival have in common, or casually portray a source of tension—a particular initiative, employee, or event—in a more favorable light. It sounds obvious. But redirection will shift negative emotions away from you and lay the groundwork for Step 2: reciprocity.

Reciprocity

The essential principle here is to *give before you ask*. Undoing a negative tie begins with giving up something of value rather than asking for a "fair trade." If you give and then ask for something right away in return, you don't establish a relationship; you carry out a transaction.

When done correctly, reciprocity is like priming the pump. In the old days, pumps required lots of exertion to produce any water. You had to repeatedly work a lever to eliminate a vacuum in the line before water could flow. But if you poured a small bucket of water into the line first, the vacuum was quickly eliminated, enabling the water to flow with less effort. Reciprocity with a rival works in much the same way.

Reflect carefully on *what* you should give. Ideally, choose something that requires little effort from the other party to reciprocate. Clendenin moved from redirection to reciprocity at the lunch by promising to support Gunning's leadership development and future advancement at Xerox. But, recognizing that mere promises of future returns wouldn't be enough to spark collaboration, he also offered Gunning something concrete: the chance to attend executive-level meetings. This was of immediate value, not a distant, murky benefit. Gunning could gain visibility, credibility, and connections.

The arrangement also ensured reciprocity. Gunning's presence at the meetings furnished Clendenin with on-hand technical expertise and organizational knowledge while giving him "reputation points" with Gunning's contacts. Thus, Clendenin's offer created the purest form of reciprocity; if Gunning attended the meetings, Clendenin would never have to explicitly request a quid pro quo.

Reciprocity involves considering ways that you can immediately fulfill a rival's need or reduce a pain point. Live up to your end of the bargain first, but figure out a way to ensure a return from your rival without the person's feeling that pressure. Another example comes from Brian's colleague Adam Galinsky, who advises leaders in contentious restructurings and business closings to generate goodwill among outgoing employees by offering professional references or placements at other companies as long as the employees continue to meet or exceed expectations until their office closes. The employees see immediate value, and although they don't consciously pay back the organization, the firm nonetheless benefits by maintaining continuity in its workforce until the scheduled closure.

Similarly, a colleague who helps an adversary complete a project or a subordinate who stays overtime to finish a task for a difficult boss not only help themselves but can reap rewards when other teammates or superiors benefit from that effort, too. Here the judicious giving before asking sets a foundation for reciprocity with third parties, whose buy-in can positively assist in reshaping the adversarial relationship. (See the sidebar "Rivalries Don't Exist in a Vacuum.")

Rationality

Step 3, rationality, establishes the expectations of the fledgling relationship you've built using the previous steps so that your efforts don't come off as dishonest or as ineffective pandering. What would have happened if Clendenin had left the lunch without explaining how he wanted to work with Gunning going forward? Gunning might have begun to second-guess his new boss's intentions and resumed his adversarial stance. If a rival is worried about the other shoe dropping, his emotional unease can undermine the trust you've built.

To employ rationality, Clendenin told Gunning that he needed him, or someone like him, to reach his goals at Xerox. This made it clear that he saw Gunning as a valuable, but not indispensable, partner. Another, softer approach might have involved Clendenin's

Rivalries Don't Exist in a Vacuum

EVEN WHEN A LEADER EXECUTES the 3Rs flawlessly to end a rivalry, his work isn't necessarily done. That's because the relationship is often about more than just the two individuals. We all know people who seek to play to their advantage antagonism between others; some third parties might even view a blossoming partnership with trepidation or envy, triggering new negative emotions and rivalries.

You can head off this problem, as John Clendenin did, by framing your work as beneficial not just to you and your adversary but to the whole organization, which makes the reversal of rivalry in everyone's interest. When Clendenin brought Tom Gunning into those executive-level meetings, he made it clear that Gunning was going to be a "poster child" for a new age at Xerox, in which talented, long-term employees could find new paths to leadership in a time of corporate transition. Even if the conflictmongers didn't care about Clendenin's and Gunning's success, it would be far more difficult for them to sabotage an effort that was obviously good for the company.

---

giving Gunning "the right of first refusal" to collaborate with him, making the offer seem special while judiciously indicating that there were others who could step in. Just to be clear, Clendenin was not asking Gunning for a specific favor in exchange for the one he'd granted in Step 2. He was simply saying that he wanted him to become an ally.

Clendenin also reinforced the connection between the three steps by making his offer time-limited, which raised the perception of the value of the deal without changing its content. He told Gunning he needed an answer before they left the restaurant. "I needed to nip this in the bud," Clendenin recalls. "He knew I didn't care if we sat in that restaurant until midnight if we had to."

When rationality follows redirection and reciprocity, it should push your adversary into considering the situation from a reasoned standpoint, fully comprehending the expectations and benefits, and recognizing that he is looking at a valued opportunity that could be lost. Most people are highly motivated to avoid a loss, which complements their desire to gain something. Rationality is like offering medicine after a spoonful of sugar: It ensures that you're getting the benefit of the shifted negative emotions, and any growing positive ones, which would otherwise diffuse over time. And it avoids the ambiguity that clouds expectations and feedback when flattery and favors come one day, and demands the next.

Of course, Clendenin and Gunning did not walk out of the restaurant as full-blown collaborators. But both accepted that they should give each other the benefit of the doubt. Over the following weeks, this new mindset allowed them to work as allies, a process that deepened trust and resource-sharing in a self-reinforcing cycle. In this way, a potentially debilitating rivalry was transformed into a healthy working relationship and, in time, a strong partnership. Several years later, when Clendenin moved to another Xerox unit, he nominated Gunning as his replacement—and Gunning excelled in the position. The foundation for that remarkable shift had been established during the span of a single lunch.

Adapting the 3Rs

A key advantage of the 3Rs is that the method can work to reverse all kinds of rivalries, including those with a peer or a superior. Later in Clendenin's tenure at Xerox, he noticed an inefficiency in the company's inventory systems. At the time, Xerox was made up of semi-autonomous international units that stockpiled excess inventory to avoid shortages. Clendenin proposed that the units instead share their inventories through an intrafirm network that would improve resource use and lower carrying costs for the company as a whole. Although the idea was objectively good for Xerox, it threatened the power of some unit vice presidents, so when Clendenin floated his idea, they shot it down.

A short time later, however, following an unexpected announcement by the CEO that the company needed better asset management, Clendenin found a way to reintroduce his proposal to the VPs. Because he knew they viewed him as an unwelcome challenger—or rival—he used the 3Rs.

His first move was to redirect their negative emotions away from him by planning a lunch for them at the regional office and serving

What If the 3Rs Fail?

THE 3RS ARE EFFECTIVE, but they aren't a guarantee of defusing resistance. What should you do if the strategy isn't working?

Strive for collaboration indirectly. For example, work well with a third party whom your rival trusts. A common ally can highlight to him the benefits of working with you.

Remember that timing matters. People in power need a reason to interact. This was certainly the case with John Clendenin's inventory-management pitch to the Xerox VPs: At first rebuffed, he was able to refloat his idea when the CEO called for a new strategy.

Recognize when to look elsewhere. Sometimes the effort needed to reverse a rivalry is so great, and the returns so low, for you and your company that you're better off deploying the same resources in another relationship.

---

them himself. This showed deference. He also presented himself not as an individual pushing a proposal but as someone who could expedite organizational change, shifting the reference point of his rivals' tension. "With all of those egos and personalities, I never said, 'This is my idea,'" Clendenin recalls. "I always said 'we.'"

Applying the reciprocity principle of "give before you ask," he requested nothing from them at the meeting. Instead, he facilitated a discussion about the CEO-led initiative. Inventory management was, unsurprisingly, a problem cited by many of the VPs, and Clendenin's facilitation brought that to light. He then took on the luster of the person who had illuminated a generic problem, rather than someone who wanted to lessen the VPs' autonomy.

That allowed him to present the rationality of his original idea. All of a sudden, it looked like an opportunity—rather than a threat—to the formerly antagonistic group. Clendenin indicated that he would be willing to coordinate a new system more cheaply than anyone else in the market could offer, while also noting that he might not have time to do so in the future, which raised the perceived value of his offer. The VPs agreed to execute the plan in stages and put Clendenin in charge. The initiative grew in small but steady steps, eventually saving Xerox millions. Equally important, Clendenin's embrace by his rivals positioned him as a broker in the company and burnished his reputation as an institution builder.

John Clendenin understood that rivalries help no one; indeed, success often depends on not just neutralizing your foes but turning them into collaborators. By using the 3Rs to build trust, Clendenin made sure everyone in his network thrived—including himself, Gunning, their team, the VPs, and Xerox—forming the basis for long-term ties and shared success. Years later, Clendenin started his own international logistics company. His partner in this new endeavor was his old rival, Tom Gunning, and the lead investors were none other than the unit VPs from Xerox who had once shot down his ideas.

―――――――――

Brian Uzzi is the Richard L. Thomas Professor of Leadership and Organizational Change at Northwestern's Kellogg School of Management and the codirector of the Northwestern Institute on Complex Systems (NICO). **Shannon Dunlap** is a journalist and writer based in New York City.

## CHAPTER 17

How to Deal with a Passive-Aggressive Colleague

by Amy Gallo

YOUR COLLEAGUE SAYS ONE THING in a meeting but then does another. He passes you in the hallway without saying hello and talks over you in meetings. But when you ask to speak with him about it, he insists that everything's fine and the problem is all in your head. Argh! It's so frustrating to work with someone who is acting passive-aggressively. Do you address the behavior directly? Or try to ignore it? How can you get to the core issue when your colleague pretends that nothing's going on?

What the Experts Say

It's not uncommon for colleagues to occasionally make passive-aggressive remarks to one another over particularly sensitive issues or when they feel they can't be direct. "We're all guilty of doing it once in a while," says Amy Su, coauthor of *Own the Room: Discover Your Signature Voice to Master Your Leadership Presence.*

Adapted from content posted on hbr.org on January 11, 2016 (product #H02LQP)

But persistent passive-aggressive behavior is a different ball game. "These are people who will often do anything to get what they need, including lie," says Annie McKee, founder of the Teleos Leadership Institute and coauthor of *Primal Leadership: Unleashing the Power of Emotional Intelligence.* In these cases, you have to take special precautions that help you and, hopefully, your counterpart both get your jobs done. Here are some tips:

Don't Get Caught Up

When your coworker pretends nothing is going on or accuses you of overreacting, it's hard not to get angry and defensive. But, McKee says, "This is not one of those situations to fight fire with fire." Do your best to remain calm. "The person may want you to get mad so they can then blame you, which is a release of their own anxiety," Su explains. "Responding in an emotional way will likely leave you looking—and feeling—like the fool. This is your opportunity to be the bigger person."

Consider What's Motivating the Behavior

People who routinely act in a passive-aggressive way aren't necessarily complete jerks. It could be that they don't know how to communicate or are afraid of conflict. McKee says that passive-aggressive behavior is often a way for people to "get their emotional point across without having true, healthy conflict." There's also a self-centeredness to it. "They make the flawed assumption that others should know what they're feeling and that their needs and preferences are more important than others'," says Su. Understand this, but don't try to diagnose all your colleague's problems. "You just have to see it for what it is," Su adds, "an unproductive expression of emotions that they can't share constructively."

Own Your Part

Chances are that you're not blameless in the situation. Ask yourself if something you're doing is contributing to the dynamic or causing the person to be passive-aggressive. "Own your half," says Su. Also, consider whether you've dished out the same behavior. "It can happen to even the best of us, whether we're procrastinating or wanting to avoid something. We might leak emotions in a way that's hurtful to others," says Su.

Focus on the Content, Not the Delivery

It might be the last thing you want to do, but try to see the situation from your colleague's perspective. What is the underlying opinion or perspective she's attempting to convey with her snarky comment? "Analyze the position the person is trying to share with you," says McKee. Does she think that the way you're running the project isn't working? Or does she disagree about your team goals? "Not everyone likes or knows how to publicly discuss or express what they think," says Su. If you can focus on the underlying business concern or question rather than the way she's expressing herself, you can move on to addressing the actual problem.

Acknowledge the Underlying Issue

Once you're calm and able to engage in a productive conversation, go back to the person. Say something like: "You made a good point in that exchange we had the other day. Here's what I heard you saying." This will help them talk about the substance of their concerns. "By joining *with* them, you have a better chance of turning the energy around," McKee explains. Do this in a matter-of-fact way, without discussing how the sentiment was expressed. "Don't listen or give any credence to the toxic part," advises Su. "Sometimes it's that they just want their opinion heard."

Watch Your Language

Whatever you say, don't accuse the person of being passive-aggressive. "That can hurt your cause," says McKee. Su agrees: "It's such a loaded word. It would put someone who's already on the defensive into a more angry position. Don't label or judge them."

Instead, McKee suggests recounting how some of your previous in-teractions have played out and explaining the impact it's having on you and possibly others. If feasible, show that the behavior is work-ing against something your counterpart cares about, like achieving the team's goals.

Find Safety in Numbers

You don't have to deal with this situation alone. "It's OK to reality-check with others and have allies in place to say you're not crazy," says Su. But be sure to frame your discussions as an attempt to constructively improve the relationship, so it doesn't come across as gossiping or bad-mouthing your colleague. Su suggests you ask something like: "I was wondering how Susan's comment landed with you. How did you interpret that?"

Set Guidelines for Everyone

You might also enlist the help of others in coming up with a long-term solution. "As a team, you can build healthy norms," McKee says. Together, you can agree to be more up-front about frustrations and model the honest and direct interactions you want to happen. You can also keep one another accountable. If your problematic col-league tends to ignore agreements, you might take notes in meetings about who's supposed to do what by when, so there are clear action items. The worst offenders are likely to give in to the positive peer pressure and public accountability.

Get Help in Extreme Situations

When a colleague persistently tries to undermine you or prevent you from doing your job, and outside observers confirm your take on the situation, you might have to go further. "If you share the same manager, you may be able to ask for help," says McKee. You might tell your boss: "A lot of us have noticed a particular behavior, and I want to talk about how it's impacting my ability to do my work." But she warns, "Step into those waters carefully. Your manager may be hoodwinked by the person and may not see the same behaviors, or be conflict-averse himself and not want to see it."

Protect Yourself

"If there's an interdependence in your work, make sure you're meeting your commitments and deadlines," Su says. "Copy others on important emails. Don't let that person speak for you or represent you in meetings. After a meeting, document agreements and next steps." McKee also suggests keeping records: "Track specific behaviors so that you have examples if needed. It's hard to argue with the facts." She also recommends you try to avoid working with the person and "keep contact to a minimum. If you have to work together, do it in a group setting" where your colleague is likely to be on better behavior. You might not be able to break their passive-aggressive habits, but you can control your reaction to any incidents.

Principles to Remember

Do:

- Understand why people typically act this way—their needs probably aren't being met

- Focus on the message your colleague is trying to convey, even if their delivery is misguided

- Take a step back and ask yourself if you're contributing to the issue in some way

Don't:

- Lose your cool—address the underlying business issue in a calm, matter-of-fact way

- Accuse the person of acting passive-aggressively—that will only make them madder

- Assume you can change your colleague's behavior

Case Study #1: Make Your Coworker Publicly Accountable

One of Neda Khosla's coworkers (names and details have been changed) in the student guidance office of the public high school where she worked was making things difficult for her. "He would agree to a plan in a meeting but then sabotage it by not following through," she explains. Her colleague, Gareth, defended himself by saying things like "That's not how I remember it" or "I didn't think we had finalized the plan." She tried to talk about these "misunderstandings" with him, but he always shrugged her off: "He'd say he was busy or didn't have time to talk," she recounted.

When Neda told Jim, her and Gareth's boss, that a certain project hadn't gotten done because of this strange dynamic, Jim said that he had noticed the pattern too. Together, they devised a plan to make Gareth more accountable. "He and I agreed that he would publicly ask for a volunteer to take notes on each meeting, [documenting] who would be responsible for accomplishing each task and by when," Neda recalls. She was the first volunteer.

And the approach worked. After Neda sent around the task list, Gareth couldn't make excuses. He was accountable to everyone who attended the meetings. And Neda didn't mind the additional work: "The extra effort I put in was less than the time I was spending fuming about my coworker and running around to pick up the pieces of the things he didn't complete. It actually helped everyone in our department be more productive and was something we should have done a long time ago."

Case Study #2: Get Help Sooner Rather Than Later

James Armstrong, a digital marketing consultant for Roman Blinds Direct, used to manage an eight-person team at a digital marketing agency. He had gotten the promotion three months after one of his direct reports, Violet, joined the agency, and she clearly wasn't thrilled to suddenly have him as a new boss. But "she was a top performer and extremely competent," James recalls, and since they'd worked "fairly harmoniously together as colleagues," he was happy to have her in the group.

Unfortunately, Violet became very difficult to manage. She didn't communicate with him unless absolutely necessary; she didn't actively engage in training sessions that he offered; and she "poked holes" in his initiatives. "She took every opportunity to make it clear that she didn't value my input," he explains.

Surprised and dismayed by her attitude, he decided to address it as he would with any other team member: "directly and clearly." He started by asking her in their one-on-one meetings whether something was wrong. She said there wasn't, but the behavior persisted, so he tried taking her out to coffee and asking whether he had unknowingly offended her or if she wanted to be managed in a different way. She acknowledged that there was a "personality clash," but she ended the conversation there and continued to treat him dismissively at the office. He heard from other staff members that she had even called him "lazy and useless."

"The last thing I wanted was to pass the issue further up the chain and potentially harm Violet's career," he says. After all, she was a valuable team member and he wanted to protect her. But, he reflects, "I should have immediately approached my manager." When he eventually did, she pointed out that his failure to effectively manage a key team member amounted to poor performance on his part.

Within a year, both James and Violet voluntarily left the agency, but neither was happy with the circumstances. He says that if he could do it over again, he would have talked to his manager sooner, kept better records on Violet's "toxic attitude," and when there weren't drastic improvements, fired her "without hesitation."

––––––

Amy Gallo is a contributing editor at *Harvard Business Review* and the author of the *HBR Guide to Dealing with Conflict*. She writes and speaks about workplace dynamics. Follow her on Twitter @amyegallo.

## CHAPTER 18

What to Do If You're a Toxic Handler

by Sandra L. Robinson and Kira Schabram

DIVANI (NOT HER REAL NAME) is a senior analyst at a large telecommunications firm. She proudly describes herself as her department's "resident cheer-upper." As she says, "I have always been the person that people turn to for support . . . I listen really well and I like to listen, I like to help." But the year before I spoke to her, Divani's organization was going through a major change initiative: "I already had so much on my plate, and so many colleagues were leaning on me—turning to me to process, commiserate, ask for advice. It was hard to get through my own deadlines and also be there for my coworkers. I was drowning in stress and nearing burnout." She told us about feeling down on Sunday nights, feeling increasingly angry and cynical, and having trouble sleeping because she couldn't "shut my mind off." She took up smoking again after having given it up for four years and let her exercise routine falter.

Divani is what former Sauder School of Business professor Peter Frost and one of us (Sandra) have termed a *toxic handler*, someone who voluntarily shoulders the sadness, frustration, bitterness, and anger that are endemic to organizational life just as joy and success

---

Adapted from "When You're the Person Your Colleagues Always Vent To" posted on hbr.org on January 11, 2016 (product #H03A8W)

are. Toxic handlers can be found at all levels of the organization, particularly in roles that span disparate groups. And they are by no means confined to management roles. Their work is difficult and critical even if it often goes uncelebrated; it keeps organizations positive and productive even as the individuals within them necessarily clash and tussle. By carrying others' confidences, suggesting solutions to interpersonal issues, working behind the scenes to prevent pain, and reframing difficult messages in constructive ways, toxic handlers absorb the negativity in day-to-day professional life and allow employees to focus on constructive work.

This isn't easy work. And as Sandra's and Peter Frost's research of over 70 toxic handlers (or those who managed them) revealed, individuals in these roles frequently experience untenably high levels of stress and strain, which affect their physical health and career paths and often mean they have a diminished capacity to help others in the long run—a side effect that is most troubling for handlers.

But if handlers can recognize that they're playing a role that is both highly valuable *and* burdensome, they can see their own emotional competence in a new light and recognize the signs of serious strain while there's still something they can do about it.

How do you know if *you're* a toxic handler? Here are some questions to ask yourself:

- Are you working in an organization characterized by lots of change, dysfunction, or politics?

- Are you working in a role that spans different groups or different levels?

- Do you spend a lot of time listening to and offering advice to colleagues at work?

- Do people come to you to unload their worries, emotions, secrets, or workplace problems?

- Do you have a hard time saying "no" to colleagues, especially when they need you?

- Do you spend time behind the scenes, managing politics and influencing decisions so others are protected?

- Do you tend to mediate communication between a toxic individual and others?

- Are you that person who feels compelled to stand up for the people at work that need your help?

- Do you think of yourself as a counselor, mediator, or peacemaker?

If you've answered "yes" to four or more of these questions, then you may be a toxic handler. Before you panic at that label, recognize that there are both positives and negatives to fulfilling this role. On the positive side, being a toxic handler means you have valuable emotional strengths: You're probably a good listener; you're empathetic; you're good at suggesting solutions instead of piling on problems. The people around you value the support you provide. It's important, too, to understand that this role is strategically critical to organizations: You likely defuse tough situations and reduce dysfunction.

Now for the bad news. Chances are that you're taking on more work than is covered in your formal job description (and in fact, as an unsung hero, you may not be getting any kind of formal credit from the organization for these efforts and how much you bring to them). Listening, mediating, and working behind the scenes to protect others takes important time away from your other responsibilities. More importantly, it also takes tremendous emotional energy to listen, comfort, and counsel. As you are not a trained therapist, you may also be inadvertently taking on others' pain and slowly paying a price for it. Sandra's research shows that toxic handlers tend to take on others' emotions but have no way to offload them. Quite likely, as a person who is constantly helping others, you may be unlikely to be seeking support for yourself. And lastly, this role may be part of your identity, something that brings you fulfillment and in which you take satisfaction—and so it is difficult to step away from.

Consider Sheung-Li (not his real name). His manager was a star with a great track record, but he created a lot of turmoil. He wouldn't take the time to get to know anyone on Sheung-Li's team personally and totally disregarded more junior members. He was also obsessed with lofty performance goals that seemed to come out of nowhere. "My main role became protecting my team, reassuring them, keeping them focused on our objectives and away from the tensions this guy continually created," Sheung-Li described. "I spent an inordinate amount of time massaging the message, trying to convince my boss to reconsider his decisions so as to avoid the obvious fallout they would bring, playing mediator when our team was not delivering. I felt like I was treading water all the time. And I'm not even sure I was protecting my team from the pain he was causing. I was losing sleep over what was happening to my team, I had lost weight, and I was starting to get sick with one bug after another. I don't know if that was the cause but I know this was a really tough time in my life. It was hard to concentrate on anything else."

So if Sheung-Li's and Divani's stories sound familiar, how can you continue to help to your colleagues (and your organization!) while also protecting yourself? How can you keep playing your valuable role in a *sustainable* way?

Start by assessing whether the role is indeed taking a toll. Some toxic handlers are able to naturally take on more than others; you need to know what's right for you at any given time. Look for evidence of strain and burnout: physical symptoms like insomnia, jaw pain and TMJ, heart palpitations, more sickness than usual. Do you have a shorter fuse than you used to, or an inability to concentrate? Sometimes these symptoms can sneak up on you, so it may help to check in with others to see if they've noticed a change. If you're not experiencing stress as a result, there's nothing you need to change other than being aware and keeping an eye out. Being a toxic handler only needs to be "fixed" if it's actually hurting you. Here's how:

Reduce symptoms of stress
Turn to tried-and-true methods for stress relief: meditation, exercise, enough sleep, and healthful eating. Because toxic handlers have trouble doing things just for themselves, keep in mind that you're helping your colleagues by taking care of yourself. Set your colleagues as your intention for your meditation or yoga practice.

Pick your battles
It's hard to ask yourself where you'll have the most impact if you're emotionally drawn to every problem, but it's an exercise that will allow you to be more helpful where you can actually make a difference. Who is likely to be fine without your help? In which situations have you not even made a dent, despite your best efforts? Step away from these interactions.

Learn to say "no"
It's hard to say no to things you want to do, but it's important. Here's how to do it while still being supportive:

- Convey empathy. Make it clear that you feel for your colleague in their pain—you're not denying that they are having a legitimate emotional response to a situation.

- Tell them you're currently not in a position to be most helpful to them right now and, to the extent you are comfortable, explain the reasons why.

- Consider alternative sources of support. Refer your colleague to another person in the organization, or someone having a similar experience (so they can provide mutual support to one another). Suggest an article, book, or other resource on the topic (e.g., something on managing conflict or handling office politics). Or, if you know from experience that the person is good at coming up with creative solutions themselves, you can simply offer them encouragement to do so.

Let go of the guilt

If you feel guilty that you're not stepping in to help someone, here are some things to consider:

- Recognize that conflicts are often better solved by the parties directly involved. If you're stepping in repeatedly, you're not helping people acquire the skills and tools they need to succeed.

- Question whether you are truly the only one that can help in a particular situation. Enlist trusted others in the organization to help you think through this—you may identify a way to share the load.

- Remember that there is only so much of you to go around: Saying yes to one more person necessarily means that you are agreeing to do less for those people and projects you have already committed to.

Form a community

Find other toxic handlers to turn to for support—these could be others in similar roles in your organization, or other team members whom you see dealing with the fallout from the same toxic leader. You can also identify a pal to vent to or create a more formal group that comes together regularly to share their experiences. This is a particularly good option if your whole team or organization is going through turmoil and you know there are others experiencing the same challenges. Keep these outlets from turning into repetitive venting sessions by focusing the conversation on creative problem solving and advice.

Take breaks

These can be as small or as dramatic as you need. Divani started working with her door closed, which she had never done before. "I felt terrible about this, as if I was abandoning my coworkers who needed me. But if I lost my job, I wasn't going to be much good to anybody," she explained. Consider giving yourself a mental health day off of work or planning a significant vacation. In more dramatic situations, you could also consider a temporary reassignment of your role; because jobs that require you to mediate between multiple teams or groups tend to come under particular fire, you're more likely to get the respite you need if you are able to step away from that role for a time.

These breaks don't need to be forever, though. "Things have since calmed down at work," Divani has reported, "and I find I have gravitated back to being the person people lean on for emotional support, but at this point it is totally doable."

Make a change

If nothing you are doing has resulted in a shift, your best option may be to leave. Sheung-Li explained: "After two years of this [toxic situation], and at the encouragement of my wife, I saw a therapist. It then became clear to me this work reality was not going to change, this toxic manager was not going anywhere, the stress was eating me alive, and I am the one that needed to change. I did a bunch of things, but I think the key thing I did was I ended up making a lateral move in our company to escape this role and to protect my long-term well-being. It was the best decision I ever made."

Consider therapy

It may sound dramatic, but Sheung-Li's decison to talk to a therapist is a highly useful one. A trained psychologist can help you identify burnout, manage your symptoms of stress, help you learn to say "no," and work through any guilt. Not only can they help you protect yourself from the emotional vagaries of being a toxic handler; they can also assist you in your role. Clinical psychologists themselves are trained to listen to their clients empathetically without taking on their emotions. They can help you build the skills you need to help others without absorbing as much of the emotional burden yourself.

Lastly, here are some things we suggest you avoid. While they seem like good solutions on the surface, they often aren't as helpful as you'd think.

Just venting

While it's good to unburden yourself of your emotions—catharsis *can* reduce aggression—too much venting can actually increase stress levels. You want to move forward, rather than dwelling on problems. And this is as true for those confiding in you as it is for you! When people come to you to vent, consider saying something like, "I hear you! How about we think about what we can change to make this better?"

Going to your boss or HR

Sadly, the role of toxic handler is often underrecognized and underappreciated in organizations, despite its tremendous value. This means that while your boss may want to help, it can be risky for them in many organizational cultures. Similarly, many firms are unlikely to intervene in a toxic situation on behalf of the handler.

Yet toxic handlers are critical to the emotional well-being of organizations and the people in them. If you're a toxic handler, learn to monitor yourself for signs of emotional or physical fatigue—and know how to step away when you need to—so that you can keep doing what you do best.

_____

Sandra L. Robinson is a professor of organizational behavior at the University of British Columbia's Sauder School of Business. Kira Schabram is an assistant professor of organizational behavior at the University of Washington's Foster School of Business.

Understand Empathy

## CHAPTER 19

What Is Empathy?

by Daniel Goleman

THE WORD "ATTENTION" COMES from the Latin *attendere*, meaning "to reach toward." This is a perfect definition of focus on others, which is the foundation of empathy and of an ability to build social relationships—the second and third pillars of emotional intelligence (the first is self-awareness).

Executives who can effectively focus on others are easy to recognize. They are the ones who find common ground, whose opinions carry the most weight, and with whom other people want to work. They emerge as natural leaders regardless of organizational or social rank.

The Empathy Triad

We talk about empathy most commonly as a single attribute. But a close look at where leaders are focusing when they exhibit it reveals three distinct kinds of empathy, each important for leadership effectiveness:

- **Cognitive empathy:** the ability to understand another person's perspective.

Excerpted from "The Focused Leader" in *Harvard Business Review*, December 2013 (product #R0205B)

- **Emotional empathy:** the ability to feel what someone else feels.

- **Empathic concern:** the ability to sense what another person needs from you.

Cognitive empathy enables leaders to explain themselves in meaningful ways—a skill essential to getting the best performance from their direct reports. Contrary to what you might expect, exercising cognitive empathy requires leaders to think about feelings rather than to feel them directly.

An inquisitive nature feeds cognitive empathy. As one successful executive with this trait puts it, "I've always just wanted to learn everything, to understand anybody that I was around—why they thought what they did, why they did what they did, what worked for them and what didn't work." But cognitive empathy is also an outgrowth of self-awareness. The executive circuits that allow us to think about our own thoughts and to monitor the feelings that flow from them let us apply the same reasoning to other people's minds when we choose to direct our attention that way.

Emotional empathy is important for effective mentoring, managing clients, and reading group dynamics. It springs from ancient parts of the brain beneath the cortex—the amygdala, the hypothalamus, the hippocampus, and the orbitofrontal cortex—that allow us to feel fast without thinking deeply. They tune us in by arousing in our bodies the emotional states of others: I literally feel your pain. My brain patterns match up with yours when I listen to you tell a gripping story. As Tania Singer, the director of the social neuroscience department at the Max Planck Institute for Human Cognitive and Brain Sciences, in Leipzig, Germany, says, "You need to understand your own feelings to understand the feelings of others." Accessing your capacity for emotional empathy depends on combining two kinds of attention: a deliberate focus on your own echoes of someone else's feelings and an open awareness of that person's face, voice, and other external signs of emotion. (See the sidebar "When Empathy Needs to Be Learned.")

When Empathy Needs to Be Learned

EMOTIONAL EMPATHY CAN BE DEVELOPED. That's the conclusion suggested by research conducted with physicians by Helen Riess, the director of the Empathy and Relational Science Program at Boston's Massachusetts General Hospital. To help the physicians monitor themselves, Riess set up a program in which they learned to focus using deep, diaphragmatic breathing and to cultivate a certain detachment—to watch an interaction from the ceiling, as it were, rather than being lost in their own thoughts and feelings. "Suspending your own involvement to observe what's going on gives you a mindful awareness of the interaction without being completely reactive," says Riess. "You can see if your own physiology is charged up or balanced. You can notice what's transpiring in the situation." If a doctor realizes that she's feeling irritated, for instance, that may be a signal that the patient is bothered too.

Those who are utterly at a loss may be able to prime emotional empathy essentially by faking it until they make it, Riess adds. If you act in a caring way—looking people in the eye and paying attention to their expressions, even when you don't particularly want to—you may start to feel more engaged.

Empathic concern, which is closely related to emotional empathy, enables you to sense not just how people feel but what they need from you. It's what you want in your doctor, your spouse—and your boss. Empathic concern has its roots in the circuitry that compels parents' attention to their children. Watch where people's eyes go when someone brings an adorable baby into a room, and you'll see this mammalian brain center leaping into action.

Research suggests that as people rise through the ranks, their ability to maintain personal connections suffers.

One neural theory holds that the response is triggered in the amygdala by the brain's radar for sensing danger and in the prefrontal cortex by the release of oxytocin, the chemical for caring. This implies that empathic concern is a double-edged feeling. We intuitively experience the distress of another as our own. But in deciding whether we will meet that person's needs, we deliberately weigh how much we value his or her well-being.

When Empathy Needs to Be Controlled

GETTING A GRIP ON OUR IMPULSE to empathize with other people's feelings can help us make better decisions when someone's emotional flood threatens to overwhelm us.

Ordinarily, when we see someone pricked with a pin, our brains emit a signal indicating that our own pain centers are echoing that distress. But physicians learn in medical school to block even such automatic responses. Their attentional anesthetic seems to be deployed by the temporal-parietal junction and regions of the prefrontal cortex, a circuit that boosts concentration by tuning out emotions. That's what is happening in your brain when you distance yourself from others in order to stay calm and help them. The same neural network kicks in when we see a problem in an emotionally overheated environment and need to focus on looking for a solution. If you're talking with someone who is upset, this system helps you understand the person's perspective intellectually by shifting from the heart-to-heart of emotional empathy to the head-to-heart of cognitive empathy.

What's more, some lab research suggests that the appropriate application of empathic concern is critical to making moral judgments. Brain scans have revealed that when volunteers listened to tales of people being subjected to physical pain, their own brain centers for experiencing such pain lit up instantly. But if the story was about psychological suffering, the higher brain centers involved in empathic concern and compassion took longer to activate. Some time is needed to grasp the psychological and moral dimensions of a situation. The more distracted we are, the less we can cultivate the subtler forms of empathy and compassion.

Getting this intuition-deliberation mix right has great implications. Those whose sympathetic feelings become too strong may themselves suffer. In the helping professions, this can lead to compassion fatigue; in executives, it can create distracting feelings of anxiety about people and circumstances that are beyond anyone's control. But those who protect themselves by deadening their feelings may lose touch with empathy. Empathic concern requires us to manage our personal distress without numbing ourselves to the pain of others. (See the sidebar "When Empathy Needs to Be Controlled.")

Daniel Goleman is a codirector of the Consortium for Research on Emotional Intelligence in Organizations at Rutgers University, co-author of *Primal Leadership: Leading with Emotional Intelligence* (Harvard Business Review Press, 2013), and author of *The Brain and Emotional Intelligence: New Insights* and *Leadership: Selected Writings* (More Than Sound, 2011). His latest book is *A Force for Good: The Dalai Lama's Vision for Our World* (Bantam, 2015).

## CHAPTER 20

Beyond Empathy: The Power of Compassion

An interview with Daniel Goleman by Andrea Ovans

TWO DECADES BEFORE DANIEL GOLEMAN first wrote about emotional intelligence in the pages of HBR, he met the Dalai Lama at Amherst College. The Dalai Lama mentioned to the young science journalist for the *New York Times* that he was interested in meeting with scientists. Thus began a long, rich friendship as Goleman became involved over the years in arranging a series of what he calls "extended dialogues" between the Buddhist spiritual leader and researchers in fields ranging from ecology to neuroscience. On the occasion of his friend's 80th birthday, he was asked to write a book describing the Dalai Lama's compassionate approach to addressing the world's most intractable problems. *A Force for Good: The Dalai Lama's Vision for Our World*, which draws both on Goleman's background in cognitive science and his long relationship with the Dalai Lama, is both an exploration of the science and the power of compassion and a call to action. Curious about the book and about how the Dalai Lama's views on compassion informed Goleman's thinking on emotional intelligence, I caught up with Goleman over the phone. What follows are edited excerpts from our conversation.

Adapted from content posted on hbr.org on May 4, 2015, as "What the Dalai Lama Taught Daniel Goleman About Emotional Intelligence" (product #H021KQ)

HBR: Let's start with some definitions here. What is compassion, as you are describing it? It sounds a lot like empathy, one of the major components of emotional intelligence. Is there a difference?

Goleman: Yes, an important difference. Three kinds of empathy are important to emotional intelligence: *cognitive empathy*—the ability to understand another person's point of view, *emotional empathy*—the ability to feel what someone else feels, and *empathic concern*—the ability to sense what another person needs from you [see chapter 19, "What Is Empathy?"]. Cultivating all three kinds of empathy, which originate in different parts of the brain, is important for building social relationships.

But compassion takes empathy a step further. When you feel compassion, you feel distress when you witness someone else in distress—and because of that you want to help that person.

Why draw this distinction?

Compassion makes the difference between understanding and caring. It's the kind of love that a parent has for a child. Cultivating it more broadly means extending that to the other people in our lives and to people we encounter.

I think that in the workplace, that attitude has a hugely positive effect, whether it's in how we relate to our peers, how we are as a leader, or how we relate to clients and customers. A positive disposition toward another person creates the kind of resonance that builds trust and loyalty and makes interactions harmonious. And the opposite of that—when you do nothing to show that you care—creates distrust and disharmony and causes huge dysfunction at home and in business.

When you put it that way, it's hard to disagree that if you treat people well things would go better than if you don't or that if you cared about them they would care a lot more about you. So why do you think that doesn't just happen naturally? Is it a cultural thing? Or a misplaced confusion about when competition is appropriate?

I think too often there's a muddle in people's thinking that if I'm nice to another person or if I have their interests at heart it means that I don't have my own interests at heart. The pathology of that is, "Well, I'll just care about me and not the other person." And that, of course, is the kind of attitude that leads to lots of problems in the business realm and in the personal realm. But compassion also includes yourself. If we protect ourselves and make sure we're okay—and also make sure the other person is okay—that creates a different framework for working with and cooperating with other people.

Could you give me an example of how that might work in the business world?

There's research that was done on star salespeople and on client managers that found that the lowest level of performance was a kind of "I'm going to get the best deal I can now, and I don't care how this affects the other person" attitude, which means that you might make the sale but that you lose the relationship. But at the top end, the stars were typified by the attitude, "I am working for the client as well as myself. I'm going to be completely straight with them, and I'm going to act as their advisor. If the deal I have is not the best deal they can get I'm going to let them know because that's going to strengthen the relationship, even though I might lose this specific sale." And I think that captures the difference between the "me first" and the "let's all do well" attitude that I'm getting at.

How would we cultivate compassion if we just weren't feeling it?

Neuroscientists have been studying compassion recently, and places like Stanford, Yale, UC Berkeley, and the University of Wisconsin, Madison, among others, have been testing methodologies for increasing compassion. Right now there's a kind of a trend toward incorporating mindfulness into the workplace, and it turns out there's data from the Max Planck Institute showing that enhancing mindfulness does have an effect in brain function but that the circuitry that's affected is not the circuitry for concern or compassion. In other words, there's no automatic boost in compassion from mindfulness alone.

Still, in the traditional methods of meditation that mindfulness in the workplace is based on, the two were always linked, so that you

would practice mindfulness in a context in which you'd also cultivate compassion.

Stanford, for example, has developed a program that incorporates
secularized versions of methods that have originally come from religious practices. It involves a meditation in which you cultivate an
attitude of loving-kindness or of concern, or of compassion, toward
people. First you do this for yourself, then for people you love, then
for people you just know. And finally you do it for everyone. And
this has the effect of priming the circuitry responsible for compassion within the brain so that you are more inclined to act that way
when the opportunity arises.

*You've remarked that the Dalai Lama is a very distinctive kind of
leader. Is there something we could learn as leaders ourselves from
his unique form of leadership?*

Observing him over the years, and then doing this book for which I
interviewed him extensively, and of course being immersed in leadership literature myself, three things struck me.

The first is that he's not beholden to any organization at all. He's
not in any business. He's not a party leader. He's a citizen of the
world at large. And this has freed him to tackle the largest problems
we face. I think that to the extent that a leader is beholden to a particular organization or outcome, that creates a kind of myopia of
what's possible and what matters. Focus narrows to the next quarter's results or the next election. He's way beyond that. He thinks
in terms of generations and of what's best for humanity as a whole.
Because his vision is so expansive, he can take on the largest challenges, rather than small, narrowly defined ones.

So I think there's a lesson here for all of us, which is to ask ourselves if there is something that limits our vision—that limits our
capacity to care. And is there a way to enlarge it?

The second thing that struck me is that he gathers information
from everywhere. He meets with heads of state, and he meets with
beggars. He's getting information from people at every level of society worldwide. This casting a large net lets him understand situations in a very deep way, and he can analyze them in many different

ways and come up with solutions that aren't confined by anyone. And I think that's another lesson everyday leaders can take from him.

The third thing would be the scope of his compassion, which I think is an ideal that we could strive for. It's pretty unlimited. He seems to care about everybody and the world at large.

Daniel Goleman is the codirector of the Consortium for Research on Emotional Intelligence in Organizations at Rutgers University, a coauthor of *Primal Leadership: Leading with Emotional Intelligence* (Harvard Business Review Press, 2013), and the author of *The Brain and Emotional Intelligence: New Insights* (More Than Sound, 2011). His latest book is *A Force for Good: The Dalai Lama's Vision for Our World* (Bantam, 2015). **Andrea Ovans** is a former senior editor at *Harvard Business Review*.

Build Your Resilience

## CHAPTER 21

Resilience in the Moment

DURING DIFFICULT INTERACTIONS, you may begin to question your perceptions about yourself. For example, suppose a direct report says, "I didn't attend the meeting because I didn't think you valued my ideas." In response, you wonder to yourself, "Maybe I'm not a competent manager after all."

For many people, the sense that their self-image is being challenged creates intense emotions. These feelings can become overwhelming, making it virtually impossible to converse productively about *any* subject. For this reason, be sure to address feelings about self-image—in yourself and in the other person—during tough conversations.

Understand Self-Image

Your self-image comes from many different assumptions that you've made about yourself:

- "I'm an effective manager."

- "I'm a good person."

Adapted from "Address Emotions" in the Harvard ManageMentor topic "Difficult Interactions" (Harvard Business Publishing, 2016, electronic)

- "I care about my employees."

- "I'm committed to my organization's success."

This set of assumptions may help you meet a need for self-esteem, competence, and appreciation from others. Few people like to view themselves in a negative light—as incompetent, uncaring, or disloyal.

Why Denial Is Common

Many people view self-image from an "either/or" mindset: "I'm either loyal or disloyal" or "I'm either caring or uncaring." Unfortunately, this perspective makes it impossible for people to tolerate criticism and negative feedback from others.

For instance, if a colleague says, "I was really disappointed when you didn't support my proposal," you might conclude, "I can't possibly be a loyal person if I don't support my peer's ideas." If deciding that you're disloyal feels intolerable, you may practice *denial* and shoot back with something like, "I *did* support your proposal."

Other Reactions to Threats

Other reactions to self-image challenges include:

- **Burying the feelings, adopting a detached manner, and resorting to generalizations:** "Let's calm down and establish precise standard operating procedures here."

- **Striking back at the other person defensively:** "Are you calling me a liar?!"

- **Refusing to face the disagreement directly:** "Let's just forget about it and move on."

None of these responses enables you to listen to feedback and make the changes needed to improve the way you interact with others.

How to Respond to Criticism

by Peter Bregman

AT ONE POINT OR ANOTHER, we've all been blindsided by criticism and reacted poorly. I remember once leading a project that I thought was going great—until my two colleagues took me aside to tell me I was being controlling and overbearing. I immediately became defensive. I had trouble listening to them, and I became self-conscious and awkward for the rest of the project.

Surprise criticism about an issue you haven't perceived yourself often has that effect. It emotionally overpowers you. But you can respond more productively. As you listen to the feedback and your adrenaline starts to flow, pause, take a deep breath, and then follow this game plan.

Acknowledge and set aside your feelings. We call it *constructive* criticism, and it usually is, but it can also feel painful, destabilizing, and personal. Notice and acknowledge to yourself the hurt, anger, embarrassment, or insufficiency you might feel. Recognize the feelings, label them as feelings, and then put them aside so the noise doesn't crowd out your hearing.

Also, look beyond the delivery of the criticism. Feedback is hard to give, and your critic may not be skilled at doing it well, but that doesn't mean it's not valuable and insightful. Avoid confusing the package with the message.

Next, don't agree or disagree. Just collect the data. Ask questions. Solicit examples. Recap what you're hearing, all in the spirit of understanding. Let go of the need to respond. That will reduce your defensiveness and give you space to really listen.

Criticism, especially surprise criticism, is useful information about how someone else perceives you. Following these steps will help make sure you can fully understand it and can learn from it.

Peter Bregman is CEO of Bregman Partners, Inc., a global management consulting firm that advises CEOs and their leadership teams.

Handle Threats to Your Self-Image

Several strategies can help you effectively handle challenges to your self-image:

- **Understand your self-image.** List all the assumptions that influence your perception of yourself. By anticipating that you might experience defensiveness over threats to these particular beliefs, you may be better able to control negative feelings if they do arise.

- **Adopt a "both/and" mindset.** Instead of assuming that you can be, for example, either competent or incompetent, remind yourself that you and others are a mixture of positive and negative. You're likely competent at some things and not so skilled at others.

- **Accept imperfection.** Acknowledge that everyone makes mistakes at times. The key is to learn from them.

## CHAPTER 22

Cultivate Resilience in Tough Times

A summary of the full-length HBR article "How Resilience Works" by Diane Coutu, highlighting key ideas and examples

Idea in Brief

Resilient people possess three defining characteristics:

- They coolly accept the harsh realities facing them.

- They find meaning in terrible times.

- They have an uncanny ability to improvise, making do with whatever's at hand.

Fortunately, you can learn to be resilient. To cultivate resilience, apply these practices.

Face Down Reality

Instead of slipping into denial to cope with hardship, take a sober, down-to-earth view of the reality of your situation. You'll prepare yourself to act in ways that enable you to endure—training yourself to survive before the fact.

Example: Admiral Jim Stockdale survived being held prisoner and tortured by the Vietcong in part by accepting he could be held for a long time. (He was held for eight years.) Those who didn't make it out of the camps kept optimistically assuming they'd be released on shorter timetables—by Christmas, by Easter, by the Fourth of July. "I think they all died of broken hearts," Stockdale said.

Adapted from "How Resilience Works" in *Harvard Business Review*, May 2002 (product #R0205B)

Search for Meaning

When hard times strike, resist any impulse to view yourself as a victim and cry, "Why me?" Rather, devise constructs about your suffering to create meaning for yourself and theirs. You'll build bridges from your present-day ordeal to a fuller, better future. Those bridges will make the present manageable, by removing the sense that the present is overwhelming.

Example: Austrian psychiatrist and Auschwitz survivor Victor Frankl realized that to survive the camp, he had to find some purpose. He did so by imagining himself giving a lecture after the war on the psychology of the concentration camp to help outsiders understand what he had been through. By creating concrete goals for himself, he rose above the sufferings of the moment.

Continually Improvise

When disaster hits, be inventive. Make the most of what you have, putting resources to unfamiliar uses and imagining possibilities others don't see.

Example: Mike founded a business with his friend Paul, selling educational materials to schools, businesses, and consulting firms. When a recession hit, they lost many core clients. Paul went through a bitter divorce, suffered from depression, and couldn't work. When Mike offered to buy him out, Paul slapped him with a lawsuit claiming Mike was trying to steal the business.

Mike kept the company going any way he could—going into joint ventures to sell English-language training materials to Russian and Chinese competitors, publishing newsletters for clients, and even writing video scripts for competitors. The lawsuit was eventually settled in his favor, and he had a new and much more solid business than the one he started out with.

Diane Coutu is the director of client communications at Banyan Family Business Advisors, headquartered in Cambridge, Massachusetts, and is a former senior editor at *Harvard Business Review*.

## CHAPTER 23

Practice Self-Compassion

by Christopher Germer

IF A GOOD FRIEND TELLS YOU about an ordeal they're facing or a mistake they've made, how do you typically respond? In all likelihood, you'll offer kindness and comfort, perhaps speaking in a warm and soothing tone, and maybe offering a hug to show how much you care. When your friend recovers and the conversation continues, chances are that you'll expand your support by encouraging your friend to take necessary action or try to discover how to steer clear of similar difficulties in the future.

Now reflect for a moment how you might you treat *yourself* when *you* make a big mistake or experience a setback. It's likely that you'd be much tougher on yourself—that you'd spring to self-criticism ("I'm such an idiot!"), hide in embarrassment or shame ("Ugggh!"), or ruminate for a long time about your perceived shortcomings or bad luck ("Why me? Why did this happen to me?"). When things go wrong in our lives, we tend to become our own worst enemy.

To recover emotionally and get back on your feet, however, there's a different approach you can take: *self-compassion.*

Adapted from content posted on hbr.org on January 5, 2017, as "To Recover from Failure, Try Some Self-Compassion" (product #H03E32)

I've been working with mindfulness in my psychotherapy practice for over 30 years. It is a powerful resource that helps us stay present and focused on the task at hand. I've come to realize, however, that a component of mindfulness that is essential for emotional resilience is often overlooked. In particular, when we fail in a big way, we're likely to become engulfed in shame and our sense of self is dismantled. We all know what this feels like—we're unable to think straight, temporarily suspended in time and place, dislocated from our bodies, and uncertain who we really are. Shame has a way of wiping out the very observer who is needed to be mindful of our situation.

What does it take to rescue yourself and begin to address the situation in an effective manner? You need to treat yourself with the same kindness and support as you'd provide for a dear friend.

A substantial and growing body of research shows that this self-compassion is closely associated with emotional resilience, including the ability to soothe ourselves, recognize our mistakes and learn from them, and motivate ourselves to succeed. Self-compassion is also consistently correlated with a wide range of measures of emotional well-being such as optimism, life satisfaction, autonomy, and wisdom, and with reduced anxiety, depression, stress, and feelings of shame.[1]

To achieve these benefits, self-compassion must include three components, according to my colleague and pioneering self-compassion researcher, Kristin Neff:

- **Mindfulness:** Awareness of what's going on in the present moment. To be kind to ourselves, first we need to *know* that we're struggling *while* we're struggling. It also helps to name the emotions we're feeling in tricky situations and to ground ourselves in the here and now (sensations, sounds, sights). These are all skills associated with mindfulness that make space for a compassionate response.

- **Common humanity:** Knowing we're not alone. Most of us tend to hide in shame when things go really wrong in our lives, or we hide from *ourselves* through distraction or with a few stiff drinks. The antidote is recognizing our common humanity—understanding that many others would feel the same way in similar situations, and that we're not the only ones who suffer in life.

- **Self-kindness:** A kind and warm-hearted response to ourselves. This can take many forms, such as a gentle hand over the heart, validating how we feel, talking to ourselves in an encouraging manner, or by a simple act of kindness such as drinking a cup of tea or listening to music.

  When we feel threatened, our nervous system is awash in adrenaline and thus goes into overdrive. When we're in this state, showing ourselves care and kindness is usually the last thing we're inclined to do. When we experience positive, warm connections, however, our system releases oxytocin instead, a feel-good hormone that downregulates the effects of adrenaline. Taking a mindful pause and then bringing kindness to ourselves seems to activate our innate caregiving system and the calming effect of oxytocin, allowing the mind to clear and giving us a chance to take rational steps to resolve the issue.

Even though self-compassion is not the default option for most of us when things go wrong, anyone can learn to do it. Neff has developed an exercise you can use in everyday life when you need self-compassion the most—the Self-Compassion Break (see the sidebar "Self-Compassion Break")—which is based on the three components of self-compassion described above. (This is just one exercise we offer as part of our empirically supported Mindful Self-Compassion training program.)

Consider the following example of the Self-Compassion Break in action: Your boss gave you a stretch assignment to lead a large and critical project. The project was a great success, due in large part to your skillful leadership, and you believe you demonstrated that you're ready for a promotion. But when you raise the idea with your boss, she laughs dismissively and changes the subject. Livid with anger, you retreat from the conversation, asking yourself why you bothered to work so hard in the first place, since you would never be

Self-Compassion Break

WHEN YOU NOTICE THAT YOU'RE under stress or are emotionally upset, see if you can locate where the emotional discomfort resides your body. Where do you feel it the most? Then say to yourself, slowly:

1. **"This is a moment of struggle."** That's mindfulness. See if you can find your own words, such as:

   - "This hurts."

   - "This is tough."

   - "Ouch!"

2. **"Struggle is a part of living."** That's common humanity. Other options include:

   - "Other people feel this way."

   - "I'm not alone."

   - "We all struggle in our lives."

Now, put your hands over your heart, or wherever it feels soothing, sensing the warmth and gentle touch of your hands, and say to yourself:

3. **"May I be kind to myself. May I give myself what I need."** Perhaps there are more specific words that you might need to hear right now, such as:

   - "May I accept myself as I am."

   - "May I learn to accept myself as I am."

   - "May I be safe."

   - "May I be strong."

   - "May I forgive myself."

If you're having trouble finding the right language, it can help to imagine what you might say to a close friend struggling with that same difficulty. Can you say something similar to yourself, letting the words roll gently through your mind?

---

recognized for it. *Of course* your boss wasn't going to support you, or even notice—she just wanted someone to do the heavy lifting to promote her own selfish agenda. Or maybe you're hopelessly out of touch and your performance really wasn't as good as you thought it was? When we're in the grip of strong emotions, our minds run wild.

As a savvy businessperson, you might think that this would be the perfect moment to advocate for yourself if it were only possible to make a balanced, compelling case for your promotion. But without a moment of self-compassion, your emotional reactivity is likely to stand in your way—you'd put your anger on display instead of showing off your leadership skills, or you'd let self-doubt eat at your resolve to see the discussion through to an acceptable conclusion.

How do you activate self-compassion in the heat of the moment? Begin by acknowledging how you feel; for example, recognizing that you might still feel angry ("She's terrible, and I hate her"), see yourself as the victim ("She made me go through all of that—for what?!"), or doubt yourself ("Maybe she's right—maybe I don't deserve a promotion—I didn't do that great a job after all").

Next, acknowledge that others would probably have similar feelings in this situation: requesting a promotion after you've expanded your skills and taken on more responsibility is a reasonable thing to do, and your emotional reaction to the rejection of that request is not out of line. Consider any examples you know of others in similar situations—perhaps Rob in the finance department told you last year that his promotion was also denied and you noticed how angry he was and how he doubted his own worth. You are not alone.

Finally, express kindness to yourself: What would you say to a friend in your shoes? Perhaps you'd say, "It's rough being taken for granted." "Whatever comes of it, that project *was* a huge success— look at the numbers." Also think about how you care for yourself already. Do you go for a run, pet your dog, call a friend? If you do that when you're suffering, that's self-compassion.

Once you've shifted your frame of mind from a threat state to self-compassion, you're likely to find yourself calmer and in a place that you can sit down and write a thoughtful and persuasive proposal about your promotion—one that builds on your project success and exhibits your leadership potential under stress.

Lastly, a warning: Many people dismiss self-compassion because they think it flies in the face of their ambition or hard self-driving attitude—qualities that they feel have made them successful. But being self-compassionate doesn't imply that you shouldn't be ambitious or push yourself to succeed. Rather it's about *how* you motivate yourself. Instead of using a whip—motivating yourself with blame and harsh self-criticism—self-compassion motivates like a good coach, with encouragement, kindness, and support. It's a simple reversal of the Golden Rule—learning to treat *ourselves* as we naturally treat others in need—with kindness, warmth, and respect.

Christopher Germer is a clinical psychologist and part-time lecturer on psychiatry at Harvard Medical School. He is a co-developer of the Mindful Self-Compassion (MSC) program, author of *The Mindful Path to Self-Compassion*, co-editor of *Mindfulness and Psychotherapy*, and *Wisdom and Compassion in Psychotherapy*, and a founding faculty member of the Institute for Meditation and Psychotherapy and the Center for Mindfulness and Compassion, Cambridge Health Alliance/Harvard Medical School.

Note

1. See, for example: L. K. Barnard and J. F. Curry, "Self-Compassion: Conceptualizations, Correlates, and Interventions," *Review of General Psychology* 15, no. 4 (2011): 289–303; K. D. Neff, S. S. Rude, and K. Kirkpatrick, "An Examination of Self-Compassion in Relation to Positive Psychological Functioning and Personality Traits," *Journal of Research in Personality* 41 (2007): 908–916; F. Raes, "The Effect of Self-Compassion on the Development of Depression Symptoms in a Non-clinical Sample," *Mindfulness* 2 (2011): 33–36; D. L. Zabelina and M. D. Robinson, "Don't Be So Hard on Yourself: Self-Compassion Facilitates Creative Originality Among Self-Judgmental Individuals," *Creativity Research Journal* 22 (2010): 288–293; E. Schanche et al., "The Relationship Between Activating Affects, Inhibitory Affects, and Self-Compassion in Patients with Cluster C Personality Disorders," *Psychotherapy* 48, no. 3 (2011): 293–303.

CHAPTER 24

Don't Endure; Recharge

by Shawn Achor and Michelle Gielan

AS CONSTANT TRAVELERS AND PARENTS of a two-year-old, we sometimes fantasize about how much work we could do if we could just get on a plane, undistracted by phones, friends, or *Finding Nemo*. And so in advance of a trip, we race to get all our groundwork done: packing, going through TSA, doing a last-minute work call, calling each other, boarding. But then when we try to have that amazing in-flight work session, we find that we get nothing done. Even worse, after refreshing our email or reading the same studies over and over, we are too exhausted when we land to soldier on with the emails that have inevitably still piled up.

Why can't we be tougher—more resilient and determined in our work—so we can accomplish all of the goals we set for ourselves? Through our current research, we have come to realize that the problem comes from a cultural misunderstanding of what it means to be resilient, and the resulting impact of overworking.

As a society, we often associate "resilience" and "grit" with a militaristic, "tough" approach to our work. We imagine a Marine slogging through the mud, a boxer going one more round, or a football player picking himself up off the turf for one more play. We believe

---

Adapted from content posted on hbr.org on June 24, 2016, as "Resilience Is About How You Recharge, Not How You Endure" (product #H02Z3O)

that the longer we tough it out, the tougher we are, and therefore the more successful we will be.

However, this entire conception is scientifically inaccurate. In fact what's holding back our ability to be resilient and successful is the lack of any kind of recovery period. Resilience is defined as the ability to quickly bounce back from stressful situations—no matter what problems are thrown at us, we continually get back up, ready for the next one. But even for the most resilient person, getting ready doesn't happen instantly. It is a process—and an important one. Research has found that there is a direct correlation between lack of recovery and increased incidence of health and safety problems. And lack of recovery—whether it disrupts our sleep with thoughts of work or keeps us in continuous cognitive arousal as we obsessively watch our phones—is costing our companies $62 billion a year (that's *billion*, not million) in lost productivity.[1]

Misconceptions about resilience as nonstop activity and energy are often bred into us from an early age. For instance, parents might praise the resilience of their high school student who stays up until 3 a.m. to finish a science fair project. But when that exhausted student drives to school, his impaired driving poses risks for himself and others; at school, he doesn't have the cognitive resources to do well on his English test and has lower self-control with his friends; and at home, he is moody with his parents.

The bad habits we learn when we're young only magnify when we hit the workforce. In a study released last month, researchers from Norway found that 7.8% of Norwegians have become workaholics, where *workaholism* is defined as "being overly concerned about work, driven by an uncontrollable work motivation, and investing so much time and effort to work that it impairs other important life areas."[2] And in fact that drive can backfire in the very area for which we're sacrificing ourselves: In her excellent book *The Sleep Revolution: Transforming Your Life, One Night at a Time*, Arianna Huffington wrote, "We sacrifice sleep in the name of productivity, but ironically our loss of sleep, despite the extra hours we spend at work, adds up to 11 days of lost productivity per year per worker, or about $2,280."[3]

The key to resilience is *not* working really hard all the time. It is actually found in the time that we stop working and recover. Ideally, we need to create cycles for ourselves in which we work hard, then stop and recover, and then work again.

This conclusion is based on biology. *Homeostasis*, a fundamental biological concept, is the ability of the body to continuously restore and sustain its own well-being. When the body is out of alignment and therefore in a state of stress or exhaustion from overworking, we waste a vast amount of mental and physical resources trying to return to balance before we can move forward. As Jim Loehr and Tony Schwartz have written in *The Power of Full Engagement*, the more time you spend in the performance zone, the more time you need in the recovery zone; otherwise you risk burnout.

And if, instead of taking a break, you muster your resources to continue to "try hard," you need to burn ever more energy in order to overcome your currently low arousal level, which only exacerbates your exhaustion. It's a vicious downward spiral.

But the more imbalanced we become due to overworking, the more value there is in activities that allow us to return to a state of balance.

So what are those activities that allow us to return to homeostasis and thereby increase our resilience? Most people assume that if you stop doing a task like answering emails or writing a paper, that your brain will naturally recover, so that when you start again later in the day or the next morning, you'll have your energy back. But stopping work doesn't mean you're actually recovering: If after work you lie around on the couch and check your phone and get riled up by political commentary, or get stressed thinking about decisions about how to renovate your home, your brain has not received a break from high mental arousal states. And surely everyone reading this has occasionally lain in bed for hours, unable to fall asleep because their brain is thinking about work, even if they don't have a device in hand. If you're in bed for eight hours, you may have rested, but you can still feel exhausted the next day. That's because rest and recovery are not the same thing.

If you're trying to build resilience at work, you need adequate internal and external recovery periods. As researchers F. R. H. Zijlstra, M. Cropley, and L. W. Rydstedt wrote in a 2014 paper: "Internal recovery refers to the shorter periods of relaxation that take place within the frames of the workday or the work setting in the form of short scheduled or unscheduled breaks, by shifting attention or changing to other work tasks when the mental or physical resources required for the initial task are temporarily depleted or exhausted. External recovery refers to actions that take place outside of work—e.g., in the free time between the workdays, and during weekends, holidays or vacations."[4]

There are four main researched ways to increase your resilience. First, start by deliberately opening a space for recovery to happen. We've worked with several companies that tout the benefits of investing in employee well-being, but fail to create tangible results because they don't carve out time for their workers to devote part of their workday to those rejuvenating activities. Adding more activities to an already full plate of work increases the stress load.

Second, it is crucial that you take *all* of your paid time off. As we described in a previous HBR article entitled "The Data-Driven Case for Vacation," taking your days off not only gives you recovery periods to recharge, but in fact significantly raises your productivity and the likelihood of promotion.

Third, while it might sound counterintuitive, it is possible to use technology to limit tech use while building internal recovery periods into your daily routine. The average person turns on their phone 150 times every day.[5] If every distraction took only 1 minute (which would be seriously optimistic), that would account for 2.5 hours of every day. In her upcoming book *The Future of Happiness*, based on her work at Yale Business School, Amy Blankson suggests downloading the Instant or Moment apps to see how many times *you* turn on your phone each day; using the app reminds you to make a choice in those moments when you grab your phone—and choose to stay away. You can also use apps like Offtime or Unplugged to create tech-free zones by strategically scheduling automatic airplane modes. In addition, you can take a cognitive break every 90 minutes to recharge your batteries. Try to not have lunch at your desk, but instead spend time outside or with your friends—*not* talking about work.

Fourth, now that you have carved out time for rejuvenation, it's time to engage in an activity or two that make you feel happy and replenished. Take the pressure off and just do something for the fun of it! Go on a walk or run, call an old friend, meditate by watching your breath go in and out for five minutes, try a new recipe, or do something nice for someone else. Choose to do something that makes you feel alive, gives you a mental break from work, and keeps you fully engaged the whole time. Not only does spending your time this way help you come back stronger, oftentimes these activities are more memorable in the long run.

As for us, we've started using our plane time as a work-free zone, and thus as time to dip into the recovery phase. The results have been fantastic. We are usually tired already by the time we get on a plane, and the cramped space and spotty internet connection make work more challenging. Now, instead of swimming upstream, we relax, meditate, sleep, watch movies, journal, or listen to entertaining podcasts. And when we get off the plane, instead of being depleted, we feel rejuvenated and ready to return to the performance zone.

Shawn Achor is *New York Times* best-selling author of *The Happiness Advantage* and *Before Happiness*. His TED talk is one of the most popular, with over 14 million views. He has lectured or researched at over a third of the *Fortune* 100 and in 50 countries, as well as for the NFL, NASA, and the White House. He is leading a series of courses on "21 Days to Inspire Positive Change" with the Oprah Winfrey Network. **Michelle Gielan**, a national CBS News anchor turned UPenn positive psychology researcher, is the best-selling author of *Broadcasting Happiness*. She is partnered with Arianna Huffington to research how a solution-focused mindset fuels success, and shares her research at organizations including Google, American Express, and Boston Children's Hospital. Michelle is the host of the *Inspire Happiness* program on PBS.

Notes

1. J. K. Sluiter, "The Influence of Work Characteristics on the Need for Recovery and Experienced Health: A Study on Coach Drivers," *Ergonomics* 42, no. 4 (1999): 573–583; and American Academy of Sleep Medicine, "Insomnia Costing U.S. Workforce $63.2 Billion a Year in Lost Productivity," *ScienceDaily*, September 2, 2011.

2. C. S. Andreassen et al., "The Relationships Between Workaholism and Symptoms of Psychiatric Disorders: A Large-Scale Cross-Sectional Study," *PLoS One* 11, no. 5 (2016): e0152978.

3. Ronald C. Kessler et al., "Insomnia and the Performance of US Workers: Results from the America Insomnia Survey," *Sleep* 34, no. 9 (2011): 1161–1171.

4. F. R. H. Zijlstra et al., "From Recovery to Regulation: An Attempt to Reconceptualize 'Recovery from Work'" (special issue paper) (Hoboken, NJ: John Wiley & Sons, 2014), 244.

5. J. Stern, "Cellphone Users Check Phones 150x/Day and Other Internet Fun Facts," *Good Morning America*, May 29, 2013.

## CHAPTER 25

How Resilient Are You?

by Manfred F. R. Kets de Vries

WE ALL FACE SETBACKS from time to time, and the ability to bounce back stronger than before is something we envy in others. So how can we develop that ability in ourselves?

A large body of research shows that resilient people are generally strong in three areas: challenge, control, and commitment. They accept that change, not stability, is the norm; they believe they can influence events in their lives; and they are engaged with the world around them.

This test will help you assess your strengths and weaknesses in these areas and provide feedback on ways to improve.

Circle your reaction to each statement, then follow the instructions below to score yourself.

Challenge

1. You're told that you won't be getting the promotion you sought, because another candidate is more qualified.

   a. Although you are upset, you say nothing.

   b. You acknowledge that you are disappointed and request a fuller explanation.

Adapted from material originally published on hbr.org on January 20, 2015

    c. You ask what you need to do to improve your chances for advancement in the future.

2. You learn that your company will be opening an office in Beijing. Succeeding in that market would be difficult, but you know that you have the right experience to lead the office.

    a. You consider the risks and decide not to pursue the opportunity.

    b. You discuss the pros and cons with some of the people in your network.

    c. You throw your hat into the ring.

3. A major client tells you that a contract you worked hard to win has been given to a competitor.

    a. You tell your team that you made every effort to land the client.

    b. You put the setback out of your mind, accepting that some factors in the client's decision were beyond your control.

    c. You reflect on the experience, realizing that you now have a much better understanding of how to deal with this client in the future.

Control

4. You overhear an unflattering conversation about yourself.

    a. You pretend it doesn't bother you.

    b. You remind yourself that the speakers don't know you very well.

    c. You approach the speakers calmly and express your desire to understand why they see you that way.

5. Your boss comes to you on Friday afternoon with an emergency: He wants to meet with a client on Monday morning and

needs you to prepare a feasibility study first. You have a family camping trip planned for the weekend.

a. You accept the assignment, not mentioning your weekend plans.

b. You mention the camping trip but agree to the assignment after your boss emphasizes its importance.

c. You tell your boss that you have made a commitment to your family and ask if he can schedule the meeting for Tuesday instead.

6. Work has become increasingly stressful. There are too many deadlines, too many requests, too many late nights.

a. You tell yourself, "This, too, shall pass."

b. You try to give some of your work to a colleague.

c. You request a vacation or a leave of absence to recharge.

Commitment

7. Your best friend says that he is worried about your health and suggests that you join his fitness club.

a. You say, "No, thanks. I'm fine."

b. You agree that the fitness club is a good idea and make a note in your calendar to look into it.

c. You take his concern to heart and arrange to visit the club together.

8. Your company's subsidiary in Africa requests financial and technical support for a high school in the region. Although there would be no immediate monetary benefit to the firm, this is a valuable opportunity to build a reputation as a socially responsible employer.

a. You decline the request on cost grounds.

b. You agree to give the matter serious consideration.

c. You give your consent and call a friend at the World Bank for suggestions on how to launch the initiative.

9. Early in your career you had set a goal to become general manager at a *Fortune* 1000 company by age 50. The clock is ticking: You're 48, and you're a division head.

a. You accept your current role and decide to make the best of it.

b. You continue striving for advancement but lower your ambitions a bit.

c. You figure out a way to reach your goal.

Score Yourself

For each area, record the number of each answer below and add up your total score for that area.

Challenge

of a ____ = _____

# of b ____ x 2 = _____

# of c ____ x 3 = _____

Total = _____ = Challenge Score

If you had a high challenge score (7-9): You turn difficult events to your advantage and view setbacks as learning opportunities. You have positive relationships with others.

If you had a low challenge score (1-6): You need to work on turning difficult events to your advantage and reframing them in a constructive light. If you experience setbacks in the process, regard them as learning opportunities, not failures. Remember the importance of positive relationships with others.

Control

of a ___ = _____

# of b ___ x 2 = _____

# of c ___ x 3 = _____

Total = _____ = Control Score

If you had a high control score (7–9): You can distinguish between things you can and can't control, and you deal with emotionally difficult problems proactively. You see things in perspective and know how to set boundaries.

If you had a low control score (1–6): Work on distinguishing between things you can and can't control, perhaps with the help of an executive coach or a therapist. Try to deal with emotionally difficult problems proactively. Use humor to "roll with the punches." Set boundaries in both your professional life and your personal life to avoid burnout. Delegate more responsibilities to your direct reports.

Commitment

of a ___ = _____

# of b ___ x 2 = _____

# of c ___ x 3 = _____

Total = _____ = Commitment Score

If you had a high commitment score (7–9): You pursue goals that are meaningful to you and maintain positive relationships with people who matter to you. You recognize the importance of health and balance and have an active life outside of work.

If you had a low commitment score (1–6): Clarify what is important to you and pursue those activities. Make an effort to spend time with people who are meaningful in your life. Develop healthy habits, including daily exercise, regular sleep, and relaxation techniques. Don't ignore problems.

———————————

To take this assessment online and compare your results to those of other HBR readers, visit https://hbr.org/2015/01/assessment-how-resilient-are-you.

———————————

Manfred F. R. Kets de Vries is the Distinguished Professor of Leadership Development and Organizational Change at INSEAD in France, Singapore, and Abu Dhabi. His most recent book is *Riding the Leadership Roller Coaster: An Observer's Guide* (Palgrave Macmillan, 2016).

Developing Emotional Intelligence on Your Team

## CHAPTER 26

How to Help Someone Develop Emotional Intelligence

by Annie McKee

IT'S EASY TO POINT FINGERS at those in the office who lack basic self-awareness or social skill. Whether clueless colleagues or brutish bosses, these people make life challenging for the rest of us, ruining the dynamic of work teams and shattering productivity and morale. But in fact most of us can stand to improve our emotional intelligence. Even those of us who are adept extroverts can learn how to become more empathetic; those who are kind givers can learn to be more persuasive.

As a manager, it's up to you to develop the emotional intelligence of your direct reports—whether they are socially awkward, downright nasty, or simply looking to become more influential. In doing so, you'll help them grow in their careers—and make your workplace a healthier, happier, more productive place to be.

Here's the problem: Emotional intelligence is difficult to develop because it is linked to psychological development and neurological pathways created over an entire lifetime (to learn more, see Daniel

Adapted from content posted on hbr.org on April 24, 2015 (product #H0216Z)

Goleman's book *The Brain and Emotional Intelligence: New Insights*). It takes a lot of effort to change long-standing habits of human interaction—not to mention foundational competencies like self-awareness and emotional self-control. People need to be invested in changing their behavior and developing their emotional intelligence, or it just doesn't happen. What this means in practice is that you don't have even a remote chance of changing someone's emotional intelligence unless *they* want to change.

Most of us assume that people will change their behavior when told to do so by a person with authority (you, the manager). For complicated change and development, however, it is clear that people don't *sustain* change when promised incentives like good assignments or a better office.[1] And when threatened or punished, they get downright ornery and behave really badly. Carrot-and-stick performance management processes and the behaviorist approach on which they are based are deeply flawed; yet most of us start (and end) there, even in the most innovative organizations.

What *does* work is:

> First, helping people find a deep and very personal vision of their own future.

> Then, helping them see how their current ways of operating might need a bit of work if that future is to be realized.

These are the first two steps in Richard Boyatzis's *intentional change* theory—which we've been testing with leaders for years. According to Boyatzis—and backed up by our work with leaders—here's how people really can begin and sustain change on complex abilities linked to emotional intelligence:

First, find the dream

If you're coaching an employee, you must *first* help them discover what's important in life. Only then can you move on to aspects of work that are important to them. Help your employee craft a clear and compelling vision of a future that includes powerful and positive relationships with family, friends, and coworkers. Notice that I'm talking about *coaching*, not *managing*, your employee. There's a big difference.

Next, find out what's really going on
What's the current state of your employee's emotional intelligence? Once people have a powerful dream to draw strength from, they're strong enough to take the heat—to find out the truth. If you are now truly coaching, you're trusted and your employee will listen to you. Still, that's probably not enough. You will want to find a way to gather input from others, either through a 360-degree feedback instrument like the ESCI (Emotional and Social Competency Inventory), or a Leadership Self-Study process (as described in our book, *Becoming a Resonant Leader*), which gives you the chance to talk directly to trusted friends about their emotional intelligence and other skills.

Finally, craft a gap analysis and a learning plan
Note that I did not say "performance management plan," or even "development plan." A learning plan is different in that it charts a direct path from the personal vision to what must be learned over time to get there—to actual skill development.

Learning goals are *big*. Take, for example, one executive I know. Talented though he was, his distinct lack of caring about the people around him had placed him in danger of being fired. He wanted what he wanted—and watch out if you were in his way. He couldn't seem to change until it finally dawned on him that his bulldozer style was playing out at home too, with his children. That didn't fit at all with his dream of a happy, close-knit family who would live close to each other throughout their lives. So, with a dream in hand and the ugly reality rearing its head at work and at home, he decided to work on developing empathy. As a learning goal, empathy is one of the toughest and most important competencies to develop. The capacity for emotional and cognitive empathy is laid down early in life, and then reinforced over many years. This exec had a good foundation for empathy in childhood, but intense schooling and a stint at an up-or-out management consulting firm had driven it out of him. He needed to relearn how to read people and care about them. He was able to succeed—yes, it took a good while, but he did it.

———————

This sounds like a lot of hard work for your employee, and it can be. Here's where a final important piece of the theory comes into play. They—and you—can't do it alone. People need people—kind and supportive people—when embarking on a journey of self-development. Are you there for your employees? Do you help them find other supporters, in addition to yourself, who will help when their confidence wanes or when they experience inevitable setbacks?

Developing one's emotional intelligence can make the difference between success and failure in life and in work. If you're the one responsible for people's contributions to the team and your organization, you are actually on the hook to try to help those (many) people who are emotional-intelligence-challenged, deficient, and dangerous. It's your job.

But what if you're not the boss? You can still make a difference with colleagues. All of the same rules apply to how people change. You just need to find a different entry point. In my experience, that entry begins with you creating a safe space and establishing trust. Find something to like about these people and let them know it. Give them credit where credit is due, and then some (most of these folks are pretty insecure). Be kind. In other words, use your emotional intelligence to help them get ready to work on theirs.

And finally, if none of this works, these "problem people" don't belong on your team—or maybe even in your organization. If you're a manager, that's when it's time to help them move on with dignity.

———————

Annie McKee is a senior fellow at the University of Pennsylvania and the director of the PennCLO Executive Doctoral Program. She is the author of *Primal Leadership* (with Daniel Goleman and Richard Boyatzis), as well as *Resonant Leadership* and *Becoming a Resonant*

Leader. Her new book, *How to Be Happy at Work,* is forthcoming from Harvard Business Review Press in September 2017.

Note

1. "What Motivates Us?" interview between Daniel Pink and Katherine Bell, *HBR Ideacast* (podcast), February 10, 2010.

## CHAPTER 27

Handling Emotional Outbursts on Your Team

by Liane Davey

DO YOU HAVE A CRIER on your team—you know, the one with tissue-thin skin who expresses frustration, sadness, or worry through tears? Maybe you have a screamer, a table pounder who is aggressively invested in every decision. These kinds of emotional outbursts are not just uncomfortable; they can hijack your team, stalling productivity and limiting innovation.

Don't allow an emotional person to postpone, dilute, or drag out an issue that the business needs you to resolve. Instead, take the outburst for what it is: a communication. Emotions are clues that the issue you are discussing is touching on something the person values or believes strongly in. So look at outbursts as giving you three sets of information: emotional data; factual or intellectual data; and motives, values, and beliefs.

We get stuck when we only focus on the first two—emotions and facts. It's easy to do. When someone starts yelling, for instance, you

---

Adapted from content originally posted on hbr.org on April 24, 2015, as "Handling Emotional Outbursts on Your Team" might think he's mad (emotion) because his project has just been defunded (fact). And many managers stop there, because they find feelings uncomfortable or aren't sure how to deal with them. That's why the first step is to become more self-aware by questioning your mindset around emotions. There are several myths that often get in a team leader's way:

Myth #1: There is no place for emotion in the workplace. If you have humans in the workplace, you're going to have emotions too. Ignoring, stifling, or invalidating them will only drive the toxic issues underground. This outdated notion is one reason people resort to passive-aggressive behavior: Emotions will find their outlet; the choice is whether it's out in the open or in the shadows.

Myth #2: We don't have time to talk about people's feelings. Do you have time for backroom dealings and subterfuge? Do you have time to reopen decisions? Do you have time for failed implementations? Avoiding the emotional issues at the outset will only delay their impact. And when people don't feel heard, their feelings amplify until you have something really destructive to deal with.

Myth #3: Emotions will skew our decision making. Emotions are already affecting your decision making. The choice is whether you want to be explicit about how (and how much) of a role they play or whether you want to leave them as unspoken biases.

With your beliefs in check, you'll be better able to get beyond the emotion and facts to the values the person holds that are being compromised or violated. This is critical because your criers and screamers are further triggered when they don't feel understood. The key is to have a discussion that includes facts, feelings, *and* values. People will feel heard and the emotion will usually dissipate. Then you can focus on making the best business decision possible.

Here's how.

Spot the emotion. If you wait until the emotion is in full bloom, it will be difficult to manage. Instead, watch for the telltale signs that something is causing concern. The most important signals will come from incongruence between what someone is saying and what their body language is telling you. When you notice someone is withdrawing eye contact or getting red in the face, acknowledge what you see: *"Steve, you've stopped midsentence a couple of times now. What's going on for you?"*

Listen. Listen carefully to the response, both to what is said and what you can infer about facts, feelings, and values. You will pick up emotions in language, particularly in extreme words or words that are repeated: *"We have a $2 million budget shortfall and it's our fourth meeting sitting around having a lovely intellectual discussion!"* Body language will again provide clues. Angry (leaning in, clenched jaw or fists) looks very different from discouraged (dropping eye contact, slumping) or dismissive (rolling eyes, turning away).

Ask questions. When you see or hear the emotional layer, stay calm, keep your tone level, and ask a question to draw the person out and get them talking about values: *"I get the sense you're frustrated. What's behind your frustration?"* Listen to their response and then go one layer further by testing a hypothesis: *"Is it possible that you're frustrated because we're placing too much weight on the people impact of the decision and you think we need to focus only on what's right for the business?"*

Resolve it. If your hypothesis is right, you'll probably see relief. The person might even express their pleasure: *"Yes, exactly!"* You can sum it up: *"We've talked about closing the Cleveland office for two years and you're frustrated because you believe that the right decision for the business is obvious."* You've now helped them articulate the values they think should be guiding the decision. The team will now be clear on why they are disagreeing. Three people might jump in, all talking at once: *"We* are *talking about people who have given their lives to this organization!" "Here we go again . . ."* Use the same process to reveal the opposing points of view.

Once everyone is working with the same three data sets—facts, emotions, and values—you will be clear what you need to solve for— in this case, *"How will we weigh the financial necessity against the impact on people?"* Although taking the time to draw out the values might seem slow at first, you'll see that issues actually get resolved faster. And ironically, as you validate emotions, over time people will tend to be less emotional because it's often the suppression of emotions or attempts to cobble together facts to justify those emotions that was causing irrational behavior.

If you're leading a high-performing team, you'd better be ready to deal with uncomfortable, messy, complex emotions. If there's a situation you have failed to address because of an emotional team member, spend some time thinking about how you will approach it and then go have the conversation. Today. You can't afford to wait any longer.

Liane Davey is the cofounder of 3COze Inc. She is the author of *You First: Inspire Your Team to Grow Up, Get Along, and Get Stuff Done* and a coauthor of *Leadership Solutions: The Pathway to Bridge the Leadership Gap.* Follow her on Twitter @LianeDavey.

## CHAPTER 28

How to Manage Your Emotional Culture

by Sigal Barsade and Olivia A. O'Neill

WHEN PEOPLE TALK ABOUT "corporate culture," they're typically referring to *cognitive* culture: the shared *intellectual* values, norms, artifacts, and assumptions that serve as a guide for the group to thrive. Cognitive culture sets the tone for how employees think and behave at work—for instance, how customer-focused, innovative, team-oriented, or competitive they are or should be.

Cognitive culture is undeniably important to an organization's success. But it's only part of the story. The other critical part is what we call the group's *emotional* culture: the shared *affective* values, norms, artifacts, and assumptions that govern which emotions people have and express at work and which ones they are better off suppressing. Though the key distinction here is thinking versus feeling, the two types of culture are also transmitted differently: Cognitive culture is often conveyed verbally, whereas emotional culture tends to be conveyed through nonverbal cues such as body language and facial expression.

Adapted from "Manage Your Emotional Culture" in *Harvard Business Review*, January 2016 (product #R0601C).

In our research over the past decade, we have found that emotional culture influences employee satisfaction, burnout, teamwork, and even hard measures such as financial performance and absenteeism. Countless empirical studies show the significant impact of emotions on how people perform on tasks, how engaged and creative they are, how committed they are to their organizations, and how they make decisions. Positive emotions are consistently associated with better performance, quality, and customer service—this holds true across roles and industries and at various organizational levels. On the flip side (with certain short-term exceptions), negative emotions such as group anger, sadness, fear, and the like usually lead to negative outcomes, including poor performance and high turnover.

So when managers ignore emotional culture, they're glossing over a vital part of what makes people—and organizations—tick. They may understand its importance in theory but can still shy away from emotions at work. Leaders expect to influence how people think and behave on the job, but they may feel ill-equipped to understand and actively manage how employees feel and express their emotions at work. Or they may regard doing so as irrelevant, not part of their job, or unprofessional.

Emotional Cultures in Action

Nearly 30 years ago, the social psychologist Phil Shaver and his colleagues found that people can reliably distinguish among 135 emotions. But understanding the most basic ones—joy, love, anger, fear, sadness—is a good place to start for any leader trying to manage an emotional culture. Here are a few examples to illustrate how these emotions can play out in organizations.

A culture of joy
Let's begin with one that's often clearly articulated and actively reinforced by management—above the surface and easy to spot. Vail Resorts recognizes that cultivating joy among employees helps customers have fun too, which matters a lot in the hospitality business.

It also gives the organization an edge in retaining top talent in an extremely competitive industry. "Have fun" is listed as a company value and modeled by Vail's CEO, Rob Katz—who, for instance, had ice water dumped on his head during a corporate ALS Ice Bucket Challenge and then jumped fully clothed into a pool. About 250 executives and other employees followed his lead.

This playful spirit at the top permeates Vail. Management tactics, special outings, celebrations, and rewards all support the emotional culture. Resort managers consistently model joy and prescribe it for their teams. During the workday, they give out pins when they notice employees spontaneously having fun or helping others enjoy their jobs. Rather than asking people to follow standardized customer service scripts, they tell everyone to "go out there and have fun." Mark Gasta, the company's chief people officer, says he regularly sees ski-lift operators dancing, making jokes, doing "whatever it takes to have fun and entertain the guest" while ensuring a safe experience on the slopes. On a day-to-day basis, Vail encourages employees to collaborate because, as Gasta points out, "leaving people out is not fun." At an annual ceremony, a Have Fun award goes to whoever led that year's best initiative promoting fun at work. The resort also fosters off-the-job joy with "first tracks" (first access to the ski slopes for employees), adventure trips, and frequent social gatherings.

All this is in service to an emotional culture that makes intuitive sense. (Joy at a ski resort? Of course.) But now consider an organization where the demand for joy wasn't immediately visible. When we surveyed employees at Cisco Finance about their organization's emotional culture, it became clear to management that fostering joy should be a priority. The survey didn't ask employees how they felt at work; it asked them what emotions they saw their coworkers expressing on a regular basis. (By having employees report on colleagues' emotions, researchers could obtain a more objective bird's-eye view of the culture.) It turned out that joy was one of the strongest drivers of employee satisfaction and commitment at the company—and more of it was needed to keep up engagement.

So management made joy an explicit cultural value, calling it "Pause for Fun." This signaled that it was an important outcome to track—just like productivity, creativity, and other elements of performance. Many companies use annual employee engagement surveys to gauge joy in the abstract, often in the form of job satisfaction and commitment to the organization. But Cisco Finance measured it much more specifically and is conducting follow-up surveys to track whether it is actually increasing. In addition, leaders throughout the organization support this cultural value with their own behavior— for example, by creating humorous videos that show them pausing for fun.

A culture of companionate love

Another emotion we've examined extensively—one that's common in life but rarely mentioned by name in organizations—is *companionate love*. This is the degree of affection, caring, and compassion that employees feel and express toward one another.

In a 16-month study of a large long-term-care facility on the East Coast, we found that workers in units with strong cultures of companionate love had lower absenteeism, less burnout, and greater teamwork and job satisfaction than their colleagues in other units.[1] Employees also performed their work better, as demonstrated by more-satisfied patients, better patient moods, and fewer unnecessary trips to the emergency room. (Employees whose dispositions were positive to begin with received an extra performance boost from the culture.) The families of patients in units with stronger cultures of companionate love reported higher satisfaction with the facility. These results show a powerful connection between emotional culture and business performance.

Because this study took place in a health-care setting, we wondered whether companionate love matters only in "helping" industries. So we surveyed more than 3,200 employees in 17 organizations spanning seven industries: biopharmaceutical, engineering, financial services, higher education, public utilities, real estate, and travel. In organizations where employees felt and expressed companionate love toward one another, people reported greater job satisfaction, commitment, and personal accountability for work performance.

Creating an Emotional Culture

To cultivate a particular emotional culture, you'll need to get people to feel the emotions valued by the organization or team—or at least to behave as if they do. Here are three effective methods:

Harness what people already feel

Some employees will experience the desired emotions quite naturally. This can happen in isolated moments of compassion or gratitude, for example. When such feelings arise regularly, that's a sign you're building the culture you want. If people have them only periodically and need help sustaining them, you can try incorporating some gentle nudges during the workday. You might schedule some time for meditation, for instance; or provide mindfulness apps on people's work devices to remind them to simply breathe, relax, or laugh; or create a kudos board, like the one in an ICU we studied, where people can post kind words about other employees.

But what can you do about emotions that are toxic to the culture you're striving for? How can you discourage them when they already exist? Expecting people to "put a lid" on those feelings is both ineffective and destructive; the emotions will just come out later in counterproductive ways. It's important to listen when employees express their concerns so that they feel they are being heard. That's not to say you should encourage venting, or just let the emotions flow without attempting to solve the root problems. Indeed, research shows that extended venting can lead to poor outcomes. You're better off helping employees think about situations in a more constructive way. For example, loneliness, which can eat away at employee attitudes and performance, is best addressed through cognitive reappraisal—getting people to reexamine their views of others' actions. Considering plausible benign motivations for their colleagues' behavior will make them less likely to fixate on negative explanations that could send them into a spiral.

Model the emotions you want to cultivate

A long line of research on emotional contagion shows that people in groups "catch" feelings from others through behavioral mimicry and subsequent changes in brain function.[2] If you regularly walk into a room smiling with high energy, you're much more likely to create a culture of joy than if you wear a neutral expression. Your employees will smile back and start to mean it.

But negative feelings, too, spread like wildfire. If you frequently express frustration, that emotion will infect your team members—and their team members, and so on—throughout the organization. Before you know it, you'll have created a culture of frustration.

So consciously model the emotions you want to cultivate in your company. Some organizations go a step further and explicitly ask employees to spread certain emotions. Ubiquity Retirement + Savings says, "Inspire happiness with contagious enthusiasm. Own your joy and lend it out." Vail Resorts says, "Enjoy your work and share the contagious spirit."

Get people to fake it 'til they feel it

If employees don't experience the desired emotion at a particular moment, they can still help maintain their organization's emotional culture. That's because people express emotions both spontaneously and strategically at work. Social psychology research has long shown that individuals tend to conform to group norms of emotional expression, imitating others out of a desire to be liked and accepted. So employees in a strong emotional culture who would not otherwise feel and express the valued emotion will begin to demonstrate it—even if their initial motivation is to be compliant rather than to internalize the culture.

This benefits the organization, not just the individuals trying to thrive in it. In early anthropological studies of group rituals, strategic emotional expression was found to facilitate group cohesion by overpowering individual feelings and synchronizing interpersonal behavior.

So maintaining the appropriate culture sometimes entails disregarding what you are truly feeling. Through "surface acting," employees can display the valued emotion without even wanting to feel it. Surface acting isn't a long-term solution, though. Research shows that it can eventually lead to burnout—particularly in the absence of any outlet for authentic emotions.[3]

A better way to cultivate a desired emotion is through "deep acting." With this technique, people make a focused effort to feel a certain way—and then suddenly they do. Imagine that an employee at an accounting firm has a family emergency and requests a week off work at the height of tax audit season. Although his boss's first thought is *No—not now—no!* she could engage in deep acting to change her immediate feelings of justifiable panic into genuine caring and concern for her subordinate. By trying hard to empathize, saying "Of course, you should go be with your family!" and using the facial expressions, body language, and tone of voice she would use when actually feeling those emotions, she could coax herself into the real thing. She would also be modeling a desired behavior for the subordinate and the rest of the team.

Fortunately, all these ways of creating an emotional culture—whether they involve really feeling the emotion or simply acting that way—can reinforce one another and strengthen the culture's norms. People don't have to put on an act forever. Those who begin by expressing an emotion out of a desire to conform will start to actually feel it through emotional contagion. They'll also receive positive reinforcement for following the norms, which will make them more likely to demonstrate the emotion again.

Of course, the culture will be much stronger and more likely to endure if people truly believe in the values and assumptions behind it. Someone who is uncomfortable with an organization's emotional culture and has to keep pretending in order to be successful would probably be better off moving to a different work environment. Companies often have more than one emotional culture, so another unit or department might be a good fit. But if the culture is homogeneous, the employee may want to leave the company entirely.

Implementation Matters at All Levels

Just like other aspects of organizational culture, emotional culture should be supported at all levels of the organization. The role of top management is to drive it.

349

Leaders are often insufficiently aware of how much influence they have in creating an emotional culture. Traci Fenton is the founder and CEO of WorldBlu, a consulting firm that tackles fear at work. She shares this example: At one *Fortune* 500 company, unbeknownst to the CEO, senior employees regularly use text message codes to describe his nonverbal expressions of anger in meetings. "RED" means he is getting red in the face. "VEIN" means his veins are popping out. "ACP," which stands for "assume the crash position," means he is about to start throwing things. This leader is very effective at creating an emotional culture—but it's probably not the one he wants.

So don't underestimate the importance of day-to-day modeling. Large, symbolic emotional gestures are powerful, but only if they are in line with daily behavior. Senior executives can also shape an emotional culture through organizational practices. Take "compassionate firing," which is common at companies that build a strong culture of companionate love. Carlos Gutierrez, the vice president of R&D systems at Lattice Semiconductor, was deeply concerned about the impact of layoffs on his employees. He recognized that the traditional HR protocol of asking terminated employees to clean out their desks immediately and leave the premises would be especially painful to people who had worked side by side for 10–20 years. Along with his partners in HR and R&D, he implemented a protocol whereby employees had an extended time to say good-bye to their colleagues and to commemorate their time together at the company. Also, although two-thirds of the R&D workforce is outside the United States, Sherif Sweha, the corporate vice president of R&D, believed it was important for the affected team members in each region to receive the news from a senior leader face-to-face. So he and members of his staff flew to the company's sites in Asia to have in-person conversations with all the employees to be laid off—and also those who would remain with the company.

Though top management sets the first example and establishes the formal rules, middle managers and frontline supervisors ensure that the emotional values are consistently practiced by others. Because one of the biggest influences on employees is their immediate boss, the suggestions that apply to senior executives also apply to those managers: They should ensure that the emotions they express at work reflect the chosen culture, and they should speak explicitly about what is expected from employees.

It's also important to link the emotional culture to operations and processes, including performance management systems. At Vail Resorts, the culture of joy has been incorporated into the annual review, which indicates how well each employee integrates fun into the work environment and rates everyone on supporting behaviors, such as being inclusive, welcoming, approachable, and positive. Someone who exceeds expectations is described as not only taking part in the fun but also offering "recommendations to improve the work environment to integrate fun."

Decades' worth of research demonstrates the importance of organizational culture, yet most of it has focused on the cognitive component. As we've shown, organizations also have an emotional pulse, and managers must track it closely to motivate their teams and reach their goals.

Emotional culture is shaped by how all employees—from the highest echelons to the front lines—comport themselves day in and day out. But it's up to senior leaders to establish which emotions will help the organization thrive, model those emotions, and reward others for doing the same. Companies in which they do this have a lot to gain.

Sigal Barsade is the Joseph Frank Bernstein Professor of Management at Wharton. **Olivia A. O'Neill** is an assistant professor of management at George Mason University and a senior scholar at the school's Center for the Advancement of Well-Being.

Notes

1. Sigal Barsade and Olivia A. O'Neill, "What's Love Got to Do with It? A Longitudinal Study of the Culture of Companionate Love and Employee and Client Outcomes in a Long-Term Care Setting," *Administrative Science Quarterly* 59, no 4. (2014).

2. Sigal Barsade, "The Ripple Effect: Emotional Contagion and Its Influence on Group Behavior," *Administrative Science Quarterly* 47, no. 4 (2002).

3. Alicia A. Grandey, "When 'The Show Must Go On': Surface Acting and Deep Acting as Determinants of Emotional Exhaustion and Peer-Rated Service Delivery," *Academy of Management Journal* 46, no. 1 (February 2003): 86–96.

Index

The most important management ideas all in one place.

We hope you enjoyed this book from *Harvard Business Review*. Now you can get even more with HBR's 10 Must Reads Boxed Set. From books on leadership and strategy to managing yourself and others, this 6-book collection delivers articles on the most essential business topics to help you succeed.

HBR's 10 Must Reads Series

The definitive collection of ideas and best practices on our most sought-after topics from the best minds in business.

- Change Management
- Collaboration
- Communication
- Emotional Intelligence
- Innovation
- Leadership
- Making Smart Decisions

- Managing Across Cultures
- Managing People
- Managing Yourself
- Strategic Marketing
- Strategy
- Teams
- The Essentials

hbr.org/mustreads

Buy for your team, clients, or event.
Visit hbr.org/bulksales for quantity discount rates.

Harvard
Business
Review
Press

BOOST YOUR EMOTIONAL INTELLIGENCE— AND YOUR PROFESSIONAL SUCCESS

The **HBR Emotional Intelligence Series**, features smart, essential reading on the human side of professional life. Each book offers proven research showing how our emotions impact our work lives, practical advice for managing difficult people and situations, and inspiring essays on what it means to tend to our emotional well-being at work. Uplifting and practical, these books describe the social skills that are critical for ambitious professionals to master.

Harvard Business Review Emotional Intelligence Collection

THIS FOUR-VOLUME SET INCLUDES:
Empathy
Happiness
Mindfulness
Resilience

COMING SOON

Authentic Leadership
Influence + Persuasion

Buy for your team, clients, or event.
Visit hbr.org/bulksales for quantity discount rates.